An Experts' Guide to International Protocol

An Experts' Guide to International Protocol

Best Practice in Diplomatic and Corporate Relations

Gilbert Monod de Froideville and Mark Verheul

LONDON AND NEW YORK

First published in 2021 by Amsterdam University Press Ltd.

Published 2025 by Routledge
4 Park Square, Milton Park, Abingdon, Oxon OX14 4RN
605 Third Avenue, New York, NY 10158

Routledge is an imprint of the Taylor & Francis Group, an informa business

© Gilbert Monod de Froideville, Mark Verheul / Taylor & Francis Group, 2021

All rights reserved. No part of this book may be reprinted or reproduced or utilised in any form or by any electronic, mechanical, or other means, now known or hereafter invented, including photocopying and recording, or in any information storage or retrieval system, without permission in writing from the publishers.

Trademark notice: Product or corporate names may be trademarks or registered trademarks, and are used only for identification and explanation without intent to infringe.

ISBN: 9789463727167 (hbk)
ISBN: 9781041175520 (pbk)
ISBN: 9781003690757 (ebk)

NUR   754

Cover illustration: Elmer Dumlao
Cover design: Elmer Dumlao, Jordan

DOI   10.5117/9789463727167

For Product Safety Concerns and Information please contact our EU representative: GPSR@taylorandfrancis.com
Taylor & Francis Verlag GmbH, Kaufingerstraße 24, 80331 München, Germany

Table of Contents

**Preface to the original edition by His Royal Highness
  Prince Carlos de Bourbon de Parme**   9

Prologue   11

Acknowledgements   13

1. **International protocol**   17
   Introduction   17
   Protocol vs Etiquette   17
   Etiquette and its History   18
   Protocol and its History   20
   Protocol and cultural differences   24

Interview with Professor Jaap de Hoop Scheffer, former Secretary-General of NATO   29

2. **Precedence**   41
   Introduction and history   41
   Comparison of countries around the world   44
   Various facts, trivia, and guidelines   48

Protocol and the International Court of Justice by Dame Rosalyn Higgins, DBE, QC, former President of the International Court of Justice in The Hague   53

3. **Seating arrangements and order of processions**   59
   Introduction   59
   Tables   60
   Conference settings   70
   Posing for official group photographs   74
   Seating plans during audiences and press conferences   74
   Order of receiving lines   74
   Order of processions   75
   Seating in vehicles   76

Protocol at the United Nations and at Think Tanks – A Comparative Perspective by Dr Abiodun Williams, former President of The Hague Institute for Global Justice   77

4. **Flag protocol**   87
   Introduction   87
   Designs and colours   91
   Flag Codes   95
   Rules for using flags   97
   Flag protocol and flag order   98
   Application of flag protocol   100
   Trivia   116

A genuine experience, protocol in an international institution, the European Parliament by Mr François Brunagel, former Head of Protocol of the European Parliament   117

5. **Invitations and dress codes**   125
   History and introduction   125
   General guidelines for composing an invitation   127
   Forms of address   130
   Examples of invitation texts   131
   Dress codes   140

Diplomatic language and formal language: a code with a double meaning by Professor Olivier Arifon, former Professor at the Université libre de Bruxelles in charge of the chair in communication   152

6. **Gifts and honours**   165
   Gifts   165
   Honours   167

State visits by His Excellency Mr José de Bouza Serrano, former Ambassador of the Portuguese Republic to the Netherlands   176

7. **Ceremonies**   183
   Introduction   183
   Meaning of a Ceremony   183
   Organising a Ceremony   184

Components of a Ceremony	185
State Ceremonies	186
State Visits	188
Laying of wreaths	197
Presentation of credentials	199
State funerals	204
Inauguration / Swearing-In and Coronation	206
Gun salutes	208
Guard of Honour / Ceremonial Guard	212
Escorts of Honour	214
Suite of Honour	215
Silent processions	216

Protocol at the Olympic Games by Mr Andrea Miliccia, former Protocol Manager for the London 2012 Opening Ceremony — 217

8. The protocol officer — 225
Introduction	225
The focus of a protocol officer	226
Four stages for a successful high-level event	230
Unforeseen circumstances	234
Speech by Ivo van Vliet, Jeroen Koks, and Ruben Nederpel	236

Protocol is a basic principle of professional success by Mr Jean Paul Wijers, Managing Director and founder of the Protocolbureau, and the Institute of Strategic Relationship Management — 239

Presidential Protocol by Mr Lahoud Lahoud, Director-General, Chief of Protocol & Public Relations Department of the Presidency of the Council of Ministers of the Republic of Lebanon — 245

9. Guest and host — 249
Role of host	249
Mutual interest	249
Guest list	253
Guest's checklist in order to facilitate strategic networking	254

Interview with Mr Martin van Pernis, former President of the Board of Siemens, the Netherlands — 257

Protocol and Dance by Mr Samuel Wuersten, Artistic Director Holland Dance, and former Member of the Executive Board of Codarts Rotterdam   269

10. Protocol and stakeholder engagement during and after the COVID-19 pandemic   273
    Introduction   273
    Contributions from around the world   276
    Overall Top 40 lessons learned as well as predictions and recommendations for the (near) future   316

Authors' biographies   323

Bibliography   329

Websites   331

Illustrations and photographs   333

Index   337

Preface to the original edition by His Royal Highness Prince Carlos de Bourbon de Parme

During the heyday of the Age of Discovery, voyagers like Christopher Columbus and Vasco da Gama explored totally new lands, peoples, and practices around the globe at the command of the Spanish and Portuguese kings. Two centuries earlier, the Venetian tradesman Marco Polo had travelled the renowned Silk Road to finally reach the Mongol Empire. From formal procedures at the court of Kublai Khan to prayers in colourful Hindi temples in India to more basic rituals of the Indians in North America, they experienced that international communication and cooperation were becoming more important than ever. Even though protocol had already been part of life for thousands of years in different parts of the world, the expansion of diplomatic relations and global commerce in the following centuries increased the relevance of good knowledge and understanding of the practices in international protocol.

As it was in former days, protocol still plays an important role in the twenty-first century in the social and diplomatic traffic among heads of state, government officials, and authorities. As reflected in this book, protocol can be seen in the corporate world as conducted attention not only based on international practices and respect, but also as a means to acquire important orders and to meet with the right people. Over the years, my family and I have encountered many occasions where protocol plays a pivotal role. With deep-rooted ties with Italy, Spain, France, and the Netherlands, I have experienced many similarities in the use of protocol within these countries, but there are certainly subtle differences as well.

Numerous books have been written on protocol with most often a particular focus on the practices in the specific author's country. However, the authors of this book provide an overview of the implementation of protocol as practiced around the world. Drawing upon the extensive experience they gained during their careers, which eventually took them to every continent, they provide their unique insights into a wide range of subjects related to international protocol. Experiences of other experts as well as influential persons in diplomacy, business, culture, and sports from around the world are also shared which adds personal touches to the content. Due to the involvement of persons from different generations with various cultural and educational backgrounds, I am convinced that this book will be a valuable guide for anyone in the public, private, or academic sector in the future.

Prologue

In the spring of 2001, a long-lasting collaboration began between Gilbert Monod de Froideville and Mark Verheul. It was at the wedding of TTRRHH Prince Constantijn and Princess Laurentien of the Netherlands, where Gilbert was responsible for the overall programme as Master of Ceremonies and Mark assisted him, along with many others from the *Protocolbureau*, as usher in the Grote Kerk in The Hague. Shared involvement in several other royal events followed over the years, and after Mark's graduation in Sydney in 2005, he started working as a right-hand to Gilbert at Noordeinde Palace in The Hague. Gilbert retired a year and a half later and had the privilege of working in the Middle East as consultant and trainer for a royal court, an experience that provided him with valuable insights into the Middle Eastern culture. Mark joined him there in 2008, and it was then that the initial plans arose to write a book together, but it still took a couple of years before actually deciding to give it a try. In March 2014, on the eve of the start of the Nuclear Security Summit in The Hague, Gilbert was one of Eva Jinek's guests on the Dutch talkshow *Jinek* to elaborate on the many protocol aspects related to such a high-level conference with world leaders attending from around the globe. After the programme she mentioned that Gilbert should consider writing a book and that was the trigger for a brainstorm with Mark about what such a book should cover.

They soon agreed that the book should give an overview of the implementation of protocol as practiced around the world, since every organisation and government is dealing with aspects of international protocol as an instrument of relationship management. In this respect, they talked about the importance of diplomatic hospitality in international relations and international business, seen from a protocol perspective. And although modern life grows increasingly casual, in many sectors, protocol still reigns supreme. The book therefore offers an overview of its associated practices, including those found within the context of diplomatic relations and the business world. Focusing on a wide range of countries and cultures, the book covers topics like precedence, seating arrangements, the history and use of flags, ceremonies, invitations, dress codes, gifts, and decorations. Media and security aspects, instructions for the protocol officer, guest engagement, and the role of the host in strategic networking are also covered. To make it a true experts' guide, Gilbert and Mark have asked numerous influential diplomatic, business, and cultural figures to share their own experiences with protocols around the world.

Gilbert and Mark are grateful that Amsterdam University Press in partnership with The University of Chicago Press shared their enthusiasm, and they were delighted that the book was published in April 2016, exactly two years after the brainstorm and fifteen years after their first encounter.

Gilbert and Mark can proudly look back on five successful years in which their book has grown in prominence and was published in Spanish in collaboration with the Comillas Pontifical University in Madrid in September 2019 and in Mandarin in collaboration with the National Administration Press in Beijing in June 2020. With the fourth edition of the English version going to press, they expect an Arabic edition of the book anytime soon in collaboration with 3zProtocol, a Riyadh-based protocol institute.

The year 2020 was very exceptional, as we were confronted with the COVID-19 pandemic, which had a profound impact on our social manners and the implementation of protocol practices. We have therefore added an extra chapter in this fourth edition devoted to the effects of this pandemic on the execution of events and ceremonies and the implementation of protocol guidelines. The chapter also includes the lessons learned and predictions for the (near) future. Although we are all in this situation together, a one-size-fits-all solution does not exist. International protocol and strategic networking need to adapt to a 'new normal' around the world. But that is not a novelty. Developments in protocol have taken place over the centuries. And creativity, technology, political reality, and common sense have all contributed to keeping protocol relevant in modern days. Therefore, international cooperation and the sharing of experiences might be even more essential than ever during this unprecedented period.

The Hague, March 2021

Acknowledgements

You do not write an expert's guide on your own. Nor with just two of you. For that reason, Gilbert and Mark are extremely grateful for the tremendous contribution of numerous diplomatic and business relations, friends, relatives, and family members. Due to all their individual expertise, tireless assistance, perseverance and/or critical advice, the book receives its truly enhanced and international look and feel. All the flags on the cover of the book represent one or more of the people Gilbert and Mark will thank below.

***

We are extremely honoured that HRH Prince Carlos de Bourbon de Parme accepted our invitation to write a preface. With deep-rooted ties with Italy, Spain, France and the Netherlands, he truly represents the international character of the book.

We are very grateful for the opportunities we had to interview two dignified individuals with a diplomatic and corporate background. The diplomatic perspective was provided by Professor Jaap de Hoop Scheffer, former Secretary-General of NATO, and the corporate approach came from Mr Martin van Pernis, former President of the board of Siemens, the Netherlands. Thank you very much for sharing the experiences of your interesting careers with us.

We also would very much like to thank all the distinguished professionals who contributed to the original version of our book by writing an article about their own experiences, whether these are personal, academic, or more of a business philosophy point of view. In alphabetical order, they are:

Professor Olivier Arifon, former Professor at the *Université libre de Bruxelles* in charge of the chair in communication, writing on diplomatic and formal language.

Mr José de Bouza Serrano, former Ambassador of the Portuguese Republic to the Netherlands, writing on state visits.

Mr François Brunagel, former Head of Protocol of the European Parliament, writing on protocol at the European Parliament.

Dame Rosalyn Higgins, DBE, QC, former President of the International Court of Justice, writing on protocol and precedence related to the International Court of Justice.

Mr Lahoud Lahoud, Director-General, Chief of Protocol & Public Relations Department of the Presidency of the Council of Ministers of the Republic of Lebanon, writing on presidential protocol.

Mr Andrea Miliccia, former Protocol Manager for the London 2012 Olympic Games opening ceremony, writing on protocol at the Olympic Games.

Mr Jean Paul Wijers, Managing Director and founder of the Protocolbureau and the Institute of Strategic Relationship Management, writing on protocol as a basic principle of professional success.

Dr Abiodun Williams, former President of The Hague Institute for Global Justice, writing on a comparative perspective on protocol at the United Nations and at think tanks.

Mr Samuel Wuersten, Artistic Director Holland Dance and former member of the Executive Board of Codarts Rotterdam, writing on protocol and dance.

Once more, thank you very much for writing your interesting articles.

The new generation of protocol officers is represented in this book by Jeroen Koks, Ruben Nederpel, and Ivo van Vliet, former ushers of the Protocolbureau, by a speech they provided on a modernised view on protocol. We really appreciate it that we could include the full text in our book.

We are extremely grateful as well that this fourth edition contains an extra chapter on the pandemic with contributions from professionals in over 25 cities around the world ranging from Accra, Beijing, Dubai, and Geneva to Rio de Janeiro, Sydney, and Washington, D.C. After a year heavily affected by COVID-19, a multitude of personal examples, struggles, creative solutions, and lessons learned related to protocol, high-level event management, and stakeholder engagement are shared. Whether the experiences come from a national chief of protocol, a chef de cabinet of an international organisation, a CEO of a renowned hotel chain, a board member of a large protocol association, a seasoned business consultant, an associate professor at a leading university, or a youthful trainee at a diplomatic mission, they all provide valuable insights into how their organisations arranged effective pivots to keep their network in shape in this unprecedented period. Thank you very much!

Next to the written contributions, we could not have completed such a comprehensive and practical guide without the enormous creativity and devotion of Elmer Dumlao, an esteemed artist and graphic designer from the Philippines who is working in Jordan. Thank you very much for designing the cover and the dozens of illustrations throughout the book.

A big expression of gratitude is also applicable to HE Mr Floor Kist, former Grand Master of the Royal Household of the Netherlands. With his critical eye for detail, he read and reviewed many chapters of the book and has provided valued advice for changes.

We further appreciate the efforts of Mr Klaas van der Tempel, former Consul General of the Netherlands in Chicago, who supported us in a very generous manner to promote our book in the United States of America, in particular with Ambassador Ivo H. Daalder, President of the Chicago Council on Global Affairs. We feel privileged to have received the following remarks by Ambassador Daalder during the book launch in Chicago after he received the first copy of the book in April 2016: *'Proper protocol is essential to effective diplomacy and business. This important and illuminating book shows why and how protocol is necessary to conduct diplomacy and global business around the world.'*

Since we both are not native speakers of English, we could not have written this book without the exhaustive work of Carrie Ballard, Susan Hunt, Joshua Sherrington, Louise Vines and Wilkens c.s. Without their linguistic advice and translation services, the book would not have been as professional as it is now. On top of that, a special thanks to Joshua for coming up with the title of the book.

Last but definitely not least, our book would never have been published without the loving support we both got from our partners Nan and Freek. Over the years, many spare moments had to be dedicated to our book, and obviously many conversations with them turned to the topic. Not only at home in the Netherlands, but also during holidays in Belgium, France, the Far East, Iceland, Scotland, and along the Silk Road in Central Asia.

Heel veel dank voor jullie liefde, begrip, steun en klankbord!

Le congrès de Vienne, Jean-Baptiste Isabey

1. International protocol

Introduction

Why write a book on international protocol at a time when people often speak negatively about protocol, etiquette, and codes of conduct? The writers of this book are very aware of these tendencies but hope that this book will clarify the use of protocol, its development, and the particularities of the role it plays in the international world, where it reveals a respect for the traditions and cultures of others.

Protocol is no longer just the catch-all term for the written and unwritten rules of diplomatic and social discourse between heads of state, heads of government, and authorities as laid out by the Treaties of Vienna (1814–1815 and 1961–1963). Today international protocol concerns itself as well with conduct between industrial partners and the cultural and sport sector.

Conduct is not only based on existing international practices and rules of respect, but also with the goal of accurately profiling countries, organisations and businesses, securing important business contracts, and meeting the right people. It can therefore be said that protocol is a tool for maintaining good relationships.

The application of international protocol focuses on three aspects. First, it is intended to minimise tedious discussions on who must sit where, in what order and in what manner flags are displayed, or in what order people must walk, stand, or greet guests. Second, it is a means of avoiding unnecessarily disturbing diplomatic relations, and third, it is intended to cultivate a climate in which everyone feels comfortable and which lends itself well to positive decision-making.

In short, we can say that protocol is the catch-all term for establishing proper conduct in order to avoid conflicts and arguments. However, maintaining functionality always prevails over carrying out the correct protocol. Nonetheless, protocol is often confused with etiquette, and it is necessary to outline the differences between the two.

Protocol vs Etiquette

What is the essential difference between protocol and etiquette? Etiquette can be defined as the rules of politeness between people, i.e. social manners.

This would include examples like opening doors for people, proper ways of greeting, pulling a chair out for a woman, and so on, while protocol tends to focus much more on the status of a person, a country, an organisation, or a business rather than societal status. In Chapter 2, we will explore extensively the nature of status, the order of precedence, which in French is called *préséance*.

Etiquette and its History

Etiquette, which encompasses the rules of politeness and good manners, is as old as humanity itself, and it changes with the times. As such, these rules are influenced by the prevailing culture in a country. Therefore, in one country, one greets with the nose, in another cheek on cheek, and in other countries by shaking each other's hands or with an appropriately low bow or a curtsy.

The oldest found document on moral conventions is the *Prisse Papyrus*, dating back to the Twelfth Dynasty Egyptian Middle Kingdom, discovered in 1856 by the French archaeologist and writer Émile Prisse d'Avennes in Thebes and now held in the Bibliothèque Nationale de France in Paris. It was written as a practical handbook for the son of a vizier, a high-ranking functionary and (sometimes religious) government advisor for a ruler such as a pharaoh. This papyrus document contains the last two pages of the *Instructions of Kagemni*, who served under the Fourth Dynasty King Snefru, and is a compilation of moral conventions and exhortations on the practice of virtue. The conclusion of this text is followed by the only surviving copy of the *Instructions of Ptahhotep*, an Egyptian philosopher and pharaoh from the Fifth Dynasty (2414–2375 BC).

When people live together in large concentrations, unwritten rules and social conventions emerge naturally. Philip the Good, Duke of Burgundy (1419–1467), was the first monarch to write codes of conduct for his royal household, on cards, in order to maintain clarity for his personal staff.

In 1529, the Dutch scholar, theologian, and philosopher Desiderius Erasmus (1469–1536) wrote a handbook on the behaviour of children. This was in fact the first book containing rules on politeness and courtesy specifically for children. This book proved to be so popular that it was translated into several languages, and it is still possible to acquire a copy today – but it is necessary to note that the rules laid out in this book no longer apply. The rules of etiquette, of course, change with the times and are constantly subject to such change.

At this point, however, the word 'etiquette' had not yet become synonymous with good manners. During the Dutch Golden Age, which fell in the seventeenth century, the upper classes and nobility created social rules in order to distinguish themselves from the lower and middle classes. These rules were called *curalia:* the practice of *comitas* and *suavitas*, of politeness and courtesy. This encompassed the titles and forms of address used before a king or queen, how ambassadors should address one another in formal situations, which in fact form the basis of the titles and forms of address that we now use with each other. In the Netherlands, for example, a complex system of rules still governs how to write to one another, but it bears remembering that every generation tends to abandon elements of this complex system for the sake of simplicity.

An important component of etiquette – table manners – was introduced later. It was very important to lay the table in a manner that was 'closed', meaning that the spoon was laid with the convex side up, and the fork with the teeth facing onto the table, so that the value and quality of the silver were clearly shown by silver content (by an engraving of a standing, walking or laying lion) or the family crest on the silverware. This style of laying a table is still sometimes used today. When invited to dinner, people would often bring their own silverware in a decorated box in order to show the other guests their own personal wealth or nobility through the value of their personal silverware.

However, this all begs the question of when the word 'etiquette' was actually introduced and what it meant. The French initially used this word to refer to an engraving on a wooden stick, then to a small plaque on a gift or object, and later, under the French King Louis XIV (1638–1715), the Sun King, the rules and signs of conduct and politeness.

It was this king who made all of the miscellaneous life rules and court etiquette or court protocol clear and visible at his court in Versailles through the placement of signs with advice and notices on how to behave at the court. The story goes that he thought of this idea together with his gardener who had become irritated by the bad behaviour of courtiers. Rubbish was thrown on the ground and people would jump over the grass and through the bushes. Through the placement of various signs, the rules on how to behave quickly gave the word *étiquette* a new meaning – namely that of the rules and signs of conduct and politeness. Many books and the records of court attendees of the period bear witness to this fact. We should note that the size of the court, and the degree to which these life rules were orchestrated, made them necessary and the rules were enforced on over 2,000 people. At every moment of the day, dozens of servants and courtiers swarmed around the king. His only refuge was the *Petit Trianon*. Even the architecture and arrangement of the royal palace of Versailles was intended to show the king clearly, as he would be seen at the opera or the royal chapel. Not all quarters of the palace were equally accessible to all courtiers; some quarters were restricted to only the highest-ranked nobles. The rules concerning the waking of the king have also been written about in detail. To be given this role was a great honour. Every morning, the king was awakened by the grand chamberlain, with the words '*Sire, voilà l'heure*', which was the start of the *petit lever*. The highest honour was to be chosen to offer a piece of clothing to the king. Each day, the king would be medically inspected by the chief royal physician who would be attended by supporters of the royal family and those who had access to the *Grande Entrée*. Afterwards, the king was dressed in the presence of several courtiers, the *Grand Lever*. The same protocol was common practice when going to bed, the *Coucher*. It was also courtly etiquette that the king gave rooms to his favourite courtiers and guests. He then attached nameplates to their doors. These varied depending on the level of prestige of the individual – just 'Cazard' or 'Monsieur Cazard' or the highest honour 'pour Monsieur Jean Cazard', for example. Another form of etiquette was the allocation of a *tabouret*, a low cushioned stool without a back or arms where one might be seated in the presence of the king. This right was often reserved for grandchildren, foreign princesses, and high-ranking nobles. Other courtiers including the cardinals, as well as men and women of high esteem, had to stand. The higher one's prestige, the better one's chair.

With the spread of French culture through the world, the meaning of 'etiquette' began to take on the definition we use today. In the last two centuries, many books on etiquette have appeared, and they are continuously adjusted to the societal conventions of the time. Etiquette was, and continues to be, indispensable in a society where social conventions and respect for one another remain of great importance.

Protocol and its History

As indicated earlier, international protocol is focused on respect and an acknowledgement of status and hierarchy.

Previously, it was the power of a country that defined the position it took in the diplomatic world. Chapter 2 goes into greater detail about this. However, we now concern ourselves with the emergence of the definition of protocol. When was protocol first spoken about, and was it then something entirely new, or had forms of respect for the status of people, countries, institutes, organisations, and industries long been considered?

Before the word protocol emerged, there were indeed everyday forms of hierarchy, which can be observed in old frescoes or wall paintings in Ancient Egypt, Asia, and in Ancient Rome, where entire processions were often depicted. Here, a focus on hierarchy is clearly visible, such as an acute attention to detail when determining who stood where and in what order. Ancient tribes had rules of respect for status such as those concerning the tribe leader.

The definition of protocol has its origin in the Greek word *protókollon*, a portmanteau of the Greek words *protos*, meaning first, and *kolla*, meaning glue. The term was used in Late Greek to indicate a leaf or tag attached to a rolled papyrus manuscript and containing notes as to contents (later it indicated the first page that was glued on top of a notarial document), and also to describe the seal on a document. Throughout history, protocol has had many definitions. These include:
- An original outline or report whereby a treaty is prepared.
- An agreement between states.
- Minutes of an international agreement, which acquires the powers of a treaty from the signatures of the participants. For example, the 9 protocols of London, the first of which was in 1814 and the last in 2000.
- The first copy of an agreement or of a similar document before it is ratified.
- A set of standard procedures for the regulation of data transmission in computer science.
- The plan for the process of a medical treatment or for a scientific experiment.
- A code for proper behaviour, such as safety protocol and academic protocol.
- An aspect of diplomatic etiquette in the form of official correspondence between ministries responsible for foreign relations.
- The forms of ceremonies and etiquette such as those practiced by heads of state and diplomats.

International protocol as we know it now focuses on respect and the creation of a good and comfortable diplomatic and business climate, as well as the minimisation of conflict and disagreement. Many of these international agreements are unwritten and based on reciprocity and a good management of relationships.

On an official visit such as a state visit, respect for the host country's protocol is essential. At the time of Queen Beatrix of the Netherlands, her husband Prince Claus emphasised time and again that the organisers of the many official visits of the royal family abroad should not attempt to enforce their own protocol, as this would imply a lack of respect for the valid standard protocol in place in the host country. This could jeopardise diplomatic relations. It goes without saying that one must respect the rules of the host country. Every country has its own local protocol which is often based on the indigenous culture. In some countries, it is customary that the most important guests are seated at a high table facing the other guests while in other countries, the head table is placed adjacent to several other round tables. Protocol at an official audience of two heads of state also differs between countries. In some countries, the two delegations sit on either side of the heads of state in a U-formation. This protocol is widely used in Asia, the Middle East, and in Eastern Europe but less often in the West. In many countries these meetings are limited to just the two heads of state. While historically it had been customary to hold a return dinner, this practice has since been changed, partly on the initiative of the Netherlands, into a return cultural event, such as a dance performance or a concert. Doing so enables countries to exhibit their own cultures. This practice appeals to many heads of state, and it has today been adopted by many other nations.

Due to the busy schedules of heads of state these days, the length of a state visit is often limited to one or two days. Historically, state visits could last up to three days.

Furthermore, each country has its own protocol concerning the minor details of speeches and state dinners. These details vary from speeches at the beginning of dinner to saving the speeches until after the main course. Protocol also varies on when and whether to play national anthems. In some countries, such as the United Kingdom, the 'loyal toast' is customary. This occurs simultaneously with a traditional ceremony. Official protocol states that the 'loyal toast' must be performed following the official introduction of honoured guests and opening remarks or the completion of all courses of the meal, that it be the first toast given, and that a glass of any beverage other than a cocktail be used. In practice, it is always the first toast of the evening.

In carrying out the toast in the United Kingdom, the event's host will rise and request the audience's attention. Once accomplished and the guests are standing, the host raises his or her glass and recites the toast –'The Queen' – without any other words or music. The audience then responds to the toast by repeating 'The Queen' or in Canada, *'La Reine'* followed by taking a sip. After this, *God Save the Queen* is played, and the guests sit down again when it is finished.

In Sweden, the toast is a formal ritual, and one does not drink until the host has personally invited every guest for a toast. They look into each other's eyes and say 'skål.'

It is important that one lets the guests and elders toast in order of hierarchy and age. When toasting, it is also important that eye contact is made and everyone nods before the glasses are lowered, and that men wait for women to put their glasses back on the table.

There are also many differences and contrasts in the area of gifts. In Western culture, it is not customary to give extremely expensive gifts. It is instead the gesture that counts. In the Middle East, however, hospitality and respect are communicated through the extravagance of the gift. At dinner, too, hospitality is communicated by an overabundance of food, something that is unfamiliar in Western culture. Another noteworthy difference is that official dinners must not last too long.

When speaking of international protocol in government relations, it is important to consider the precedence that exists between heads of state, ambassadors, authorities, and countries, but it is also of relevance to describe the nuances in arrival and departure ceremonies at official visits. These include gun salutes at official welcome ceremonies, styles of greeting, the order in which flags are displayed, exchange of gifts and honours/decorations, order of procession, laying of wreaths, and the presentation of credentials.

In a world where the global economy is ingrained in every aspect of life, international protocol is also given an extremely important place in industry as an instrument for the management of relationships based on respect, good communication, cooperation, hospitality, and the maintenance and understanding of the correct manner to conduct oneself in international business with foreign cultures.

Not only the increase in international relations and the growing role of business at home and abroad have played a role, but in particular a declining economic situation, where competition and strategic networks require attention, make protocol important. In an uncertain global economic situation, strong international communication and cooperative networks have become increasingly important, thereby increasing the need for good diplomatic relations.

These noteworthy changes have meant that the form of protocol has had to change to fit the needs of our time, which are increasingly focused on ensuring that good business is done in an environment that depends on a correct knowledge of how to deal with cultural differences.

Protocol and cultural differences

It is today much more common to travel abroad far from our own borders to other, distinct cultures. Being a guest in a foreign country means first having respect for the manner in which guests are treated in the host country. This of course varies between all countries and cultures, and in many countries it is essential to build a good relationship before business can be done.

During meetings or while doing business with foreigners, one should be aware that they might be conducting business in an environment with different values and norms from those in their culture. It is tempting to think that a single Asian culture, Middle Eastern culture, South American culture, African culture, and European culture exists, but this assumption would prove to be very wrong. In these regions, one finds several differences between countries, often based on religions or local traditions dating back hundreds if not thousands of years.

The importance of showing respect for one another's culture cannot be overstated. A lack of knowledge inhibits proper communication, which is essential when dealing with other cultures, both within our own society and outside it. Not showing interest or acknowledging cultural differences in another country can sometimes do more harm than good, causing the loss of important international agreements or orders.

In the world of protocol and etiquette, we see that differences in culture have an enormous influence on the manner in which business is conducted, and how we interact with one another in international organisations and the international community.

In the world's many cultures, protocol and etiquette often take on their own form under the influence of local values and norms. This is why doing business in Switzerland and Germany is very concrete. Business is conducted clearly and transparently, and the context of discussions does not play any kind of role in understanding. However, in other regions such as in the Arab world and parts of Asia, context plays a very significant role, little is explained 100% clearly, and meetings are often not transparent.

In the Middle East, guests at a dinner will never be seated with their backs to the head of state, and one must never show the soles of their feet to their conversation partner as this is a grave insult. In addition, the use of the left hand is limited in most situations.

Body language too differs from place to place. Every day we use our head, our hands, and our arms to express ourselves. A simple nod of the head can give the wrong impression – in some Asian countries, a nod of the head can mean 'I'm listening', and it does not automatically mean 'I agree.' In China, facial expressions are kept to a minimum in order to avoid endless misunderstandings, and gesticulations are considered bad form. The host always begins the conversation, and others must listen. Then there is a moment of silence for reflection, and only then may the others respond. The 'OK' hand sign, with the thumb and the forefinger, also has many meanings in different countries, and in some it can be an obscene insult. In the Netherlands, for example, it is customary to stick one's thumb up to indicate happiness with something. In Central Europe, as it is here, it is also used to indicate needing a lift by the side of the road. However, it is important to be careful as in many Mediterranean countries, Russia, the Middle East, and parts of Africa and Australia, the same gesture can be seen as an obscene insult. In large parts of Europe and North America, one sticks one's fist in the palm of the other hand to express anger. In a tense situation, this can inadvertently cause problems. In Africa, this gesture means agreement with something. In many Western countries, the 'V' sign is a symbol meaning peace. In Greece, it means 'go to hell.' In the United Kingdom and Australia, the same gesture, but turned around with the back of the hand shown, can cause problems. In these countries, doing so is seen as much worse than just showing the middle finger. In East Asian countries, the same gesture is used to accompany a smile in photos and videos.

An official gift-giving ceremony between heads of state is often based on international protocol and reciprocity, and it is important to think about whether gifts are appropriate for the countries receiving them. No bottles of wine in the Middle East, for example. In China, it is not acceptable to give a letter opener as a gift or a clock to an older person. In some countries white and yellow flowers should not be given as gifts, as these are connected to death. An elegant fountain pen however is a nice gift.

While doing business in the Russian Federation, it is customary to invite colleagues for a casual dinner, but showing up for such a dinner empty-handed is completely unacceptable. Wine, good whisky, chocolates, exotic fruit, and pastries are all good ideas for a gift. A bottle of vodka can be seen as something of an insult, just like a bottle of wine in France. Ordinarily, women receive flowers as gifts from their guests, but it is important to avoid giving yellow flowers in the Russian Federation as this means the end of a relationship. Flowers in an even number are only meant for deaths and should therefore also be avoided.

Chapter 6 will look more closely at gifts.

The manner of greeting also varies from country to country. In the Middle East, local men often greet one another by touching the person, and depending on how well they know one another, they might do this up to three times. In the United Arab Emirates, local men greet one another by touching their noses together. In the Mediterranean countries, France among them, hands are frequently shaken and the giving of kisses is a whole ritual that varies from region to region from one to five kisses, as can be seen in Corsica. In 2020, the world was confronted with the COVID-19 pandemic. This resulted in social distancing among people, which ruled out any physical-contact ways of greeting one another in order to limit the spread of the virus (see chapter 10).

Personal space and distance between people also varies between cultures. For example in Latin American and Middle Eastern countries, people stand closer to one another while in the United States and United Kingdom, it's customary to stand much farther apart. In one culture, looking someone in the eye while speaking to them is natural and usual, while in others it might be unthinkable.

Lastly, protocol follows the customary rules in international diplomatic intercourse concerning hierarchy, rank, and ceremony. It is therefore essential for international relations to use the protocol that is codified through international law and common international use. This governs interactions between the many official representatives of the world's countries.

Agreements are being made regularly through international treaties and reciprocity in the area of international protocol. We must continue to see them as instruments to help us build good, healthy relationships, reduce conflicts, and keep diplomacy running smoothly. First and foremost we should not lose sight of the effectiveness of international protocol. Creating a seating arrangement that is completely impractical while being correct in terms of protocol adds nothing and instead does damage to the effectiveness of an event that is intended to strengthen underlying relationships. Chapter 3 looks more closely at seating arrangements.

A subject that is deeply interwoven in protocol is diplomacy. Certainly diplomacy, beside protocol and etiquette, plays an unmistakably important role – what do we wish to achieve? And how do we wish to achieve it?

What is diplomacy? In general, we can say that diplomacy is the art of conducting negotiations between parties in order to reach a decision agreeable to everyone. In other words, it is a tactful manner by which to strike a deal. Often, international diplomacy is referred to as the conduct of international relations carried out by professional diplomats on matters such as peace, war, the economy, and culture. Winston Churchill said: 'Diplomacy is the art of telling people to go to hell in such a manner that they ask for directions.'

Experience has taught us that the correct use of international protocol has an impact on diplomatic relations. It is the means by which accidental insults and arguments about precedence and interpersonal relationships can be avoided, and as mentioned previously, it should not disturb diplomacy.

This is why countries must mutually respect international protocol and apply it as correctly as possible.

Every head of state or government representative expects to be received in a way that follows protocol correctly. Flags that are not displayed in the correct order, the use of the wrong flag, the playing of the wrong national anthem, or leaving the official welcome to a low-ranking functionary can all be interpreted as an insulting action with the intention of sending a message. It is therefore possible to say that international protocol is a powerful instrument in our international society.

Professor emeritus Jaap G. de Hoop Scheffer, former Secretary-General of NATO

Jakob Gijsbert (Jaap) de Hoop Scheffer was born in Amsterdam on 3 April 1948. After completing his secondary education, he studied law at Leiden University, graduating in 1974. From 1974 to 1976 he performed his military service in the Royal Netherlands Air Force and was discharged as a reserve officer. From 1976 to 1986, he was employed in the foreign service of the Ministry of Foreign Affairs, serving in Ghana, at the Netherlands delegation to NATO, and as private secretary to the Dutch foreign minister. Mr De Hoop Scheffer was elected to the House of Representatives of the States General for the Christian Democratic Alliance (CDA) in June 1986 and served on the Standing Committees on Foreign Affairs, Justice, European Affairs, and Defence. He was the chair of the Standing Committees for Foreign Affairs and Development Cooperation and a member of the parliamentary assemblies of NATO and the Council of Europe. He was the party leader of the CDA between 1997 and 2001. On 22 July 2002, he was appointed minister of Foreign Affairs. The Netherlands held the chairmanship of the Organization for Security and Cooperation in Europe (OSCE) in 2003. Mr De Hoop Scheffer was the chairperson-in-office of that organisation until he stepped down as foreign minister on 3 December 2003. From January 2004 to August 2009 he was Secretary-General of NATO and chairman of the North Atlantic Council. Since then, he has served on the board of Air France-KLM as a non-executive director (2011-2020) and was a member (2010-2014) and chair (2014-2018) of the supervisory board of the Rijksmuseum in Amsterdam. Until April 2020, he lectured on international relations and the practice of diplomacy in The Hague at the Faculty of Governance and Global Affairs of his alma mater Leiden University. He is the chair of the Advisory Council on International Affairs for both government and parliament. He is also a member of the Advisory Council of VNO-NCW, the Dutch Employers Organisation, a member of the Trilateral Commission, a trustee of the Brussels-based 'Friends of Europe', a member of the European Council on Foreign Relations, and he serves on the board of the Centre for European Policy Studies. He is chair of the Netherlands Civil Honours Advisory Committee. On 29 June 2018, he was appointed Minister of State.

Interview with Professor Jaap de Hoop Scheffer

Mr De Hoop Scheffer, to begin with, we would like to say how much we appreciate the opportunity to interview you on the subject of international protocol. You can look back on a fascinating career in which you served in many roles in the diplomatic and political worlds, with your ministerial appointment and ultimately your role as secretary-general of NATO as high points. Given that you are now professor of international relations and diplomacy at the University of Leiden Campus in The Hague, you are clearly still very active in the field.

We should start where your career in the foreign service began – at the Dutch Embassy in Accra, Ghana. Can you remember what aspects of protocol you came into contact with in connection with your work?

Yes, that was in a way that we Dutch rarely think about, given that we associate high temperatures with casual clothing – something that was absolutely not done in terms of protocol. Everyone had to be impeccably dressed, regardless of how high the temperature and humidity were. My wife and I also observed that in diplomatic relations and foreign affairs, as well as on national days, people attached a great deal of importance to protocol and correct etiquette.

After that and many other postings, you returned to The Hague, first in the political field and later as minister of Foreign Affairs. In your final days as minister you hosted the OSCE summit of 2003 in Maastricht. Can you tell us how, in your view, protocol played an important role in the smooth running of that conference, bearing in mind the part played by all the delegations in attendance?

At international conferences every aspect of protocol plays an essential role. When your role at foreign-minister level is that of chairperson-in-office, the situation is slightly different than when you are operating at the heads-of-state and heads-of-government level. I will return to that later. In this case we were dealing with representatives at ministerial level. An important aspect there was to keep everyone happy about the speaking order. There are of course countries with a desire to be placed high on the speakers' list, because with so many countries taking part they want to avoid being cut short after waiting three hours to speak. As chairman, with the help of your staff, you have to try to prepare this as carefully as possible, discuss it with the participating countries, and agree on how long the interventions may last. The goal is to avoid an interminable meeting that results in an unworkable situation. Because protocol does not dictate in advance what the order should be. It is necessary however to take into account the key positions held by countries like the United States and Russia in the OSCE, which should certainly not be overlooked at a conference of that nature. There are countries that prefer to speak later because they want to hear the other countries' position and tone first. In such cases it is quite possible that the Russians first want to hear what the Americans have to say, or vice versa. At the NATO-Russia Council that was sometimes a dilemma too. I should mention here that experience as chairman plays an important part in making sure everything runs smoothly, particularly knowing when to be flexible and when to be firm. Protocol also plays a role in the allotting of accommodation that sometimes may be affected by what is available in a country, as well as the desired distance from the conference location, for example. On top of this are the motorcades, the number of cars per delegation and the order. This is all the more important for heads of state and government in that seniority is extremely important in terms of order of arrival. Sometimes there are heads of government who deliberately delay leaving their hotel in order to arrive last and therefore more prominently. As the host of the conference, there is little you can do about that at the time.

During your time as secretary-general of NATO, the partnership expanded from nineteen to twenty-eight countries, with Albania and Croatia among them. We assume that such an accession is accompanied by ceremonial aspects. What stands out most for you and what was your role in this as secretary-general?

The ceremonial aspects are apparent at various stages, from the moment that the political green light is given until the accession itself at a NATO summit. At these meetings solemn statements are made by the secretary-general and the incumbent honorary ministerial chairman of the North Atlantic Council. The more visible part takes place outside in front of the main entrance with a flag ceremony, where the flags of the acceded countries are formally raised. These were often emotional events. For me, growing up on this side of the Iron Curtain, I had underestimated this, and it was only at such moments that I realised what this accession meant to these countries, with representatives often moved to tears, especially when their national anthem was played. The secretary-general naturally has a significant role in such ceremonies.

The flags are generally always raised in alphabetical order in English, although I should mention that NATO is bilingual, and uses both French and English. Something which is quite handy if you encounter a protocol problem, as you can always switch to the French alphabet and thus overcome a possible sensitivity concerning a seating plan, for example. Such sensitivities can be quite strong, as I experienced. On one occasion a certain president categorically stated that he did not wish to be seated next to another particular president. By changing the language the problem could be resolved without further ado. Ultimately, protocol is there not to be a burden, but rather to minimise conflicts and awkward situations. The meeting table, for example, is oval in order to give no one a more important position, and the English alphabet is used. For me as secretary-general this meant that Albania was seated to my left, with the United States to my right. This had the added benefit that the president of the United States was next to me at summits which sometimes provided an opportunity to be able to briefly discuss something directly.

You mentioned avoiding conflicts. We can imagine that during your time as secretary-general of NATO you often had to communicate with non-allies on politically sensitive matters. Can you give us one or two examples where you could use protocol to support you in formal and informal meetings in order to communicate such matters in a way that was both congenial and effective?

I think that your question pinpoints a crucial aspect of diplomacy. Your mission is actually from your first conversation to try to build a connection with your discussion partner, one that to some extent goes beyond the professional. What I mean by that is if I need to tell someone something less pleasing, I want to know exactly who he or she is, their life story, their background, and of course the politics of the country in question. As the English say, 'what makes someone tick?' Hobbies, for example, may offer a useful avenue. I remember a president from a particular country that actually had nothing to do with NATO, but we had one thing in common, we both owned a Labrador dog. Opening a conversation by talking about dogs, you show that you are interested in that person. You know he loves his dog as much as you do yours. If you have something difficult to communicate – this was not just in my NATO days, but when I was a minister too – for example, when a Dutch citizen was taken hostage in Russia and I had to ask President Putin if he was willing to do his utmost to secure the freedom of my countryman as quickly as possible, then it is best to follow protocol and diplomatic procedure given that we Dutch can be somewhat direct at times. In this case it wasn't so much a difficult communication but more a request for help, but here too, despite the often difficult relations between the two countries, you try to mellow the other party with the personal attention you give them. I also built up an extremely positive relationship with former President George W. Bush, and not just me, but my wife too, who exchanged books with his wife, where my wife sent books translated from Dutch which she thought Mrs Bush might be interested in, and Mrs Bush sent books in return that she thought my wife would like to read. The president would certainly be aware of something like that, and this helps to create a good relationship. Indeed, I tell my students just how important the personal aspect is and how protocol can also be used in this way to good effect. It goes beyond simply showing respect for the culture, tradition and religion, such as not showing the soles of one's feet and avoiding use of the left hand in the Arab world, for example.

In your position you have travelled widely and seen a lot of the world. Can you tell us which countries seemed extremely formal and which were less formal in terms of protocol?

There are indeed differences. A country like Turkey attaches great importance to protocol and during my visits as SG of NATO, I was always received at the same level as a prime minister. This meant that there was always a Guard of Honour. The Turkish national anthem was played, as well as the NATO anthem, which incidentally few people even know exists. As SG, you are then invited to inspect the Guard of Honour standing to attention. You stop at the flag and pay your respects by making a slight bow. There are also many well-known pictures of the Bundeskanzleramt where German Chancellor Angela Merkel receives her guests and joins them in the inspection of the Guard of Honour, and because the procedure is complicated she tries to coach them in what to do. I always made sure I was properly briefed by my military advisor.
Thus Turkey is an example, but it is certainly not the only one, of a country where protocol and military ceremony play an important role. That is less so in the United States, in the sense that when you are received at the White House there is no military ceremony, at least not during a working visit. The protocol takes a different form there, where the head of protocol is expected to select your delegation on the basis of seniority, in accordance with protocol. If you visit the Pentagon, however,

> the ceremony becomes more visible and a modest Guard of Honour is presented to you. In general, you can say that for my position as SG almost every country observes some form of protocol, including at the airplane steps. I remember a time when I alighted an aircraft but the red carpet had been rolled out to the wrong door. The Guard of Honour however was in the right place. As I recall, the East European countries and Baltic States are not generally very protocol oriented. In that respect, they are relatively young, independent countries still searching for the best form for international diplomatic discourse. Countries like New Zealand and Australia I also perceived as less concerned with protocol, unlike Japan and China that put much more emphasis on protocol.

You mentioned several times the use of flags in ceremonies. Have you ever seen flags raised incorrectly?

> Oh yes, indeed. Once a flag was raised upside down, and once the wrong flag was raised. The Dutch flag is sometimes confused with the Luxembourg flag. A flag was once blown off the flagpole while being raised. Those are awkward moments. Luckily, they don't happen too often. It shows that with international protocol you can never be too careful.

In your view, how did protocol differ most between your role as secretary-general at NATO and as the Dutch minister of Foreign Affairs?

> Actually, there was a big difference. As minister of Foreign Affairs, you are constantly making brief working visits, with a meeting, lunch or dinner, while as secretary-general you are received at a higher level, as a head of government, so official protocol then plays a much bigger role. As a minister, you fly to and from the various countries and there is no time for ceremony or anything of that nature; it is just a working visit. The exception to this is an OSCE conference, for example, where ministers meet in a more formal setting around the table, with receptions and delegations and so on. It also makes a difference whether you are visiting a country as the prime minister, when all the stops will be pulled out to highlight the visit for the purpose of building international relations between the two countries.

You have been a professor at the University of Leiden Campus The Hague since 2009, where you teach international relations and diplomacy. Can you tell us the most important piece of advice you give to students about protocol and managing relations?

> *There are two mainly. When you work with other countries, before you say or do anything, first learn something about the history, culture, traditions, geography, and religion of the country concerned. If you don't do that, you cannot pretend to understand a country like Afghanistan, or even a country closer to home, like Belgium. Look at the traditions, the culture, in Europe it may be so that religious faith is a private matter, but Europe is by far the most secular continent in the world. There are countless other countries where that is completely different. Even in the United States, the president ends speeches with the words 'God bless you, God bless the United States of America.' It would be unthinkable for the Dutch prime minister to end a speech in that way. If you don't know why the Sunnis and Shiites are in conflict with one another, you cannot understand the Middle East. A second important lesson is that when you go abroad and you are professionally involved with international relations, find out about the life of the person or people you will be talking to. As I mentioned earlier, do they have hobbies, what makes them tick? Because they are all human beings, even at the highest level, just like the rest of us, all with their own domestic concerns, children who might be doing well at school or not, and so on. You will need to know about that if you want to be a good diplomat. In my opinion, this is a major part of protocol and managing relations. The mission is 'to create a good climate.' Those are the two basic principles. Have respect for your discussion partner and his or her culture. You will never be a successful diplomat unless you have that understanding and respect.*

To continue on from that idea of respect being so important in society, this brings us to another position that you've held since 2014, chairman of the Civil Honours Advisory Commission. To many this might sound formal and ceremonial, but it is an important institution that bestows recognition on as many people as possible who have made an outstanding contribution to Dutch society. How do you perceive this formal and ceremonial image?

> *Everyone is familiar with the birthday honours list, or 'lintjesregen' as we call it in Dutch. The vast majority of people are rightly proud if a royal honour is conferred on them or a family member. The basic principle is that for someone to qualify for an honour they must be of impeccable*

character. It is, after all, a royal honour bestowed by the king. It is something special. The commission advises the minister. There are of course those honours that can be awarded without discussion, but there are also matters that need to be considered, including the 'grade' at which the honour should be awarded. Every two weeks the Advisory Commission, along with the chancellor of the Netherlands Orders of Knighthood, meet to discuss these matters. As I mentioned, we advise the minister, and our role is to protect the integrity of the system and its proceedings.

Do you see the exchange of honours during a state visit as a way of strengthening the bond between two countries and showing respect for one another?

Definitely, the exchange of honours plays an important role during state visits. The 'high grades' that are often awarded are sometimes criticized, but people should remember that this is where the idea of 'reciprocity' comes into play, which is extremely important in international diplomacy. When country x uses the occasion of a state visit to present the equivalent of a Grand Cross of the Order of Orange-Nassau to someone in the Dutch entourage, then reciprocity requires that the Netherlands does the same. There are those who say that the level of the award should be reduced slightly, and some countries do that; some countries are ready to discuss it, but there needs to be a clear understanding. However, reciprocity remains the key principle.

When you look back on all the positions you have held where protocol and ceremony played an important role, did you feel it was essential to have people around you with expertise that you could draw on, and what was it like to have such an outstanding head of protocol in both your top functions?

In my time at NATO a Dutch lieutenant colonel together with the NATO director of protocol was responsible for this. In this role it is important to have someone who is highly familiar with military protocol and ceremonial matters. And not just these aspects, but gifts too, so that the other party should feel that the gift was chosen with thought. A good example was when then Secretary of State Colin Powell retired from the NATO Council. He has a fairly unusual hobby in that he collects old Volvos and has numerous vintage Volvos in his garage that he likes to tinker with at the weekend. When someone of his standing retires, you

> scour the world to find a unique miniature, and eventually I was able to give him one. But you need to know that about a person of course. You need to have someone in the head of protocol role who knows your preferences too. There are the unwritten rules, such as the fact that I find it not fitting to inspect a Guard of Honour wearing an overcoat. This is something that a head of protocol needs to be aware of and point out to me before the inspection begins, and take my coat from me. Even if it is wet and windy, you should take your coat off as a mark of respect for the Guard of Honour standing to attention for you. It is also important that a head of protocol can inform you at the last moment of anything that may have happened that you need to know about. That last little piece of information can help you perform even better in your meetings. I attach great importance to being able to do just that little bit more when you sit together as two professionals.

Before we turn to the last question, this interview will be included in a book we are publishing on international protocol with contributions from the international community, government, and industry, as well as the cultural and sport sectors that will underline the importance of international protocol. To whom would you recommend the book? Do you think it has more to offer because, unlike books that have been published in various countries about their own protocol, this one takes a more comprehensive approach?

> Yes, I think that the many aspects covered will be useful for people in both the public and private sectors. CEOs also travel halfway around the world to do business these days and are received with due formality. They do not have to inspect a Guard of Honour, but on many fronts showing respect and the attendant protocol are still important. As I said before, they also need to know about the history, culture, traditions, geography, and religion of the country concerned, and they will be faced with the same questions and circumstances as someone in the public sector. So I can see the value of such a book for anyone who operates in the international arena and certainly not just in the public sector. I think that this book will be very useful. It has great value which will extend far beyond national borders. We were just talking about the Baltic States, but there are many other instances too where people may be searching for suitable forms of protocol like those so clearly presented in your book. I would therefore heartily recommend this volume to everyone working in an international corporate or diplomatic

environment and for any country looking for the best way to apply international protocol.

My wife once gave lessons in France to a number of diplomats, and she mentioned that when you are hosting a dinner at home for a number of international guests, you must select a seating arrangement that will cause as few social difficulties as possible. You must bear in mind the languages spoken by your guests and not seat people next to each other who cannot speak to one another for the whole evening. In these sorts of situations, practicality must prevail. Everything must be geared towards making everyone feel comfortable. In a situation where the spouse of a leader does not speak any foreign languages, then you must ensure that an interpreter is seated between you and her, so that you can still have a conversation. In the same way, you also need to bear in mind your guests' political backgrounds. When you host a dinner at home you need to avoid situations that could lead to difficulties later. Thus, even the 'lesser' protocol which might seem unimportant is actually just as important. Nor should you forget to mention specific guests in your speech. If you remember the names of eight out of ten people, and forget two, that can be very embarrassing.

To end our interview, would you share an anecdote or something else with us? Something interesting and useful for the reader?

I have a nice example. As secretary-general of NATO you have constant protection, no matter what you are doing, which is quite special. When you travel with your wife, she should be taken care of as well. When you are driven around in armoured cars weighing thousands of kilos with doors that you can't even get open yourself, you need to make sure that someone is taking care of your wife, too. This wasn't really a problem for my predecessors as their wives did not get involved. My wife, I am glad to say, came with me to Brussels. The first time we arrived in one of our member states, we stopped in front of the hotel in our armoured car and the right rear passenger door, where I was seated, was opened. As an aside, you might wonder whether the proper etiquette should be followed here, where normally in a left-hand drive car your spouse would be seated to the right of you; or whether you should follow the protocol, where the most important person on the visit is seated on the right. Thus, I sat on the right, and my wife was to my left. She sat there and could not possibly open her door herself. I made the mistake of just stepping out of the car and shaking hands, surrounded by television cameras, in a country that I had come to for a summit with everyone in attendance. My poor wife was entirely forgotten. From that moment on I always asked for someone on the left door, and remained seated in the car until the left door had been opened and my wife had left the car and come around the back of the vehicle to join me on the right. Only then would I step out, and we could be greeted together. You have to learn quickly when you are in a new position.

We would very much like to thank you for this interesting interview.

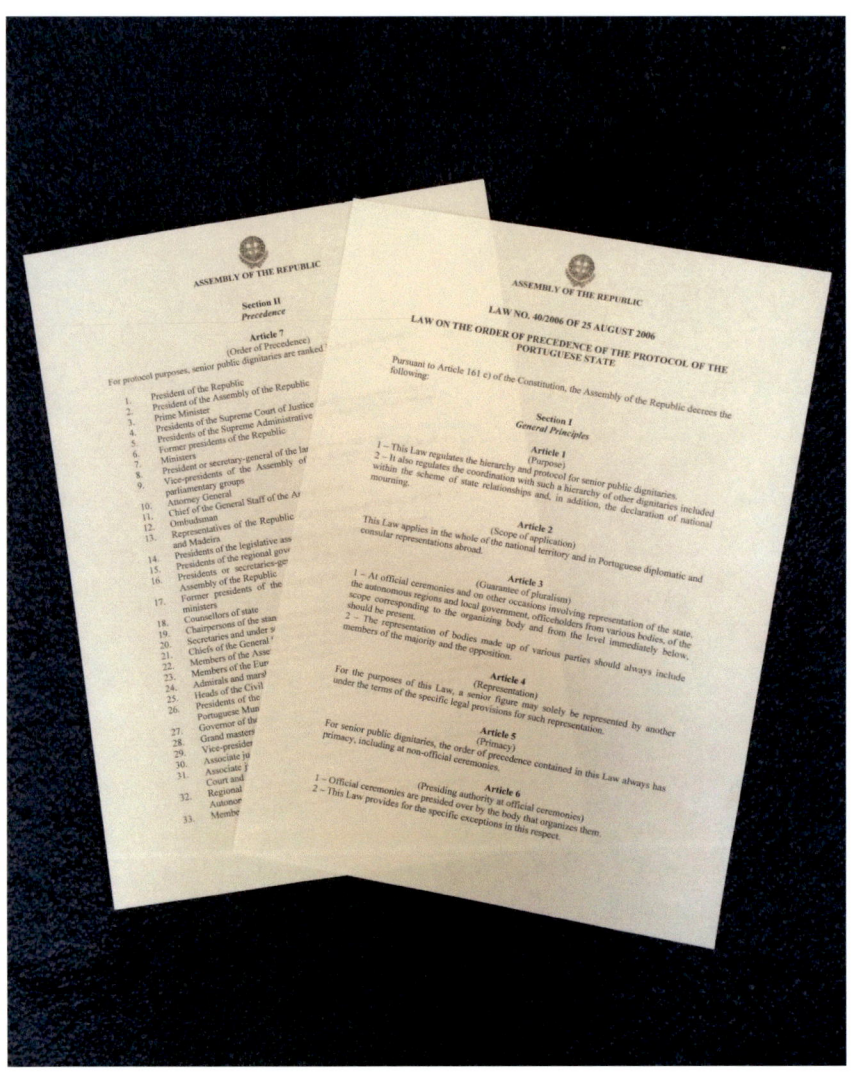

Order of precedence of Portugal

2. Precedence

Introduction and history

The most essential principle of international protocol is the showing of respect and acknowledgement of status, order, and hierarchy of functionaries and the authorities they represent. These rules of precedence are called *préséance* in French, a term that is used widely in the diplomatic world. For centuries, the power and wealth of a country, a dukedom, or a city determined the positions of their representatives. It is in this way that the Knights of the Golden Fleece, together with Philip the Good, Duke of Burgundy, held their ninth chapter meeting in The Hague, in 1456. In the *Grote Kerk* (Great Church), coats of arms were hung from the pillars above the seating places of every knight, and the quality of placement was determined by their wealth and status; the greater their wealth and status, the closer they were seated to Philip the Good. It goes without saying that over time, this led to uncomfortable or even violent situations, where one knight felt that his status was higher than another's and vice versa. In short, such a subjective way of determining the status of individuals was not ideal. In 1814 and 1815, in the aftermath of the Napoleonic Wars, the Congress of Vienna, under the leadership of the victorious powers Prussia, Austria, Russia, and Great Britain, was held to reconstruct the political and institutional order in Europe. During the congress, the Commission for Precedence According to Protocol borrowed from the notion of equality that had already been proclaimed twenty-five years earlier during the French Revolution in the second word of the motto *Liberté, Égalité, Fraternité*. On 19 March 1815, after meeting four times since December 1814, the commission decided that precedence could only be given to diplomats on the basis of their accreditation date, the date that the diplomat in question had presented his credentials to the receiving head of state. In other words, the more years of service in a country, the higher one's place on the order of precedence. Under this system, the longest-serving ambassador also acts as *doyen* (dean) of the diplomatic corps, allies or great powers are not given special status or privileges, and the papal legate, or nuncio, is given absolute priority. A nuncio is the ambassador from the Holy See to a government who advocates for the members of the Catholic Church in their host country. In countries that recognise His Holiness as pontiff and head of state, the nuncio is often the dean of the diplomatic corps and thus has priority over other ambassadors. The British representative Cathcart opposed this last point, and said that while his country would provide priority to the pope's representative as a courtesy, this priority would not be 'de jure', which was supported by the Swedish delegate. However, both powers were eventually persuaded to change their views. At the same time, some thought it absurd that the ambassador of a tiny principality should receive the same status as the ambassador from Russia or Great Britain. Others felt that republics should not be given the same status as old kingdoms. Eventually, however, the original plan was adopted, and with it the rules that define international protocol to this day. In the *Vienna Convention on Diplomatic Relations*, set up in Vienna on 18 April, 1961 at the closing of the United Nations Conference on Diplomatic Intercourse and Immunities, these guidelines were adopted once again. In Articles 13.2 and 16 of this convention, it is written:

> *Article 13.2*
> *The order of presentation of credentials or of a true copy thereof will be determined by the date and time of the arrival of the head of the mission.*
>
> *Article 16*
> *Heads of mission shall take precedence in their respective classes in the order of the date and time of taking up their functions in accordance with Article 13.*
> *Alterations in the credentials of a head of mission not involving any changes of class shall not affect his precedence.*
> *This article is without prejudice to any practice accepted by the receiving State regarding the precedence of the representative of the Holy See.*

Until the French Revolution, one's birth was deemed more important than one's function. More value was given to noble titles than to the position someone held, whether in politics, academia, or the religious worlds. In the course of the nineteenth century, this began to change as the people began to rebel against the ruling classes. In today's class system, the social position of each individual is determined by their socio-economic position, which is determined by their job or income. Since the French Revolution, in many countries and especially in Western countries, people are placed on the order of precedence by virtue of their function rather than their birth. Of course, this does not entirely apply to monarchies, whose survival is dependent on the continuation of the dynasty. The United Kingdom is an exception, placing nobility high on the order of precedence. Dukes, lords, and barons are placed directly under ambassadors and the highest-ranking functionaries of the royal household. In this case, the concept of equality is clearly not being applied, and it can therefore not be seen as a universally accepted concept. We will return to the order of precedence in different countries later in this chapter.

As for the definition of precedence, it can generally be described as 'the rules concerning priority, arrangement, or the creation of a concrete hierarchy of functionaries in public positions according to public interest.' The right of priority is based on the position that the functionaries occupy, whether in the judiciary, the military, or the civil service. The hierarchy of all public positions and official titles in a country is codified in an official order of precedence. Orders of precedence are installed and maintained by national governments and international organisations. In some countries, it is not made public, in order to prevent arguments over hierarchy. Many countries do make their order of precedence public, sending them to anyone who needs access to them in order to make applying the correct order easier. Questions or remarks about the order of precedence can be sent to the government agency responsible for keeping the list, which is often the ministry of Foreign Affairs or the cabinet of the head of state.

Generally, the higher one's political mandate or the greater one's managerial responsibility, the higher one's position in the order of precedence, but this is not always the case, such as with representatives of businesses and non-governmental organisations (NGOs). One's placement on the order of precedence is not always an indication of his or her functionary importance but in many cases an indication of ceremonial or historical relevance instead. In various countries, the order of precedence can include members of a royal household, noble families, former prime ministers, and widows of former presidents to name a few. In certain circles, great importance is attached to the order of precedence in order to avoid offending anyone or souring otherwise good relations.

On national orders of precedence, the head of state is usually at the very top. In principle, the head of state represents all citizens of that country and is therefore the highest in rank. In many countries, priority is not transferrable, except in the case of a head of state. If a head of state delegates his or her chief of the Military House to go to a remembrance ceremony, the chief then receives the place of honour that would be reserved for the head of state. If, for example, a prime minister sends his or her secretary-general, that representative would not take the same place in the ceremony as the prime minister but would be placed in his or her own spot in the order of precedence.

Comparison of countries around the world

The position in each country of the head of state is unquestionable. However, each country adjusts the order of positions below the head of state according to their own political, social, and cultural perspectives. Every country honours different functionaries and places them in various positions on the order of precedence, or perhaps even not at all. In order to provide insight into these differences and relationships, twenty-one orders of precedence have been laid next to each other and compared. In alphabetical order, the lists used were from Argentina, Australia, Belgium, Brazil, Canada, France, Germany, India, Israel, Italy, Malaysia, the Netherlands, New Zealand, Pakistan, the Philippines, South Africa, Spain, Switzerland, Turkey, the United Kingdom, and the United States. The guidelines prescribed by the United Nations and the European Commission have also been taken into account. Explanations of the differences between orders of precedence concerning various functionaries are given below.

Dean of the Diplomatic Corps

Following the Vienna Convention on Diplomatic Relations, the nuncio is the dean of the Diplomatic Corps in, among others, Argentina, Belgium, the European Commission, the Philippines, and Switzerland. In most other countries, this position is held by the longest-serving ambassador. In Italy, the system is adjusted, and the ambassadors are ordered on the basis of the date when diplomatic relations between their country and Italy were realised.

Representatives of International Organisations

Some countries do not have a single representative of an international organisation on their order of precedence, including France and the United Kingdom. However, most countries have included functionaries from international organisations. In the Netherlands, the president of the International Court of Justice, based in the Peace Palace in The Hague, is the highest-placed functionary on the order of precedence after the head of state. The International Court of Justice is the highest judicial organ of the United Nations. In Germany, the secretary-general of the United Nations, the secretary-general of NATO, the chairmen of the European Parliament, the Council of Europe, and the European Commission are on the order of precedence, as are each European commissioner and the secretary-general of the Council of Europe, even if these functionaries are not resident in Germany.

In Belgium, the chairman of the European Parliament comes directly after the nuncio, and shortly thereafter the chairman and members of the Council of the European Union, the chairman of the European Commission, the secretary-general of NATO, foreign ambassadors, the president of the International Court of Justice in The Hague, the president of the Court of Justice of the European Union, and the justices of the International Court of Justice in The Hague. The Philippines and Malaysia have several representatives of UN member states on their lists. In the United States, the secretary of state is followed by the president of the United Nations General Assembly (when the General Assembly is in session) and the secretary-general of the United Nations. In the case that the General Assembly is not in session, the secretary-general precedes the president of the General Assembly. Ambassadors then directly follow on the order of precedence. Further down, the list also includes permanent representatives of UN member states as well as the heads of several international organisations such as the Organization of American States (OAS), the IMF, the World Bank, and NATO.

Legislative, Executive, and Judiciary Order

It is also important to note the several different implementations of precedence with regards to the three branches of government – the legislature, the executive, and the judiciary. For countries with bicameral legislatures, the order of precedence for the two is given by a U for the upper house, and an L for the lower house. In Belgium (L/U), Germany (L/U), the Netherlands (U/L), and Turkey, the legislature precedes the executive, and the judiciary closes the ranks. In the vast majority of countries, however, the executive takes precedence over the legislature and the judiciary. This is the case in Argentina (U/L), Australia (U/L following date of appointment), Brazil (U/L), France (U/L), Israel (where the Knesset is the unicameral legislature), Italy (U/L), New Zealand, Pakistan (U/L), the Philippines (U/L), Spain (L/U), the United Kingdom (U/L), and the United States (U/L). An order whereby the executive takes precedence, and is then followed by the judiciary and then the legislature, is used in Canada (U/L), Malaysia (U/L), and South Africa. It is worth noting that in most of the aforementioned countries, the upper house precedes the lower house.

The Leader of the Opposition

In Australia, Canada, India, Israel, New Zealand, Pakistan, Spain, and Turkey, the leader of the opposition is also given a specific place in the order of precedence alongside the representatives in the upper and lower houses, which is usually between the head of the legislature and the rest of the members.

Defence

In the Netherlands, the commander of the armed forces comes between the representatives of the national government and the provincial representatives. The rest of the military top brass follows below. In Turkey and Argentina, the military top brass also follows almost directly after the cabinet. In France, the commander of the armed forces is placed between the senators and the mayor of Paris. In India, Malaysia, and Canada, the military top brass follows directly after the lower house of the legislature, while in Italy, they directly precede it. In Australia, the commander of the armed forces is placed between the chief justice of the Federal Court of Australia and the lower house of the legislature. In Brazil, the military top brass are placed between the state ministers and foreign ambassadors. In Pakistan, the military top brass follows directly after the advisors to the president and directly before foreign ambassadors. In the United States, the senators, governors, representatives of the House, political assistants to the president, and the directors of the FBI and CIA all precede the top military brass. In New Zealand, the military top brass are at the bottom of the order of precedence, far below representatives, justices, mayors, former prime ministers, and former ministers.

Political Advisors to Heads of State or the Court

In the Netherlands, the highest functionaries of the court are placed between the ministers and the secretaries of state. In Argentina and the Philippines, the senior advisor to the president also follows directly after the cabinet. In Belgium, they follow directly after the chairman of the Supreme Court. In the United States, political assistants to the president follow directly after senators, governors, and representatives. In Pakistan, advisors to the president follow directly after the alternating chairmen of the upper and lower houses of the legislature and precede the military top brass. In Brazil, the chief of staff is more or less equal to top military officials.

Regional and Local Governments

Directors of regional authorities (such as provinces, states, *Bundesländer*, cantons, etc.) almost always precede the directors of local authorities (such as cities and towns) due to the notion of greater responsibility. Exceptions are sometimes made for the mayors of national capitals who often take a prominent place in the order of precedence.

Former Functionaries and Widows of Former Heads of State

In countries such as Belgium, Germany, the Netherlands, and the United Kingdom, these categories are not explicitly outlined in the order of precedence. In Argentina, Australia, Canada, France, India, Malaysia, New Zealand, Pakistan, the Philippines, South Africa, Spain, and the United States, one or both of these categories have places explicitly defined in the order of precedence.

The Nobility

The United Kingdom is the only country where the nobility is specifically given places on the order of precedence where they take a prominent place. Distinctions are made between dukes, marquises, lords, viscounts, and barons. In the Netherlands, the chancellor of the Netherlands Orders of Knighthood and the chairman of the High Council of Nobility are given a place in the order of precedence.

Bearers of High Honours and Heads of National Organisations

In Australia, Belgium, France, India, Malaysia, the Netherlands, New Zealand, and the United Kingdom, the bearers of the highest national honours are honoured with prominent places in the order of precedence. In the Netherlands, for example, Knights of the Military William Order take precedence over the commander of the armed forces. In the United Kingdom, bearers of the following distinctions are named by name on the order of precedence: Baronets (bearers of the highest distinction in the British Honours system), the Victoria Cross, the George Cross, the Most Noble Order of the Garter, the Most Ancient and Most Noble Order of the Thistle, the Most Honourable Order of the Bath, the Most Distinguished Order of Saint Michael and Saint George, the Royal Victorian Order, and the Most Excellent Order of the British Empire. In India, the bearers of the *Bharat Ratna* are placed between the members of the cabinet and foreign ambassadors.

Religious Representatives

In Argentina, Belgium, Brazil, Germany, Italy, and the United Kingdom, only Christian representatives are named on the order of precedence (such as archbishops and cardinals). The archbishops of Canterbury and York are placed very high, following directly after the British royal family. In Australia, Canada, the Netherlands, and New Zealand, all religious communities are represented on the order of precedence and all share the same place. Israel has also represented all religious communities but places the chief rabbis higher than the representatives of other religious communities. In Malaysia, Pakistan, and the Philippines, representatives of Islamic communities are on the list. In India, France, and the United States, religious representatives are not on the order of precedence. For India, this is notable, since Hinduism and the caste system take important places in society.

Sociocultural Institutions

In the Netherlands, Pakistan, and Turkey, the directors of certain overarching organisations are included in the order of precedence, but not the directors of individual institutions or businesses. In Argentina, the specific directors of national museums are included.

Universities

In Argentina, Brazil, Malaysia, the Netherlands, Pakistan, and Turkey, *rectores magnifici* and chancellors are specifically named on the order of precedence. Precedence among the universities is often decided by their age.

Businesses

As mentioned earlier, orders of precedence do not include representatives from businesses. CEOs of multinationals are also not given a formal place, irrespective of their particular and important positions in society. In general, the world's top CEOs sometimes take a place in the hierarchy underneath the president of the national bank or the chairman of the national chamber of commerce. With regards to hierarchy, businesses themselves can be sorted by their entry into the stock exchange of the country in question.

Various facts, trivia, and guidelines

- Precedence of heads of state: In monarchies, the hierarchy of heads of state should follow their accession to the throne, and in republics, by the date they were elected. In many monarchies, crowned heads of state

have priority over presidents, and in several Roman Catholic countries, the Pope takes the highest possible place, above secular heads of state.
- Precedence of Dutch ministries is decided by the order in which they are placed on the State Budget.
- Precedence of Spanish ministries is decided by the date of their formation.
- Political parties can be ordered on the basis of their size.
- In equal positions on the order of precedence, precedence is often decided by age, with the oldest going first.
- At a meeting between equal functionaries in the Netherlands, the Dutch functionary is, in effect, the host. In a meeting of ministers of agriculture taking place in the Netherlands, for example, the Dutch minister of agriculture would take the highest place.
- In 1818, the Congress of Aix-la-Chapelle (modern-day Aachen) was held, where it was decided that countries should sign treaties in alphabetical order. Many international organisations still use this principle in the placement of their representatives in place of priority based on the date of presentation of credentials which is in use in bilateral diplomacy. In practice, the alphabetical order in a specific language is used. French and English are the most common of these languages. Within the European Union, it has been decided that alphabetical order is based on the name of the country in the country's own language.
- Alphabetical order is also used more frequently in the United Nations than the date of admission. For the opening of the General Assembly's regular session, lots are pulled in order to decide which country comes first, so that different countries alternate sitting in front. This is then the order used at sessions of the General Assembly, as well as other UN organs, as well as the order of precedence used with permanent representatives at other events. At UN headquarters, the English alphabetical order is used, but if the body of the UN is in a French-speaking country, the French alphabetical order is used. Countries can have different preferences for how they should be entered into the order of precedence, which makes for some notable variations in the order of countries. For example, the Democratic Republic of Congo is placed under 'C' in the alphabet, while the United Republic of Tanzania is placed under 'U.'
- Permanent representatives of NATO are seated alphabetically in English or French order. The European Council uses various orders: the council of ministers is ordered by date of accession, the assembly is ordered by age, and official meetings of the council are ordered according to French alphabetical order.

- The order of the United States' fifty states is based on the date of entry to the union. Delaware is first (8 December 1787), and Hawaii is last (21 August 1959).
- American senators are ordered according to their length of service. If they entered the Senate on the same date, they can be ordered by the date of their state's entry to the union or otherwise in alphabetical order.
- Governors of American states come after the president and vice-president on the order of precedence if they are in their own state. Otherwise, they follow senators.
- Commonwealth countries do not have ambassadors to each other's countries, but instead high commissioners.
- An ambassador-at-large is an ambassador who also represents their own country in neighbouring countries to their host country, or sometimes also in international organisations such as the UN or the EU.
- Belgium has three kinds of diplomats: bilateral ambassadors with Belgium, permanent representatives (PRs) to the European Union, and permanent representatives to NATO.

  Ambassadors take priority over permanent representatives (the same goes for the United States and Switzerland). Since 1973, the following rule is also in place in Belgium: in even years (from September 1 to August 31), PRs to NATO take priority over PRs to the EU. In odd years, the opposite is true. Order by PRs to the EU is alphabetical by the name of the country in the country's language, changing every six months by which country is currently chairman.
- On the national level, a head of state is the highest in order, but following European customs, the European Parliament is the highest institution within the EU, coming before the European Council and Commission. That means that the chairman of the European Parliament is above all national and European representatives.
- Mutual precedence between diplomats and co-workers at a diplomatic post is the responsibility of the diplomatic post itself.
- If a diplomat accredited to the EU receives heads of mission, such as bilateral ambassadors and permanent representatives to NATO or the EU, the diplomats accredited to the EU receive priority over other heads of mission.
- The principal organs of the UN in order of importance are: General Assembly, Security Council, Economic and Social Council, Trusteeship Council, International Court of Justice, and Secretariat (according to Article 7 of the UN charter).

- Precedence in the UN: president of the General Assembly, secretary-general, heads of government of member states, vice-presidents of the General Assembly, chairman of the Security Council.
- Precedence in NATO: heads of government, secretary-general, ministers of foreign affairs, permanent representatives.
- The Association of Southeast Asian Nations (ASEAN) does not make a distinction between heads of state and heads of government in its order of precedence. ASEAN summits rotate between member states in alphabetical order.
- Precedence in the Arab League: representatives are ranked according to date of entry of their country.
- Precedence at the International Criminal Court: representatives are ranked according to the date of their countries' ratification of the Rome Statute of the International Criminal Court and for representatives of non-member states the English alphabet is used.
- Precedence at the Olympic Games: description can be found in the article of Mr Andrea Miliccia after chapter 7.
- Argentina: precedence of representatives is by surname in alphabetical order, and governors are ordered by the state they represent in alphabetical order.
- Australia: the president of the Senate and Speaker of the House are in order of appointment; in the case that they share the same date, the president of the Senate has precedence. Premiers of states are ordered by population of their states. Mayors of state capitals are ordered by population of their cities. Heads of religious communities are ordered by date of appointment.
- Canada: religious leaders are equal, and ordered by seniority.
- Malaysia: the king and queen are at the top, followed by rulers in chronological order of their crowning (such as sultans and raja).
- The directors general of the UN offices in Geneva and Vienna, as official representatives of the secretary-general of the United Nations, take precedence over permanent representatives.
- Precedence of specialised agencies and UN-related organisations in Geneva: ILO, FAO, UNESCO, WHO, the World Bank, IMF, ITU, WMO, IMO, WIPO, UNIDO, IAEA, WTO.
- Precedence of UN funds and programmes in Geneva: UNDP, UNCTAD, UNEP, UNHCR, UNRWA, UNICEF, UNFPA, WFP, UNODC, OHCHR.
- Specialised agencies of the UN are ranked higher due to their higher autonomy than funds and programmes.

- In Vienna and Geneva, UN-related organisations and specialised agencies are ordered by the date that their convention bound them to the UN.
- The UN office in Geneva bases precedence of organisations on the size of the geographical outreach of the organisation's mandate:
    1. Important international organisations (with the UN at the top);
    2. Regional organisations with a political or military character;
    3. Important international organisations with an administrative, economic, social, or cultural character;
    4. Important regional organisations with a non-military character;
    5. Intergovernmental administrative organisations with worldwide or regional power;
    6. International NGOs.
- The International Committee of the Red Cross (ICRC) is the only NGO in Geneva with special status inside international humanitarian law; the chairman has precedence over permanent representatives.
- If two or more parties in Geneva operate on the same level, priority is given to the representative of Geneva as they are the 'host'. If PRs organise an event, they give priority to directors general and secretaries general as a courtesy, and vice versa.
- The area an event takes place in often dictates which PR is given priority vs another, even if there is a great difference in their date of accreditation. For example, a PR accredited to the IAEA (with letters of accreditation from January 2016) attending a conference at the UN office in Vienna (UNOV) on the safe storage of nuclear waste will most likely be given precedence over a PR accredited to UNIDO, even if their letters of accreditation date from before January 2016.
- Businesses can also rank their clients by a sort of order of precedence: big clients, medium clients, and general clients, or oldest clients, clients, and new clients.

From the text above, it should be clear that universal rules governing precedence do not exist, but that several different methods exist instead as guidelines, and these can be altered. These guidelines are extremely useful in the application of protocol for, for example, seating arrangements and the coordination of processions. In the following chapter, this will be explored in greater detail.

Dame Rosalyn Higgins, DBE, QC, former President of the International Court of Justice in The Hague

Dame Rosalyn Higgins, DBE, QC is the former President of the International Court of Justice (ICJ). She was the first female judge elected to the ICJ and was elected president in 2006. She studied at Girton College, University of Cambridge receiving her B.A. degree in 1959, an LL.B. degree in 1962, and earned a J.S.D. degree in 1962 at Yale Law School. Following her education Higgins was a practicing barrister and became a Queen's Counsel (QC) in 1986, and is a bencher of the Inner Temple. Furthermore, her professional appointments included specialist in international law, Royal Institute of International Affairs, visiting fellow, London School of Economics, professor of international law, University of Kent and University of London and vice-president of the British Institute of International and Comparative Law. Higgins is the author of several influential works on international law, including *Problems and Process: International Law and How We Use It* (1994). In October 2009 she was appointed advisor on international law to the British government's inquiry into the Iraq war.

Protocol and the International Court of Justice by Dame Rosalyn Higgins

The term 'Protocol' covers the formal etiquette and code of behaviour, including matters of procedure, of diplomacy and affairs of state.[1]

On 13 February 1946 the General Assembly adopted the Convention on Privileges and Immunities of the United Nations. But although the International Court of Justice is undoubtedly 'the United Nations', being a principal organ, it was from the outset realised that its privileges, immunities and any matters of precedence, could not appropriately be dealt with by the 1946 Convention.

---

[1] 'Protocol' may also mean a memorandum or record of an agreement, often supplementing an agreement. This is not the sense here discussed!

The Statute of the Court, which is annexed to and forms an integral part of the Charter of the United Nations, itself provides in Article 19 that, when engaged on business of the Court, members of the Court would enjoy diplomatic privileges and immunities; and Article 42 lays down that the agents, counsel and advocates of the parties before the Court shall enjoy the privileges and immunities necessary to the independent exercise of their duties.

The founding Members of the United Nations thus determined that the way forward was for there to be an agreement between the Court, and the host country, the Netherlands, on the matter of privileges, immunities and precedence.

Cordial negotiations between the Court and the Netherlands ensued. A Note attached to a letter from President Guerrero of the Court to the Minister of Foreign Affairs of the Netherlands, 26 June 1946, (which affirmed the traditional liberality of the Netherlands) stipulated:

I. As concerns the privileges, immunities, facilities and prerogatives, within the territory of the Netherlands, of members and staff of the International Court of Justice, of other than Dutch nationality:

   (a) The Members of the Court will, in a general way, be accorded the same treatment as heads of diplomatic missions accredited to Her Majesty the Queen of the Netherlands. As regards the privileges, immunities and facilities above mentioned, this provision applies also to the Registrar of the Court and to the Deputy-Registrar when acting for the Registrar.

   (b) The Deputy-Registrar of the Court will, in a general way, be accorded the same treatment as counsellors attached to the diplomatic missions at The Hague. The higher officials of the Court – first secretaries and secretaries – will, in a general way, be accorded the same treatment as secretaries attached to diplomatic missions at The Hague.

   (c) The other officials of the Court will be treated as officials of comparable rank attached to diplomatic missions at The Hague.

II. Members of the Court, the Registrar and higher officials of the Court who are of Dutch nationality, are not answerable to the local jurisdiction for acts performed by them in their official capacity and within the limits of their duties. Netherlands nationals of whatever rank are exempt from direct taxation on the salaries allotted to them from the Court's budget.

III. The wives and unmarried children of Members of the Court, the Registrar and the higher officials of the Court, when of non-Netherlands nationality, shall receive the same treatment as the head of the family, if they live with him and are without profession. The household of the family (governesses, private secretaries, servants, etc.) occupy the same position as is accorded in each case to the domestic staff of diplomatic persons of comparable rank.
IV. Privileges and immunities are granted in the administration of international justice and not in the personal interest of the beneficiary. As concerns officials of the Registry, the Registrar, with the President's approval, may withdraw their immunities, with due regard to the principle laid down in the previous paragraph. In the case of the Registrar, this duty shall rest with the Court.
V. The assessors of the Court and the agents, counsel and advocates of the parties, be accorded such privileges, immunities and facilities and travel as may be required for the independent exercise of their functions. Witnesses and experts shall be accorded the immunities and facilities necessary for the fulfilment of their mission.

The Foreign Minister of the Netherlands on the same day confirmed that this had indeed been agreed – and that the Court and the Netherlands concurred that this agreement did not cover the question of precedence.[2]

Questions of immunity and privileges have generally been unproblematic. Inevitably some unfortunate incidents have occurred in the past. On one occasion, for example, the President of the Court was refused admission to the Binnenhof to hear the Queen's *Prinsjesdag* speech; apparently he had been sent a ticket of the wrong colour.

Fortunately, in the last decade and more, things have much improved and relations between the Court and the host country now proceed on an even keel. On the few occasions that it has arisen, the Dutch Courts have respected the immunities provided for. The Court's members of senior staff are not, of course, exempt from Dutch law, even if they are immune from the jurisdiction to enforce it. Accordingly, traffic tickets have been issued...

Twenty years or more ago, Court Members were advised that the Court's immunity provisions precluded them from paying. Members often wished to pay for occasional parking transgressions, and there followed a period in which Members could pay, making clear, that this

---

2   All these documents may be found at www.icj-cij.org/docket/index.

was not to be regarded as a waiver of the immunity of the Court's Members. Yet more recently, Members simply pay, if they choose for parking offences, *simpliciter*.

Among the privileges allowed by the Netherlands government is for a judge to buy a car free of tax (within a certain period before departure). That much appreciated provision has been refined over the years.

The letters between the Court and the Netherlands Foreign Minister of 26 June 1946 explicitly stated that the question of precedence remained outside that Agreement. That matter was addressed in a later letter from the Minister of Foreign Affairs of the Netherlands to the President of the International Court, 25 February 1971.

It was agreed that 'the President of the International Court of Justice would take precedence over all diplomats, ambassadors and ministers, accredited to Her Majesty the Queen of the Netherlands, including the Dean of the Diplomatic Corps'.

The example was offered, in the text, that first would come the President of the International Court of Justice, then the Dean of the Diplomatic Corps, then the Vice-President of the Court, then the next senior diplomat, then the next senior judge, and so on.[3]

From 1971 until relatively recently, this has been acted on without difficulties at various functions in The Hague where the issue of precedence has arisen.

From the perspective of the Netherlands government, the provisions of this longstanding agreement were seen no longer to be appropriate once the ICTY and ICC were established, making their seats in The Hague. As the ICTY was to be of temporary duration, the matter was broached but never pressed to any conclusion. The arrival of the International Criminal Court was a different matter. It was a permanent court, of great legal and political importance.

Discrete enquiries were made of the International Court's President as to whether the Court might entertain the idea of the President of the International Criminal Court assuming the third place of precedence. Some in the Court's number might understand that the 1971 Agreement on precedence was now problematic for the country by 2006 was host also to other tribunals, and to the ICC. But the Court has taken the position that the 1971 Agreement is an international agreement nonetheless.

---

3   It is specified that if the President is absent, the Vice-President shall take his/her place in the precedence line.

And the International Court of Justice remained, by virtue of the Charter, the principal judicial organ of the United Nations Charter.

No proposal for revision of the 1971 letter has been made by the Netherlands. But in recent years the Netherlands Protocol has arranged matters so that the President of the International Criminal Court does indeed take the third place in the order of precedence.

This complicated matter, in which the position of all concerned may be understood, is undoubtedly awkward. At the same time, relations between the International Court of Justice – the Netherlands are excellent, as they are between the ICJ and the ICC, and among the many various judges working in the Netherlands.

Ushers of the Protocolbureau

3. Seating arrangements and order of processions

Introduction

After offering insight into the rules of precedence (*préséance*), in this chapter we describe how these rules may be applied to seating arrangements and order of processions. The main focus will be on table seating plans, assigning attendees to rows and blocks, and specific arrangements for public audiences and press conferences, processions, and vehicles.

Seating arrangements are not merely formalities, but have had for centuries a symbolic connotation that sometimes caused severe rank disputes. This is why the legendary King Arthur introduced the Round Table, around which he gathered with his knights. While we cannot establish whether there was ever an actual Round Table or a different table of this kind, according to tradition, everyone seated at this table had equal status, no one took precedence over the other attendees, and everyone had an opportunity to have their say. In the Middle Ages, guests invited to a banquet were often seated along one side of a long, rectangular table, leaving the other side free for clearing the table and entertainment. At the court of Louis XIV, they started arranging tables in a U-shaped plan so that there were more opportunities for interaction. Today, one can find a wide variety of table arrangements depending on the event's location and objective and its level of formality.

One should by no means slavishly adhere to *préséance* at all times when determining seating arrangements. The rules of precedence should be seen as an aid, since functionality prevails. A seating arrangement that conforms to protocol yet proves impractical does not contribute anything to the occasion and may well be detrimental to the success of an event that is intended to strengthen mutual relations. It is important to respect the other party's requirements. For example, avoid seating people next to one another who will be unable to converse due to language differences. In addition, one needs to take account of personal affinities or – even more important – personal antipathies and political sensitivities. A well-considered seating arrangement can make a very tangible contribution to an event's overall success. Age and seniority, position and rank, personal accomplishments, and gender may all influence where an individual is seated. The following section offers a basic introduction to the general guidelines for seating plans. These rules are adhered to by the diplomatic corps in functions more or less the world over. At all times, the host bears responsibility for where his or her guests are seated. However, to ensure, that the guests' positions and expectations are given the attention they are due, it may be useful to adhere to the following guidelines. Specific examples of socially distanced seating arrangements during the COVID-19 pandemic can be found in chapter 10.

Tables

One can distinguish two types of seating plan in Western protocol: the English arrangement and the French arrangement. In the English option, the hostess and host are seated at the head of the table; in the French variant, the hostess and host are seated opposite one another along the middle section of the table. If the company includes a guest of honour, he or she is

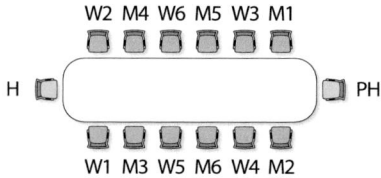

English seating according to precedence, with gender differentiation

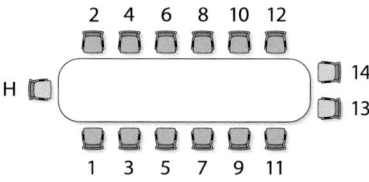

English seating with only a host

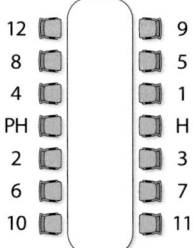

French seating according to precedence; no gender specification

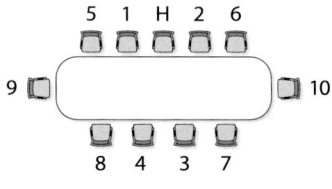

French seating with only a host

LEGEND

H	Host	HoS	Head of state
PH	Partner of host	PHoS	Partner of head of state
Co H	Co-host	M1	Male person 1
GoH	Guest of honour	W1	Female person 1
PGoH	Partner of guest of honour	D	Driver
G	Guest	PG	Partner of guest

seated directly opposite the host with the hostess on his or her right-hand side. Conversely, the partner of the guest of honour is seated to the right of the host.

The illustrations on the previous page offer examples of both variants. These examples feature seating arrangements for married couples as well as functional arrangements with no reference to gender, and seating arrangements where only a host is involved.

In other words, as a rule, the most important guests (the guest of honour and his or her spouse) are seated to the right of the host or hostess. However, in the case of a working dinner or lunch, this guest may also be seated directly opposite the host or hostess. The guest who follows in terms of precedence is seated to the left of the host or hostess, the guest who comes next is seated to the right of the guest of honour, etc. However, according to the United Nations, the place of honour can be to the left of the host or hostess in some countries as well.

One exception to the above guidelines are heads of state and their partner. In table arrangements that involve a head of state and partner, they are seated in the most prominent position, so they switch with the host and hostess. This results in placing the hostess to the right of the head of state and the host to the right of the head of state's partner.

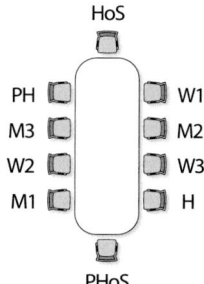

English seating with head of state

In the event that there is only a host or a hostess, he or she may choose to assign a co-host who might sit opposite him or her.

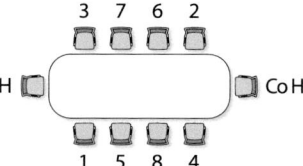

English seating with host and co-host

In the event that there is only a host or a hostess, the guest of honour might be seated across from the host or hostess.

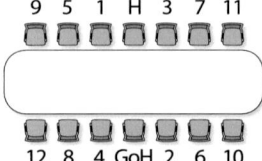

French seating with host and guest of honour

If the guest of honour is to be given the place of honour at the table, the host should avoid inviting persons of higher rank. However, when a higher-ranking guest is invited, the host may choose
- to make the senior guest the co-host, if it is a stag function (event without spouses);
- to ask the higher-ranking guest to waive his right in favour of the guest of honour;
- to divide the seating between two or more tables if there is a delicate situation regarding ranking and if the number of guests warrants it.

In general, husbands and wives are not seated next to each other and male and female guests are interspersed, including guest of honour with spouse.

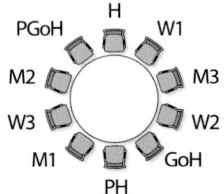

Round table with couples, including guest of honour, opposite to each other

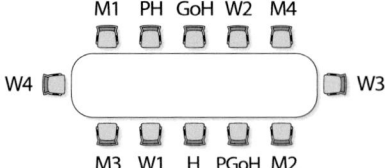

French seating with couples, including guest of honour

Unmarried or engaged couples may be seated next to each other, but could be interspersed as well. In the Middle East, Central Asia and the Far East, however, it is very common to place all couples next to each other.

As illustrated before, when attending an event with her husband, a woman is usually accorded and seated by his rank. For example, the wife of the man to the right of the hostess normally would sit at the right of the host. When the woman, attending with her husband, holds an official position herself, she would then be seated in her official place. If a non-ranking woman attends an event without her husband, she is seated as invited guest without rank.

When unmarried couples attend a function together, the non-ranking partner may be seated, as a courtesy, with equivalent rank to the ranking partner as well.

As of mid-2015, eighteen countries (Argentina, Belgium, Brazil, Canada, Denmark, France, Iceland, Luxembourg, the Netherlands, New Zealand, Norway, Portugal, South Africa, Spain, Sweden, the United Kingdom, the United States, and Uruguay) and certain sub-jurisdictions allow same-sex couples to marry. Keeping these countries in mind when making seating arrangements, treat same-sex couples in the same manner as male-female couples.

In cases where you are organising a dinner in a country where polygamy is allowed, it is customary to only invite one spouse.

If more than one table is used during an event and spouses are present, husbands and wives, including the host and hostess, normally sit at separate tables.

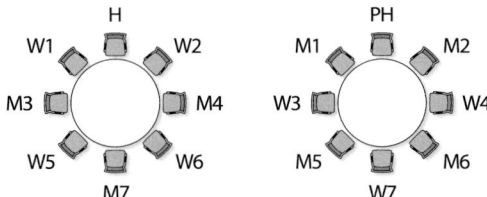

Two round tables with couples spread

In the aforementioned case where the host and hostess are seated at separate tables, they could each choose co-hosts and co-hostesses who are typically high-ranking guests or fellow colleagues.

While seating two men or women directly beside one another is not a preferable arrangement, it is considered acceptable. Placement of a woman at the end of a rectangular table is also not desirable but sometimes occurs out of necessity. To avoid this, the solution is to seat two females together; that is, move the third and seventh females together, and move the fifth male to the position of the seventh female at the end of the table.

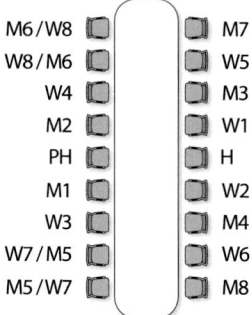

French seating with host and hostess, with option for no women on end of table

To seat eight, twelve, sixteen people (or any multiple of four) without two men or two women sitting together, the hostess sits to the right of the seat that is properly hers, so she switches with the male guest of honour.

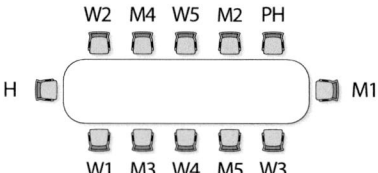

English seating with couples, host and male 1 on head of table

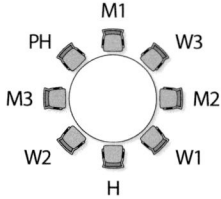

Round table with couples, host and male 1 opposite each other

Tables that are shaped like a U or a horseshoe are mainly used during gala dinners and weddings. They may be considered formal.

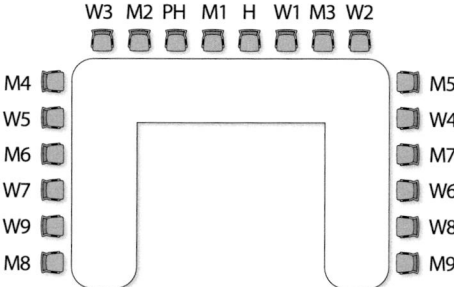

U-shape table with couples only on one side of the table

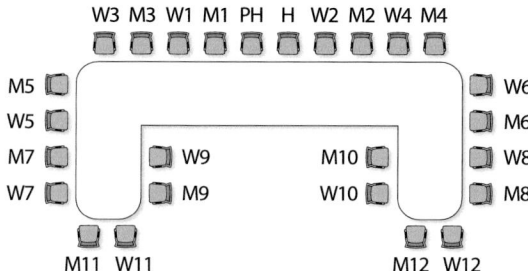

U-shape table with couples next to each other on all sides of the table

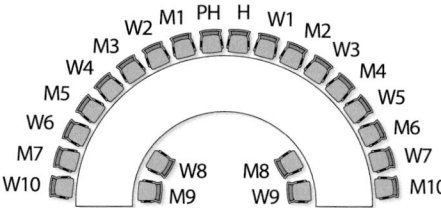

Horseshoe table with couples

If the event will be attended by a relatively large number of guests, the host may opt for a 'comb plan': a head table positioned at a ninety degree angle to a series of secondary tables. The host and hostess seat the guests of honour between them in an orderly arrangement. See illustration on the next page.

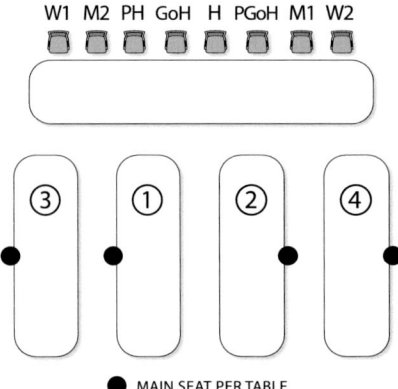

State banquet with one long main table and four other long tables

In case of a female host the seating arrangement of the main guests could also be:

PH – PGoH – GoH – H
or
GoH – H – PH – PGoH
(as seen from the observer).

In cases where the event is attended by a foreign official, this representative customarily takes precedence over his or her colleague from the host country. As such, for example, in an American home, foreign guests take precedence over Americans of comparable rank.

Delegations participating in bilateral events are often mixed during an official dinner since these occasions also have a strong social component. However, in the case of a work-oriented lunch or meeting, the delegations are generally seated opposite one another in order to emphasise the business nature of the occasion. The guests would normally be seated facing the windows. The host, on the other hand, is seated facing the room entrance, so that he or she can make eye contact with waiting staff and other support staff.

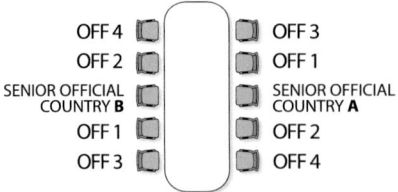

Official delegation meeting, parties opposite each other

In seating high-ranking guests, the host should not only take their position into account but also the objective of their visit and the nature of the occasion. Sensitivity to guests' interests can make the occasion much more enjoyable.

At an official dinner where there are guests without protocol ranking, the seating may be based on personal or scholastic achievement, mutual interests, social prominence, age, and closeness of friendship. When foreigners are present, linguistic ability may be a deciding factor in the seating. So, non-ranking guests may be seated between ranking guests to further interests and conversation.

As mentioned in Chapter 2, owners and/or CEOs of private sector firms do not have a specific position in the hierarchy affecting order of placement, nor are they included in any orders of precedence. However, CEOs and public officials, diplomats, and members of government are often mingled in seating arrangements, in order to encourage and intensify business and diplomatic interaction.

During dinners organised for business relations, private sector firms often seat clients next to their assigned account managers, in order to strengthen their mutual relationship.

Usually, NGO members are also not taken into account in protocol rules, but at events like diplomatic working luncheons or dinners, they are frequently invited, and the question of their seating depends very much on the nature of the discussion. If the theme of the debate is such that the NGOs may provide an important contribution, they may be seated more favourably than strict protocol rules would permit.

***

Before drawing up a seating plan, the host should establish an order for the list of invitees. In the case of official representatives, one can refer to established guidelines for order of precedence. Where required, one may start by dividing the attendees into distinct groups (the group of ambassadors, for example). After this, the host establishes the order of the respective groups, followed by the order of precedence within each individual group. In the case of a dinner where guests are seated at a number of different tables, the host first determines the seating arrangement at each individual table, after which the tables themselves are arranged in order of precedence. Determining the right seating plan is all about managing expectations. For this reason alone, it is often quite a challenge to satisfy everyone. But one should make sure that none are likely to object to the precedence that has been accorded to them. In this regard it is highly recommended not to announce the final seating plan or parts of it in advance (it is appropriate though to provide the guest list and seating arrangements to the guest of honour).

The seating plan should also appoint a co-host to each table. As a rule, the most important guests are seated at the host's table (head table). Moreover, secondary tables are also ordered according to precedence: the nearer a table is positioned to the head table, the more prominent it is.

At medium- to large-scale events, one could place a seating chart in the entrance hall so that each guest may find his or her table before entering the dining room. Seating cards are normally used when there are more than eight guests. Place them above the plates with the names (and titles if useful and appropriate) visible to the guests seated on either side. So, for the benefit of the guests across the table, consider printing the names on the back of the cards as well.

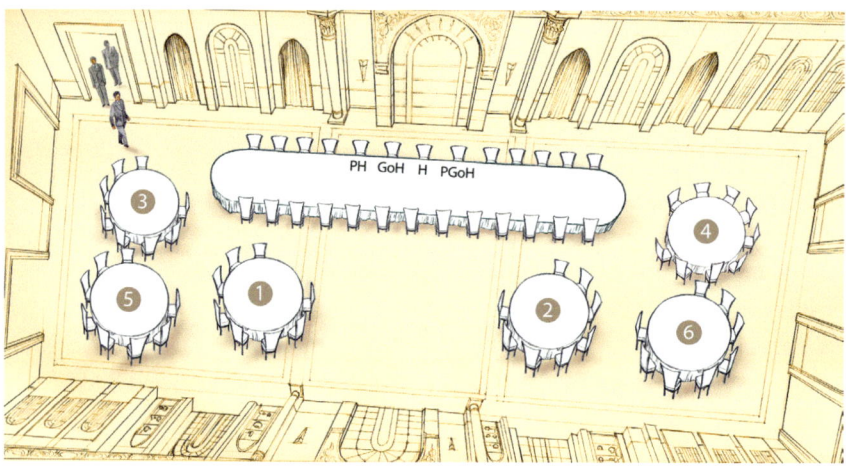

Overview room lay-out with tables numbered

In addition to the English and French options, the present process of globalisation also requires us to gain an understanding of table manners and seating plans customary to Africa, the Middle East and Asia. In the Middle East and North Africa, the guest of honour is often seated next to the host. In Asia, on the other hand, he or she is generally seated opposite the host. In some countries, it is customary to position the head table on a platform, with the main guests – seated along the length of the table – looking out over the hall and the other invitees. In others, hosts opt for a long head table combined with a large number of small round tables. In the Middle East, invitees at a formal dinner will never be seated with their backs to the head of state (see the illustration above).

Examples of seating for state banquets and official dinners / lunches

- At the White House, when more than one table is used, the president hosts one table (with foreign head of state on his right), and the first lady hosts another table (with spouse of foreign head of state on her right). The vice-president may host a table and still other tables may be hosted by the secretary of state or any high-ranking government official.
- At Buckingham Palace a U-shaped table is normally used for state banquets. The queen has the foreign head of state on her right. To her left is the Duke of Edinburgh followed by the spouse of the foreign head of state. The other members of the royal family are scattered around the table in between the other guests.
- At Windsor Castle a long table is normally used for state banquets, making use of the French, rather than the British, seating option. The foreign head of state is seated on the right of the queen and opposite them the Duke of Edinburgh with on his right the spouse of the foreign head of state.
- At many state banquets around the world, when making use of numerous tables and one main round table where both heads of state and their spouses are seated, their order is as follows (seen from the observer): spouse of host – foreign head of state – host – spouse of foreign head of state.

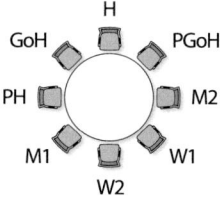

Round table with couples, including guest of honour

- The secretary-general of the United Nations hosts an official lunch (the heads of state luncheon), to which spouses are not invited, on the opening day of every year's General Debate (the lunch is replaced by a dinner if that date falls during the fast period of Ramadan). The luncheon is hosted in honour of the heads of state and government but an invitation is extended to all heads of delegations. With the exception of the five permanent members of the Security Council who can be accompanied by their minister of Foreign Affairs, only one guest per member state is invited. Taking into account the heads of the United Nations agencies present that day as well as a number of under-secretaries-general and some other selected guests, the number of participants comes close to 230, spread over twenty-three tables. The secretary-general and the president of the United States, as host country representative, are always seated together and open the *lunch each with a few remarks. The secretary-general has the president on his right. Geographical distribution for seating arrangements is taken into consideration and ensures that the same country, except for the host country, is not given a seat at the head table in consecutive years.*

Conference settings

For business-related events like conferences, symposia, lectures, annual meetings, or presentations, the organiser often positions rows of chairs in the hall for the invitees to sit on. In most cases, prominent guests are seated in the first row, but this custom may be deviated from for logistical reasons where desirable. In public theatres, for example, row ten may well offer a better view of the stage than the first row. In a case like this, the organiser may prefer to seat the host and guest of honour in row ten, to prevent them from having to strain their necks. In the following examples, however, we have assumed that the most prominent seats are in the first row.

The host is commonly seated in the middle of the first row: the most important guest is seated to his or her right. The second-most important guest is seated to the host's left. The remainder of the first row is then filled, to the left and right of the most prominent guests, with other invitees.

Front row conference seating

A member of the royal family who is not a head of state is also seated on the host's right-hand side. If the occasion is attended by a head of state, he/she is seated in the middle of the row, with the host on his/her right-hand side.

In his paper *Developments in Protocol*, Professor Goldstein describes how states regularly resort to creative approaches to protocol to resolve specific diplomatic challenges.

Creative approaches to protocol are often resorted to for particular purposes. The funeral of Japan's Emperor Hirohito became a major international event, with leaders from around the world attending. The Japanese were delighted when the United States president, George Bush, announced that he would attend. A problem was posed by traditional protocol, which dictates that heads of state be accorded precedence by the date on which they assumed their position. As Bush had only just taken office he would be the most junior in the seating arrangements. Japan, however, wanted to make the most of having the world's most powerful leader present at the funeral of its emperor. The solution hit upon was to treat the funeral as a celebration of Hirohito's life and not as a state event, and it was thus announced that heads of states would be treated in the first instance in the order of countries Hirohito had visited during his life. This resulted in placing the American president at the centre of the front row of attendant heads of state.

Supporting officials are often seated in the second row directly behind the principals, so that they can confer with the host and guest of honour in the front row when required. Members of the security staff are often positioned along the corners of the second or third row. The remaining attendees are seated between these distinct groups according to the rules of precedence.

In larger halls, attendees generally are not seated along a single row. Rather, the room may be divided into a number of blocks separated by aisles. In cases where there is only one aisle, the block to one's right when looking in the direction of the stage is the more prominent of the two. Rows may be assigned alternately from the middle seat or from the central aisle to the side of the hall.

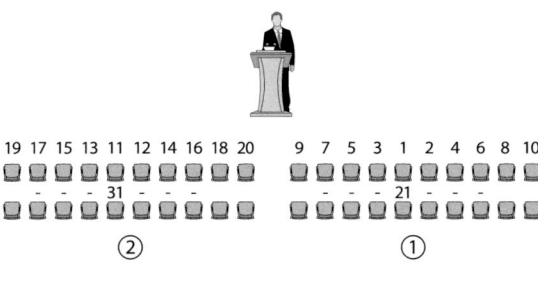

Two blocks conference seating, centred

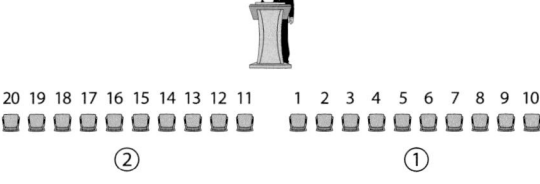

Two blocks conference seating, towards sidelines

If the rows have been ordered into three blocks (with two aisles), the central block is the most prominent of the three, followed by the block to one's right (when facing the stage) and finally the block to one's left. Once again, seating plans within the rows may be arranged in a variety of ways.

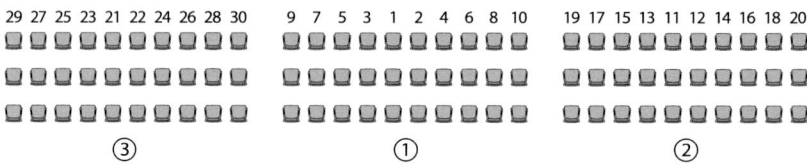

Three blocks conference seating, centred

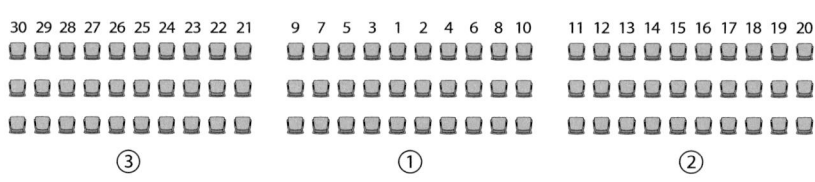

Three blocks conference seating, towards sidelines

If the hall has been divided into four blocks (with three aisles), they are given the following order of prominence from left to right, facing the stage:

Four blocks

The organiser may distinguish different guest categories when ordering the blocks. For example, he may assign one block of seats to the diplomatic corps, one to national representatives, and a third to the other invitees.

In addition to the order of the blocks, the rows and the seating of the invitees, the organiser needs to take the following guidelines into account:
- When the seat next to a head of state or a member of the royal family is temporarily vacant – because the host is called on to make a speech, for example – it is desirable for the individual placed next to this vacant seat to take the host's place during his/her absence.
- When determining the seating plan for a function that is also attended by spouses, the point of departure should be that in principle, the seating of the host authorities and officials takes precedence over the seating of couples (i.e. husband to the left, wife to the right). The organiser is consequently allowed to seat the attending spouse in one of the following rows.
- During events of a markedly social nature – a musical performance, for example – it is permitted to seat couples next to one another.
- Always take latecomers into account. In other words, be sure to reserve a number of seats in the back or along the sides of the hall for these people, so that they can easily take their seats without causing disturbance for the other attendees.
- Try to avoid seating women next to an aisle.

The private sector often also adheres to the above arrangements for economic reasons. For example, a couturier will seat his best clients and prospects in the first row during his fashion show. And during the annual general meeting of a multinational company, the supervisory board generally has pride of place, in acknowledgement of its status of supreme body within the corporation's governance structure.

Many international organisations base their seating plans for assemblies on the agreements made during the Congress of Vienna of 1815: country representatives would be seated at meetings according to alphabetical order. The UN draws lots annually before the beginning of each elected General Assembly. The first country drawn sits first in the front row (at the left-hand side facing the stage) and all other countries are seated afterwards in the alphabetical order starting with the letter of the name of the country selected first (from left to right, from the first row to the last one).

Posing for official group photographs

Generally the same rules apply to posing for official photographs, as for the basic seating arrangements in blocks. The host is commonly positioned in the middle of the first row: the most important guest is positioned to his or her right (seen from the perspective of the host). The second-most important guest is positioned to the host's left. The remainder of the first row is then filled, to the left and right of the most prominent guests, with the other attendees. If more rows are required, the same procedure applies behind the first row.

Seating plans during audiences and press conferences

Likewise, the internationally adopted rule for public audiences is that the guest is always seated to the right of the host (seen from the host's perspective, not those of the cameras), whether they are seated on separate chairs or share a sofa. The guest is also expected to stand on the host's right-hand side during press conferences. In most countries, it is customary to place one's own national flags behind the individuals in question. At the United Nations, however, the host country flag will be on a pole behind the secretary-general and the UN flag behind the government senior official.

If spouses attend the audience, there are a couple of options to seat them. They can sit beside their partners (PGoH-GoH-HoS-PHoS), be seated in a mixed format (PHoS-GoH-HoS-PGoH), be placed as partners together (PHoS-PGoH-GoH-HoS) or take their positions opposite each other (GoH-PGoH on one side and facing them HoS-PHoS).

If members of the official delegations are joining the audience, they might be seated on either side of the room and depending on the layout of the room, they can be seated on couches or chairs.

Order of receiving lines

When a reception or dinner includes a receiving line, it most often comprises, in the following order: H-GoH-PH-PGoH.

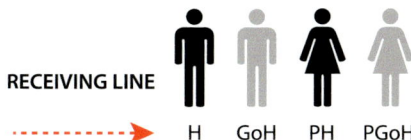

Receiving line

In this way, the host and hostess could both introduce the guest of honour and his spouse to the guests, if necessary. Occasionally, you see the following format as well, in order to keep the guest of honour's couple 'together': H-GoH-PGoH-PH. In general when the guest of honour is responsible for compiling the guest list, the host may choose to place the guest of honour in first position in the receiving line. By doing so the guest of honour can introduce the invited guests to the host: GoH – H – PGoH – PH.

If the receiving line has been assembled for a reception that the invitees can enter and leave as they please, or during a dinner at the host's home, guests generally are not required to move past this line in a specific formal order. In the case of a formal dinner, state dinner, or an official new year's reception attended by the diplomatic corps, in many cases guests receive a calling card upon their arrival, which they then hand to the master of ceremonies or the protocol officer, who reads out their name to the attendees. The guests then make their way to the host and the guest of honour. With couples, the invited guest goes first (regardless of gender) and the partner goes second. At an event hosted by a head of state for the diplomatic corps in his or her country, to avoid offence, the greeting line will be arranged according to when people took up their posts. So in the end, it all comes back to precedence again.

Order of processions

If a group of people is required to move to a different location during an official event, the attending official representatives always walk in a specific order, called a cortege. Once again, the right-hand side is considered most prominent. In other words, the guest of honour is expected to walk to the right of the host. And once again, an exception is made for heads of state: they are accorded the central position, with the host walking on their right-hand side.

The number of people moving in a cortege is often determined by the available space – for example, the width of the aisle in a hall, house of prayer, or street. Usually, the maximum number of people per row is five. In this arrangement, the place of honour is in the centre of the row, with the following order of precedence from left to right: 5-3-1-2-4. When a cortege row consists of three people, the most prominent member is also placed in the centre. In cases where rows are made up of four people, the place of honour is on the right side of the row: 4-3-2-1.

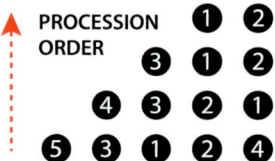

Procession order (number 1 is the host)

Seating in vehicles

In countries with right-hand traffic, the place of honour is found in the rear right-hand side of the vehicle. This is due to the fact that the right-hand side of the vehicle is closest to the pavement, making it the preferred place for alighting. In other words, the guest of honour is seated in the back, on the right. Naturally, in countries with left-hand traffic, this seating order is reversed.

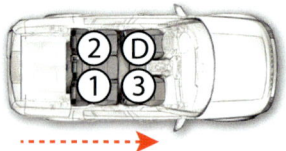 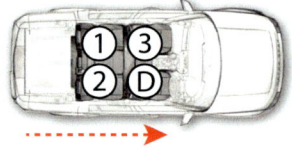

Seating car driving right	Seating car driving left

Out of courtesy, however, if a high-ranking man travels to a social event with his wife, his wife is often seated on the right hand side and he is seated on the left.

***

The above guidelines should by no means be seen as comprehensive, but they can serve as a useful guideline for functional and official occasions. Since every formal occasion is subject to new and unique factors, where this is deemed necessary, the organiser is advised to contact the protocol office of the country where the meeting will be held.

Dr Abiodun Williams, former President of The Hague Institute for Global Justice

Dr Abiodun Williams was the President of The Hague Institute for Global Justice from 2012 to 2017 and is a noted academic in conflict prevention, peacekeeping, and conflict management. Currently he is Professor of the Practice of International Politics at The Fletcher School of Law and Diplomacy, and Director of The Institute for Global Leadership at Tufts University. From 2008 to 2012 he served at the United States Institute of Peace in Washington, DC, first as vice president of the Center for Conflict Analysis and Prevention, and later as senior vice president of the Center for Conflict Management. Prior to joining USIP, Williams served as director of strategic planning for United Nations Secretaries-General Ban Ki-moon and Kofi Annan. From 1994 to 2000 he served in three peacekeeping operations in Macedonia, Haiti, and Bosnia-Herzegovina as special assistant to the special representative of the secretary-general, and political and humanitarian affairs officer. He has held faculty appointments at Georgetown and Rochester.

Protocol at the United Nations and at Think Tanks – A Comparative Perspective by Dr Abiodun Williams

Introduction

To the uninitiated, protocol may sometimes appear an extraneous or outdated aspect of international life. The codes and procedures that are set down in order to guide behaviour are often associated in the popular imagination with unnecessary formality or a preoccupation with tradition at the expense of transacting important business. Given the critical nature of decisions taken at the United Nations, does protocol therefore get in the way of achieving diplomatic breakthroughs?

My own experience in the United Nations and international think tanks suggests just the opposite. In fact, the skepticism that some show towards protocol is based on a fundamental lack of understanding of its purpose and, more broadly, of how international politics is conducted. Diplomacy is the essence of the United Nations, and rather than being superfluous, it is protocol that lubricates relations in order to achieve desired political outcomes.

In an organisation of 193 member states, each with its own assumptions, traditions, and sensitivities, the predictability that protocol brings to interstate relations goes a long way towards avoiding the perceived embarrassments or insults which can be so inimical to intercultural understanding and, ultimately, to political progress.

Those who claim the obsolescence of protocol are blind to its inherent flexibility. Protocol should not be synonymous with a rigid and complex set of rules that stands still even as empires rise and fall. The modern United Nations might share with the court of Louis XIV the operation of an established set of practices that govern its activities, but the expected behaviour at Turtle Bay, the UN's Manhattan seat, has little to do with the *moeurs* of Versailles. As protocol evolves over time, it adapts to fit a given context, as others in this volume have eloquently described.

My own vantage point in this respect has been a privileged one. After serving in UN peacekeeping missions in Macedonia, Haiti, and Bosnia, I spent seven years in the executive office of the UN secretary-general, serving first Kofi Annan and then Ban Ki-moon, as director of strategic planning. From the perspective of the UN's 38th floor – which is occupied by the secretary-general and his staff – protocol is indispensable. A typical daily schedule for the secretary-general might see him meeting with a visiting head of state or government, corresponding with or addressing diplomats in the UN General Assembly or Security Council, and delivering a speech on a contentious issue to a truly global audience.

Deftly managed, these duties can help the secretary-general perform effectively, maximising the United Nations' potential for conflict prevention, the promotion of sustainable development, and the protection of human rights. Missteps in protocol can, however, sour the secretary-general's relations with key states and lead to valuable time being allotted to mending fences rather than building bridges.

Since leaving the United Nations in 2007, I have worked at two international think tanks, the United States Institute for Peace and The Hague Institute for Global Justice. Service in these innovative institutions has given me a new perspective on the 'networked' nature of modern diplomacy, as well as new insights into the malleability of protocol, and how its application in less formal contexts than the UN can also serve policy ends. It is this comparative perspective, which evokes the fluid and 'multi-actor' nature of contemporary international relations, that this brief chapter will offer.

Protocol at the United Nations: Two Cases

Protocol at the United Nations helps to govern the relationships between its bodies as well as between member states. Its daily importance is evident to anyone who visits the organisation from the moment they apply for their credentials.

Two annual events at the UN demonstrate *par excellence* its importance; the general debate of the UN General Assembly (known to insiders as 'UNGA'), which attracts scores of heads of state and government to New York each September, and – less well-known – the annual retreat of the Security Council, organised by the Strategic Planning Unit in the Executive Office of the Secretary-General (EOSG).

The UN General Assembly General Debate
Every autumn, New York is the setting for the largest annual gathering of heads of state and government (in 2015, some 150 world leaders attended). For the United Nations Secretariat, the City of New York, and the government of the United States, this presents a gargantuan organisational undertaking, which is as much about protocol as it is about logistics.

For the host city, and its resigned inhabitants, the annual meeting presents problems of its own. Working closely with local authorities and private businesses, the protocol office of the UN Secretariat must contend with issues as varied as hotel reservations (even in a city as gilded as New York, there are only so many presidential suites), motorcade management, and security.

On the floor of the General Assembly, the speaking order must be decided, and (after speeches by Brazil, awarded this honour in perpetuity in 1947, and the United States, as host country) is subject to considerations around the level of representation, preference, and other criteria such as geographic balance. Nominally limited to fifteen minutes in length, the general debate's tendency to overrun demonstrates the pragmatic flexibility of protocol. While speakers are encouraged to be concise, in order to enable all the world's nations to have their say, the imprudence of calling time on a speech by a head of state is keenly appreciated.

It falls to the head of protocol to escort each speaker from an anteroom to the General Assembly's famous podium (in this respect, the role – whose occupant is privy to many an unguarded moment with a world leader – is one that offers an unparalleled insight into global politics). Another challenge is the organisation of the lunch that follows the opening of the general debate. In few other circumstances do 150 heads of state and government dine together.

Within the office of the UN secretary-general, there are other issues to consider. With a limited amount of time, decisions must be taken about which world leaders will be afforded the opportunity to meet the secretary-general in person. What should the duration of these meetings be, and what will be on the agenda? It is the EOSG that must manage these thorny questions, arranging meetings with around eighty delegations, and preparing talking points to guide the secretary-general's discussion with each dignitary (while taking care to ensure that the secretary-general is provided with the correct speaking notes for a given meeting!). These documents are prepared with the assistance of various UN departments, particularly the Department for Political Affairs (DPA) and the Department for Peacekeeping Operations (DPKO).

Protocol is not merely the rules governing precedence and procedure that are published in a widely-circulated manual,[4] important as these rubrics are. At the general debate, it is often the meetings on the sidelines of the formal session that allow for serious discussion of key global issues. In this sense, it is the formality of the UN's official sessions, including the sometimes dry speeches from the General Assembly floor, that creates an environment where seemingly random interactions can occur. It is, of course, the protocol office that makes these 'chance occurrences' possible, for example by setting up strategically placed cubicles in which high-level tête-à-têtes might take place.

UN Security Council Retreats
Less celebrated than the general debate, but potentially as consequential, is the annual retreat of the Security Council, hosted by the UN secretary-general and organised by the strategic planning unit in his executive office. The relationship between the secretary-general and the Security Council is a delicate and intricate one that must abide by time-honoured

---

4   See https://www.un.int/protocol/pm/manual-protocol

traditions while treading new ground.[5] The secretary-general must consider how he manages relations with the five permanent members of the Council (any of whom, if he is serving his first term, could use their veto power to scupper his chances of re-election), as well as the ten elected members who are sensitive to any suggestion of hierarchy within the Council.

The relationship between the secretary-general and the Security Council is generally governed by formal rules, such as those pertaining to communications. The secretary-general is expected, for example, to transmit communications to the president of the Council (a role that rotates on a monthly basis among the body's members), who will then consult with other missions and report back on behalf of the whole.

The annual retreat, which has taken place 'off-campus' at Greentree or Pocantico near New York City, is an informal event with the dual aim of building rapport and addressing intractable issues outside the more inflexible environment of Turtle Bay. To engender a more relaxed atmosphere, the permanent representatives who serve on the Council are invited to attend the retreat with their spouses (experience suggests that this puts even the most senior diplomats on their best behaviour). This, together with a more casual dress code, creates an informal atmosphere that has proved conducive to productive discussions.

It would be a mistake, however, to conclude that 'real business' is not transacted in settings which are informal and, therefore, devoid of protocol. In the organisation of retreats such as that of the Security Council, UN staff must still consider who should sit where at working sessions or dinners, and who should be housed closest to the secretary-general. Occasionally, practical considerations override assumptions about precedence. What to do, for example, when the bed in the room adjacent to the secretary-general's cannot accommodate the impressive dimensions of an ambassador from an important country? A habitual misunderstanding about the application of protocol is the assumption of its rigidity; in reality, protocol is equally about knowing when to break established rules in the name of good sense. In this case, the ambassador was happily housed in a nearby cottage.

The contrast between traditional communications from the UN secretary-general to the Security Council and the informality of the

---

5   See Manuel Frohlich and Abi Williams (eds.), *The UN Secretary-General and the Security Council: A Dynamic Relationship* (Oxford: forthcoming, 2016).

annual retreat shows how practices evolve in modern diplomacy, but it also evinces a critical aspect of protocol: predictability. Whether formal or informal, predictable rules of expected behaviour avoid confusion and awkwardness, allowing important discussions to take place.

Protocol in Think Tanks

In contrast to the established procedures of an international organisation like the United Nations, think tanks are in a position to make their own rules. As new actors on the international stage, serving decision-makers by producing innovative research, convening experts, and training practitioners, think tanks and other non-governmental organisations are increasingly important players in global politics.

While think tanks need not adopt the protocol practices of established organisations, they are well-served, however, by knowing when these rules are expected to be applied and where creative abandonment of traditional protocol may serve the purposes of innovation. Where think tanks serve a convening role not entirely different from that of the United Nations itself, it would, for example, be imprudent to cast aside aspects of protocol the utility of which has been discussed above.

Innovation may nevertheless be necessary. Often, think tanks are called upon to convene various actors such as government officials, academics, civil society representatives, and businesspeople. Whereas the UN's understanding on protocol is fundamentally predicated on interaction between diplomats, albeit from very different cultures, think tanks have the added challenge of fostering dialogue between agents of entirely different professions. This carries risks. Many blockages in policy implementation have resulted from civil servants and private sector contractors failing to 'speak the same language.'

Given the multidimensional aspects of most contemporary policy problems, inter-sectoral collaboration is often necessary. It is often think tanks that can provide the neutral space for such discussions to take place, and they must correspondingly facilitate discussions by making clear expected rules of conduct, such as the Chatham House Rule, which allows participants to recount others' observations from a given meeting without citing particular individuals.[6]

6   https://www.chathamhouse.org/about/chatham-house-rule?gclid=CIDosJKEnMgCFUrpwgodGtcKZQ

Think tanks are often associated with efforts to open new channels for communication between actors whose diplomatic interactions may be stymied. Whereas 'Track 1' diplomacy covers formal negotiations between official actors, 'Track 2' diplomacy convenes non-official actors such as civil society or religious leaders to build relationships and confidence. 'Track 1.5' efforts can combine official and non-official actors.[7] It may be supposed that such initiatives are inherently less formal than traditional processes, for example those convened by the United Nations. In reality, whatever the constellation of actors being convened, predictable rules of behaviour are still required to facilitate meaningful discussion.

Recent dialogues at The Hague Institute for Global Justice illustrate this reality. A mediation between two parties to a conflict over a technical issue still required careful consideration of delegation composition, speaking time, and other such factors. Similarly, two landmark conferences on the genocides in Rwanda and Srebrenica, which brought together contemporary decision-makers to consider lessons learned, may have been 'informal' in terms of dress, but the meetings were still necessarily governed by predictable processes pertaining to agendas and speaking rights.

Where think tanks interact with established institutions, they can certainly promote innovation. At the same time, established rules of protocol – such as the greetings offered to a visiting dignitary who may be speaking from a think tank's stage – ought not to be overlooked. The challenge for think tanks is to demonstrate their added value and flexibility while also adapting to the requirements intrinsic to international politics.

The world today is a networked one in which various actors collaborate to achieve desired outcomes. These actors may communicate horizontally across national boundaries, and it can often seem that communities such as lawyers, diplomats, or aid workers have more in common with each other than with those in different sectors, even within their own countries (these connections are deemed 'epistemic' in the literature[8]).

It is the role of think tanks to bring such actors together and to help them understand one another. Whereas 'speaking the same language' was once the job of UN interpreters, today it is equally about forging mutual understanding between representatives of different kinds of organisations.

---

7 http://glossary.usip.org/resource/tracks-diplomacy
8 See, for example, Anne-Marie Slaughter, *A New World Order* (Princeton: 2004)

Conclusion

The diversification and decentralisation of international relations have created new challenges for those charged with implementing protocol, but they have also presented an opportunity to reveal its natural flexibility. Diplomacy is increasingly conducted by representatives of different sectors and communities, but this does not negate the need for predictability in their interactions. If anything, the need for clear 'rules of the game' for interaction between individuals has never been greater.

It would also be wrong to assume that new actors on the world stage are innovators whereas traditional institutions are rigid, and therefore irrelevant. The retreats of the Security Council show that old organisations can develop new ways of achieving their aims, just as the application of traditional diplomatic protocol by think tanks and NGOs shows that they are adopting successful practices at the same time as they blaze a new path.

That conventional rules of international politics have not been jettisoned underlines that these expected codes of behaviour are not about tradition for its own sake. Instead, they enable diplomats to show respect to each other and to anticipate the way in which others will behave. Far from inhibiting fruitful dialogue, it is protocol that allows it to take place.

UN flag parade in the International Zone of The Hague

4. Flag protocol

Introduction

Worldwide, flags take an important place in symbols of solidarity between people living mutually under a nation, a city, an organisation, or a company – a symbol of recognition. Flags symbolise identity. They have often played an important role in the history of peoples. They are a visible sign of independence and authority and an emblem of nationalism. As such, the Dutch flag was one of the first of the 'revolutionary' banners.

Before diving into the particulars of the use of flags, it is important to outline the long-standing history of the flag and the study of flags that goes along with it. The study of flags is known as vexillology.

Vexillology is the 'scientific study of the history, symbolism and usage of flags or, by extension, any interest in flags in general.' The word is a synthesis of the Latin word *vexillum* (flag), which referred to the standards used by Roman legions, and the Greek suffix *-logia* (study).

Vexillology concerns itself with everything to do with flags, banners, standards, and pennants. In earlier times, people understood intuitively that they needed to mark out the territory belonging to them or their tribe in a particular way in order to indicate to others that they could not enter that territory without permission. Certain symbols were used to indicate this, such as the skulls of animals or painted animal hides. In warfare, when men fought with bows and arrows and spears, it was understood that using a symbol of recognition was a good way to prevent accidentally attacking friendly warriors. These men carried heraldic symbols as well as weapons on their shields and armour, but it soon became clear that it was also important to make the commander's position on the battlefield readily visible. Initially, these commanders used the aforementioned skulls, ponytails, and religious symbols for this purpose. Later, coats of arms were used for this. The Romans were in fact the first to carry a flag as demonstration of their military power. Every division of the Roman army had its own pole with a metal (often bronze) eagle affixed to the top of it. Often, as additional ornamentation, coloured ribbons or a single-coloured cloth without an emblem would be hung from a cross-post. This standard was called a *vexillum*. The only remaining Roman *vexillum*, from the third century BC, currently hangs in the Pushkin Museum in Russia.

The Roman Emperor Constantine used such a standard, decorated with the Christian Chi-Rho emblem on a purple background. Not only the Romans used military recognition symbols; the ancient Celtic and Germanic tribes also had flags specifically for war.

Approximately 300 years ago, flags and their laws and rules were categorised along with heraldry. The terminology for heraldry was, without much thought, applied to flags as well. Because of this, heraldry plays an important role in the basic design of many flags used today.

After the Second World War (1939–1945), a greater interest in flags arose, primarily due to the formation of many new states and international organisations. At that time, many emblems were used in flags that had no heraldic origin. Increasingly modern symbols began appearing on flags.

But what defines a flag? How can one describe a flag? The Oxford English Dictionary defines a flag as: 'A piece of cloth or similar material, typically oblong or square, attachable by one edge to a pole or rope and used as the symbol or emblem of a country or institution, or as a decoration during public festivities.'

Flag designers generally speak of the ratio between the height of a flag (the side running alongside the flagpole) and the length of it (the waving part of the flag). The most often-used ratio is 2:3, but this differs in some cases, such as in the flag of Switzerland, which assumes a square ratio of 1:1. In the United Kingdom, the College of Arms advises on other, alternate proportions, such as 12:15, 12:16, 12:18, 12:20 and 12:24. It is important to realise that the proportion is purely a matter of clarity and aesthetics.

Royal personal flags or royal/presidential standards are also discussed in vexillology. These distinctive flags are connected to an individual such as a head of state, governor, prince or princess and have a special design, often related to their coat of arms or a national identity. These flags are formally attached to a single person and can therefore only be used by the people upon whom they have been bestowed. This is what is meant by a royal or presidential standard. The royal standard of a monarch, being a heraldic flag, should only be flown while the royal person is on the premises, being hoisted on their arrival and lowered following their departure. In the UK the royal standards take precedence over all flags including the Union Jack.

FLAG PROTOCOL 89

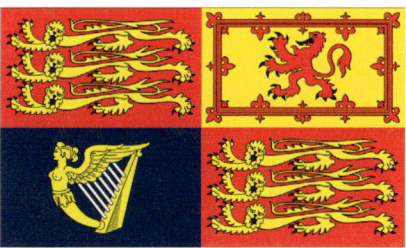

Royal Standard of HM Queen Elizabeth II

Personal flag of the president of the United States of America

Banner / Standard

In former days a banner was a flag used in square form to denote the rank or stance of the standard-bearer, often decorated with heraldic symbols and colours similar to those on their coat of arms, the buttons on their uniforms and decorative objects, and always attached to the standing pole and crossbeam with knots.

Banner vexillology refers to:
– A piece of cloth attached by one edge to a staff and used by a leader (such as a monarch or feudal lord) as his standard, sometimes with a swallowtail with two or more points;
– An ensign displaying a distinctive or symbolic device or legend especially one presented as an award of honour or distinction;
– Strip of cloth on which a sign is painted.

Mediaeval banner

Mediaeval banner

A banner that is manufactured from heavier material and flown from a pole is called a standard. Formerly, it was flown from a lance, or just the end of a lance. This cloth is mostly rounded at the end, and a fringe is attached around the edge. The symbols on the standard, as well as the colours, are usually either embroidered, gilt stamped, or painted on. In the Netherlands, the state banner / standard is seen as a state symbol.

State banner of the Netherlands

The state banner of the Netherlands is made of moiré-patterned cloth, hung from a gilded spear, and painted with the national coat of arms, as was ordained on 24 August 1815. The national coat of arms has since changed, but the picture on the state banner has remained the same. The state banner was painted by Bartholomeus Johannes van Hove (1790–1880).

In the armed forces, banners and standards are lent to military units as a reward for extraordinary acts and called 'the colours.'

Pennant

Lastly, the pennant will be discussed.

The pennant has a very special function originating from its use at sea. On specific occasions, a narrow and sometimes swallow-tailed cloth is flown from the mainmast. The pennant is much longer and narrower than a flag and ends in either a point or a swallowtail.

On land, the pennant has become a means by which to express who people fly their flags for. In the case of the Netherlands, in order to not let a flagpole stand 'empty', a long red, white, and blue pennant is left to fly. It is also customary to fly an orange pennant above the Dutch flag on special occasions related to the Dutch royal family, such as royal birthdays (see page 96). On the occasion of a death in the royal family, a black pennant is flown beside the Royal Standard at the Dutch royal palace (see page 114).

Designs and colours

As we examine the many flag developments in the world, it becomes evident that there is a complex lexicon concerning the many different parts of flags. The image below shows several different elements that can exist in flags.

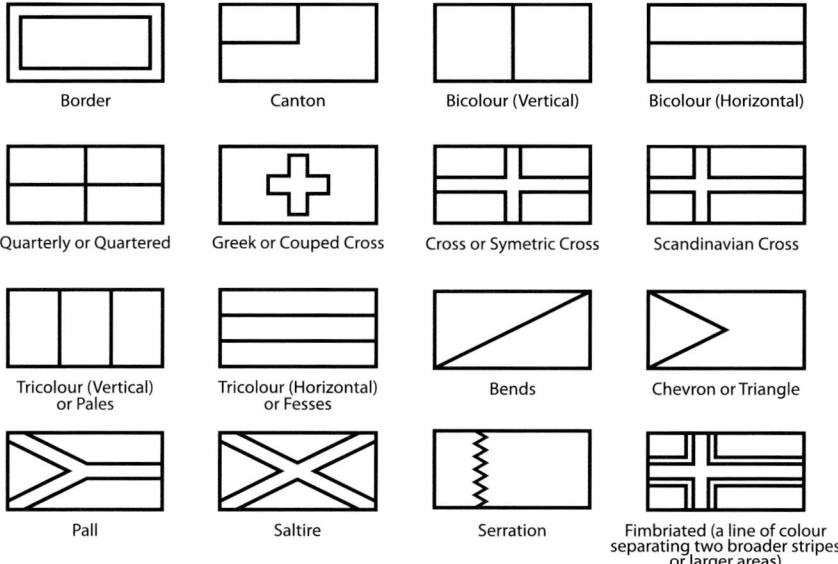

Flag elements

In his book *The Dutch Flag*, Derkwillem Visser writes the following on flag colours:

> Colours on flags often seem very colourful and decorative. In actuality, these colours are not chosen for their aesthetics, but rather for other reasons. These reasons can be historical, symbolic, or political. For this reason, every country has a flag that is derived from the history and national character of its people. Some countries' flag colours are derived from the past when their struggle for independence defined them. However, other countries such as Spain and Switzerland have clearly taken

their colours from their heraldic pasts. In Africa, it is clear that the colours red, yellow, and green stand for freedom and unity of the former colonies in that part of the world.

Below, the pan-African colours, the pan-Arabic colours and the pan-Slavic colours will be discussed. In these regions specific colours are preferred for their flags.

The pan-African colours are red, yellow, and green. These colours are derived from the flag of Ethiopia. During the decolonisation period, Ethiopia served as an inspiration for African colonies wishing to become independent because this country, except for a short period of Italian occupation, was itself never a colony. Many African countries have therefore adopted the colours red, yellow and green for their own flags. Black is also sometimes seen as a pan-African colour, especially in parts of Africa where a large portion of the population has darker skin.

Flag of Ethiopia

The pan-Arabic colours are black, red, white and green. They often appear in Arab flags. The colours go back to the flag of the Arab Revolt of 1916, and other Arab flags that were in use at that time.

Flag of the Arab Revolt

The colours white and black are the colours of the prophet Muhammad (peace be upon him). Green was his favourite colour and is the colour of the Islamic faith. In the flag of the Arab revolution, the colours stand for several caliphates, such as the Abbasid's (black), the Umayyad's (white), the Fatimid's (green), and the Hashemite's (red).

Based on the flag of the Arab Revolt, the Arab Liberation Flag emerged in 1952. This red-white-black tricolour has been used by many states since the establishment of the United Arab Republic.

Flag of the Arab Liberation

Flag of Egypt

The pan-Slavic colours, red, blue and white, are used in the flags of most of the Slavic peoples and countries.

Flag of the Czech Republic

To some readers, this might beg the question of when the Netherlands began using the three colours red, white and blue on their flag.

Research by D.G. Muller shows that the Czech flag originated in the period when the Bavarian House of Wittelsbach ruled the county of Holland (1354-1433). The colours of the flag came from the coat of arms of the counts of Holland, a combination of the coat of arms of the Bavarian House and that of the county of Holland.

This coat of arms was first used by Willem V as can be seen on the coins minted by Holland and Zeeland during this time.

Research by P.C. Guyot reveals that in 1409–1410, the treasurer of the counts of Holland purchased a 'fur-lined tabard with the colours red, white and blue' for Willem VI, Count of Holland.

It is therefore possible to say that the colours red, white, and blue had been introduced to the Netherlands. However, it is also possible that the red, white and blue comes from the blue bugle in the coat of arms of the Prince of Orange, which has a silver mouthpiece and is red gagged. Another explanation is that the Dutch flag is based on the flag of Zeeland – the traditional red lion on a gold or yellow field emerging from the sea, represented by flowing white and blue lines. At the time of the Eighty Years' War, a war between Spain and the northern part of the Netherlands, Dutch Sea Beggars introduced the colours orange, white, and blue. This flag became a symbol of the Dutch resistance and gained the name *prinsenvlag* (prince's flag) after the capture of Brielle. The name was given in homage to Prince William of Orange (1533–1584) because he had established himself as the protector of the Sea Beggars. When Spain eventually ceded sovereignty to the United Provinces, the orange colour was gradually changed to red. It is possible that there was a political reason behind this. The earliest confirmed usage of the red, white, and blue tricolour dates back to the year 1596.

In 1810, the Kingdom of the Netherlands was incorporated into the First French Empire, and the kingdom lost both its sovereignty and its flag. The flag of the First French Republic was called the *drapeau tricolore* (tricolour flag) in French, and it was the first tricolour flag to use three vertical lines.

After the French occupation, the Dutch regained their sovereignty and their flag. However, the colours were not fully standardised until 19 February 1937, when HM Queen Wilhelmina of the Netherlands issued the shortest royal decree ever: 'The colours of the flag of the Kingdom of the Netherlands are red, white, and blue.' The Dutch national flag still stands as a tricolour of bright vermillion red, clear white, and cobalt blue.

The colours red, white, and blue are, without the same meaning, also used in the flags of many other nations including but not limited to the United States, Luxembourg (identical to the Dutch flag, but with a lighter shade of blue), Norway, Iceland, and the United Kingdom.

Flag of the Netherlands

Symbolic Meanings of Colours in National Flags:

Yellow	Symbolises generosity.
White	Symbolises peace, equality and good deeds, but also submission.
Red	Symbolises toughness, courage, strength and swords.
Blue	Symbolises vigilance, truth, loyalty, endurance and justice.
Green	Symbolises hope, joy, and love. In many countries, it takes on a religious meaning. It can also symbolise fields.
Black	Symbolises determination, struggle and often reflects the ethnographic makeup of a population.

Flag Codes

A flag deserves to be handled with respect and reverence. Traditions exist that govern how flags should be raised, lowered, and stored. For this reason, every country has its own flag code.

A flag code is a law or set of instructions, usually for governments, that describe the proper way to handle the country's national flag. These codes include instructions on the manner in which the flag must be raised, when that should happen, who may use the flag, and which version of the flag may or must be used. A flag code can also determine how flags must be flown when regional, municipal, or foreign flags are also displayed with it, or how the flag must be flown during a time of mourning (often, flags are flown at half mast).

The regulations concerning these instructions can differ greatly between countries. The differences are so significant that what might be required in one country is not permitted in another. Furthermore, the authority of the flag code also varies from country to country, in the sense that in some countries the flag code is only given as advice to governmental organisations, while in others it applies to every resident. The punishments for violations of the code also differ: it might be unpunished, small fines, by prison time, or even with the death penalty.

As politically symbolic acts, flags of perceived enemy countries might be stepped on or set on fire.

The Dutch Flag Code

The Dutch flag code is established by the government and is intended for national use. The code determines when the Dutch flag must be flown and in what manner.

The dates on which the Dutch flag must be flown from official buildings were laid down in instructions from the prime minister on 22 December 1980. Individuals, businesses, and institutions are asked to follow these rules as far as possible, but in actuality they are not mandatory. These instructions have been changed several times, most recently on 17 May 2013. A quote from the instructions follows below:

> In the display of the Dutch flag, a distinction will be made between extended flags and limited flags. Extended refers to flying the flag from all official buildings, such as is done on *Koningsdag* (King's Day). Limited means flying the flag only from main buildings of departments or main buildings of institutions that do not fall directly under departments. These are the Chambers of the States General, the Council of State, the General Court of Auditors, the King's Cabinet, and the High Council of the Netherlands.

Fixed Dates for Flying Flags in the Netherlands

On the next page are printed a number of dates on which official buildings must fly extended or limited flags. If a date falls on a Sunday or a generally accepted public holiday, the flags fly on the date written in parentheses. On birthdays of members of the royal house and on *Koningsdag* (King's Day), the flag can be flown in combination with an orange pennant.

Dutch flag and orange pennant

The special members of the royal house are defined as the head of state, their spouse, the heir to the throne (the Prince or Princess of Orange) and the head of state's predecessor, but not the rest of the royal family. Therefore, Princess Amalia (the heir to the throne) is included in this list, but her sisters, Princesses Alexia and Ariane, are not.

31 January (1 February)	Birthday of Princess Beatrix – Limited, with an orange pennant.
27 April (26 April)	*Koningsdag* / Birthday of King Willem-Alexander – Extended, with an orange pennant.
4 May (4 May)	National Memorial Day – Extended, half mast from 18:00 until sundown (21:10 summer time).
5 May (5 May)	National Liberation Day – Extended.
17 May (18 May)	Birthday of Queen Máxima – Limited, with an orange pennant.
Last Saturday of June	Dutch Veterans Day – Extended.
15 August (16 August)	Formal end of the Second World War – Extended.
Third Tuesday of September	Joint Session of the States General – Extended, only in The Hague
7 December (8 December)	Birthday of Princess Amalia – Limited, with orange pennant
15 December (16 December)	*Koninkrijksdag* (Kingdom Day) – Limited

Rules for using flags

As mentioned earlier, a flag deserves to be handled with respect and reverence because it represents a country, a state, a province, municipality, organisation, a company, or a person.

For these reasons, there are several rules that are followed internationally:
- A flag needs to be flown from a flagpole or from a smaller pole attached to a house or a building. In the case of two flagpoles, of which only one is used for the national flag, it is necessary to use the leftmost flagpole viewed from the street.
- The national flag should always be displayed in a valid way and should never be allowed to touch the ground. When a flag becomes tattered or faded and is no longer in a suitable condition for use, it should be destroyed in a dignified way, for example by burning it privately, or by tearing or cutting it into strips that no longer resemble the original flag.
- Flags are normally flown from sunrise to sunset. Flags may be flown by night as well as by day as long as they are properly illuminated at all times, preferably by spotlight.
- A flag must never be used as ornamentation, as a tablecloth, or as clothing.
- Placing a signature or something similar on a flag is improper.
- When a national flag is flown with the flags of other nations, each flag should have the same width (the measurement from top to bottom) and should fly from a separate flagpole of the same height.
- According to international protocol, it is improper to place one flag in a higher position in a group of foreign flags (apart from medal ceremonies

during sporting events). This would create the unwanted impression of a privileged position for the higher flag.
- An organisational flag, such as the UN flag, can fly from the UN headquarters at a higher position and in the centre of all national flags.
- A national flag could be raised to a higher position and be placed in the middle of a circle of flags which, according to protocol, rank lower than it, such as federal state flags, provincial flags, city flags, etc.
- When flying multiple flags, the host country's national flag should always be raised first and taken down last, unless all the flags are raised and lowered simultaneously.
- In the United Kingdom, the flag is always raised in a quick, powerful manner, and lowered in a more ceremonial way. Another British tradition is to raise the flag rolled up and bound, and to deploy it with a tug of the rope. This is called 'breaking the flag.' This protocol is often used during an event or the arrival of an important guest.

Flag protocol and flag order

When presenting several international flags, these must be flown according to protocol. They are displayed in an order according to the appropriate protocol and hoisted to be seen from the street.

We will look more closely into this. What are the basic rules for presenting several flags? First, we must establish what order must be used when using multiple kinds of flags according to protocol. What is the order, the precedence of flags, the '*préséance*'?

This is the flag order that is used in most countries:
- National flag
- Foreign national flag
- Provincial flag
- City flag
- Organisational flag (in some countries, the UN flag or the EU flag follow the foreign national flags)
- Company flag
- Forces flag, such as the flag of a four star general
- Personal flag (a royal personal flag or standard)
- Other flags

A royal personal flag / standard can only be displayed separate from other flags or in combination with the national flag in second position. In the

United Kingdom an exception applies to the royal personal flag of the king or queen of the United Kingdom. This flag always takes precedence over the national flag. Furthermore, the flag order in the United Kingdom is such that the flags of England, Scotland, and Wales follow the Union Jack.

In the United Kingdom, the flag of the United Nations and the flag of the European Union follow all foreign national flags. This differs from many other European countries, where they follow the city flag.

What is the flag order of foreign national flags? In most countries, alphabetical order is used. Obviously, in French-speaking countries, the French alphabetical order is used. In the United Kingdom, the United States, and in many other countries, the English language alphabetical order is used. However, in the Middle East, the countries associated in the Gulf Cooperation Council (GCC) use Arabic alphabetic order, and in the Russian Federation, Russian alphabetical order is used. In the European Union, the alphabetical order is often determined by the countries' names in their own languages. As such, the Netherlands is under 'N' for *Nederland*, Finland is under 'S' for *Suomi*, and Greece is under 'H' for *Hellas*.

International organisations often choose English language alphabetical order. One downside of this is that, despite the countries' equality, some countries' flags are always flown first. To get around this problem, a solution used by the United Nations is to fly a different country's flag first each year. This is chosen by lottery. After the first flag, the rest of the world's flags follow in English alphabetical order. Some international organisations rotate the flags at a pace chosen by them (e.g. every week or month).

Another possibility for international organisations is to use flag orders based on:
- Date of admission to the organisation (as used by the Arab League).
- Date of ratification (however, the International Criminal Court in The Hague uses English language alphabetical order for their flags and the order of date of ratification for their meetings).

At the Olympic Games, the row of flags is headed by the Olympic flag, followed by the flag of Greece, and then the flags of all other participating countries in the alphabetical order of the language of the host country. The host country's flag is the last flag.

At the head office of an international organisation, the organisation's flag may also be flown first. It is customary to open the row of flags with the organisation's flag, and to close with it as well. This is for example used at the head office of the EU in Brussels.

At the United Nations, the UN flag flies in the centre, and from a higher flagpole. This mode of flying flags is used by many international organisations.

Application of flag protocol

Now that we have established the ways of flying flags according to protocol, the question remains as to how this protocol is applied. What is the most important place for a flag, and what is the place of honour?

Two flags

When flying two flags, the place of honour is, in principle, on the right-hand side looking out from the building, and to the left from the point of view of the street. In most countries, the place of honour is given to its own national flag, and the flag of the visiting country is displayed on the right as seen from the street.

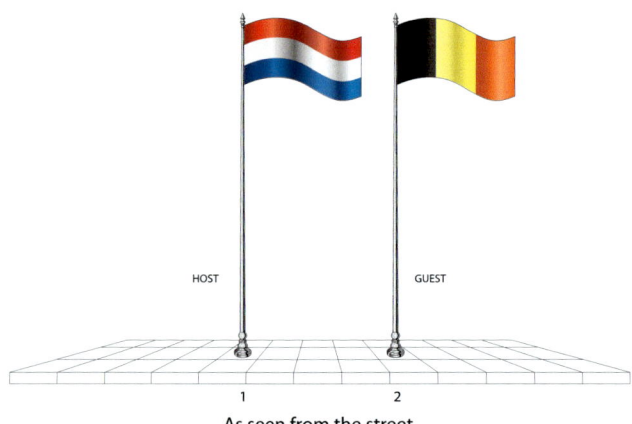

Flag of host country the Netherlands and flag of guest country Belgium

In the United States, this is codified in law. From the point of view of the building, the second flag always takes a position to the left of the national flag. This second flag can be a foreign flag, or the flag of an organisation, such as that of the Organization of American States.

In some situations, in the international world, this rule is not always followed. In photo opportunities, the guest of honour is always placed on the right of the host, and with them, most often their national flag.

Another option is to place double sets of flags behind the two authorities. In this case, it is still possible to display the national flag in the position of honour (as seen by the media on the farthest left side.) For photo opportunities, both authorities will be standing in front of their own national flags as seen by the media. This has always been done in the United States and is now used in many other countries as well.

Media picture

Double sets of flags

The European Union flag flies in the second position with the majority of the EU's countries – to the right of the national flag when observed from the street.

As seen from the street

Flag of the Netherlands with the European flag

In recent years, however, this has begun to change. The French and the Germans fly the EU flag in the position of honour on the left side when observed from the street, and the right when observed from the building.

In most countries in the Middle East, the position of honour is given to the visiting country. Here, the host country's own flag (United Arab Emirates) was placed to the left of the visiting country's (Canada), and to the right from the point of view of the street.

Flag of guest country Canada and the flag of host country the United Arab Emirates

There is much to be said for this practice. It shows more respect for the guest country, and it follows the principle of showing respect as in seating, where the guest of honour is always placed on the right.

When two flags are presented crossed, the most important flag (i.e. the national flag of Spain as host) is placed on the left side of the observer's point of view, and the second flag (Portugal as guest) on the right side. The flagpole of the most important flag is also placed above the other pole.

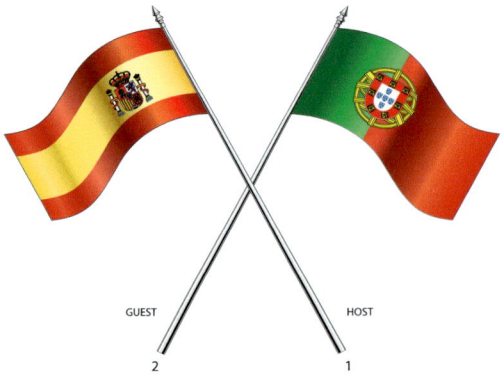

Two flags crossed, Spain and Portugal

Three flags

When presenting three flags, the country's own national flag (flag 1) is placed in the centre and flown from the middle flagpole. Following protocol, the second flag is placed to the right of the national flag (from the point of view of the building) and the third flag to the left.

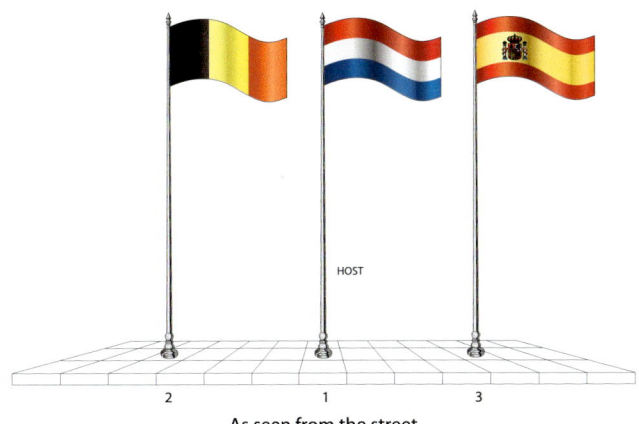

Three flags, the Netherlands host country, second flag Belgium and third flag Spain

From the point of view of the street, flag 2 (Belgium) is on the left, flag 1 (the Netherlands) in the centre, and flag 3 (Spain) is on the right.

Some countries such as the United Kingdom and the United States use another protocol. Here, from the building's point of view, the national flag (flag 1) is flown from the right (in the words of the US's protocol: from 'the flag's own right'), followed on the left side by flag 2 first (France) and then flag three (Germany). From the street's point of view, then, the national flag is on the left, and flag 2 (France) is to the right. Flag 3 (Germany) follows.

Flags number 2 and 3 can also be other types of flags such as provincial flags, city flags, or hotel flags.

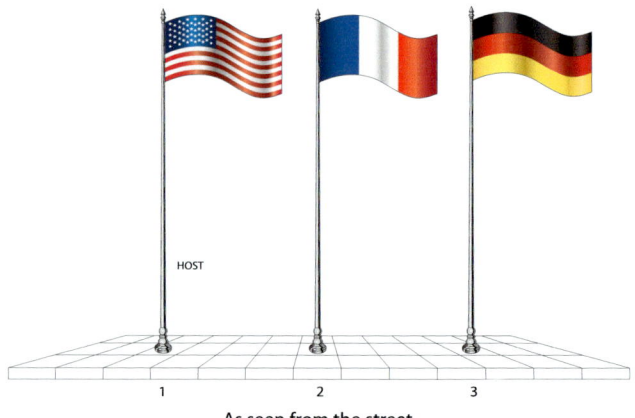

Three flags, United States host country, followed by the flag of France and the flag of Germany

Flying more than three flags in an uneven quantity

When flying more than three flags in an uneven number, the national flag always flies in the centre. The other flags fly following the order according to protocol, beginning on the right side of the national flag from the point of view of the building, then to the left of the national flag, then right again, then left, repeating ad infinitum.

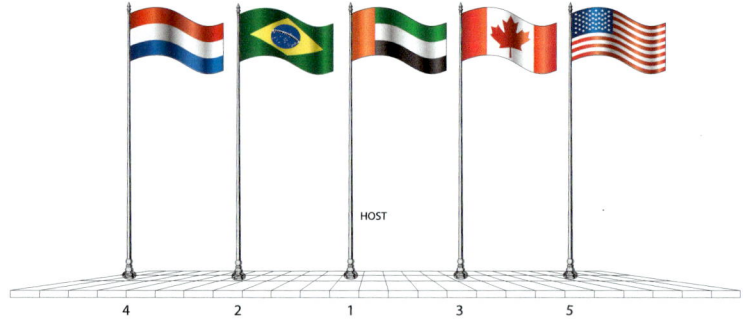

Flying more than three flags in an uneven quantity, United Arab Emirates host country and centre position, other flags in alphabetical order alternating right and left

From the street point of view, flag 2 (Brazil) flies left of the national flag (United Arab Emirates), and flag 3 (Canada) to the right. Flag 4 (the Netherlands) is to the left of flag 2 and flag 5 (United States of America) to the right of flag 3.

Sometimes, in some countries such as the United States and the United Kingdom, the flag order begins with the national flag on the rightmost flagpole (from the point of view of the building) with the following flags to the left according to the flag order. This application may also be followed by other host countries. See below.

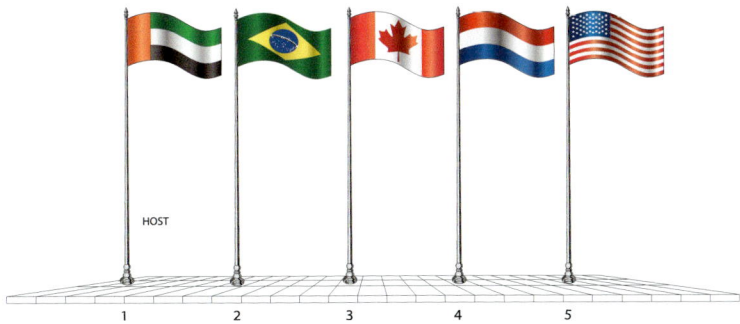

As seen from the street

Flying more than three flags in an uneven quantity, United Arab Emirates host country followed by the other countries in alphabetical order

In the United States, when displaying the national flag in combination with the state flags, the national flag will be in the centre and higher. The order of the state flags is in protocol order based on the date of statehood or ratification of the Constitution.

Flying more than three flags in an even quantity

When flying more than three flags in an even number, the national flag generally flies on the outer right from the point of view of the building and on the outer left from the point of view of the street. The other flags (Germany, Italy, and Norway) follow the national flag in order of protocol. As described earlier, this method of displaying flags is preferred by countries like the United Kingdom and United States when flying flags in uneven numbers as well.

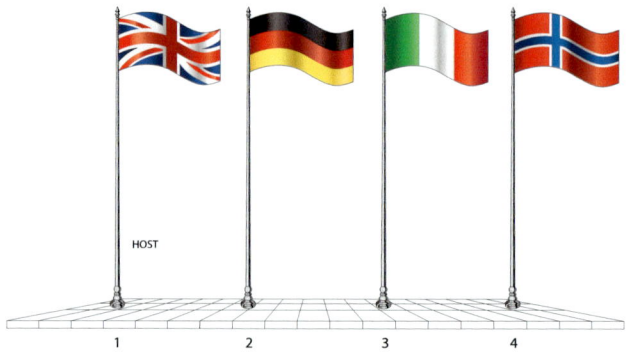

As seen from the street

Flying more than three flags in an even quantity, United Kingdom host country, other flags follow in alphabetical order

Flying two or more flags on the forecourt of a building at an angle to the main entrance

Where there are two or more flagpoles on the forecourt of a building but at an angle to the main entrance, the national flag should be flown on the outermost pole when the flagpoles are situated to the left of the main entrance and on the innermost pole when the flagpoles are to the right of the main entrance.

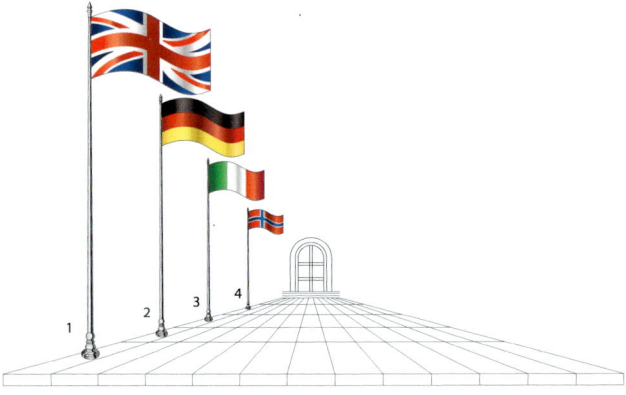

As seen from the street

Flying two or more flags on the left side of the forecourt of a building at an angle to the main entrance

FLAG PROTOCOL   107

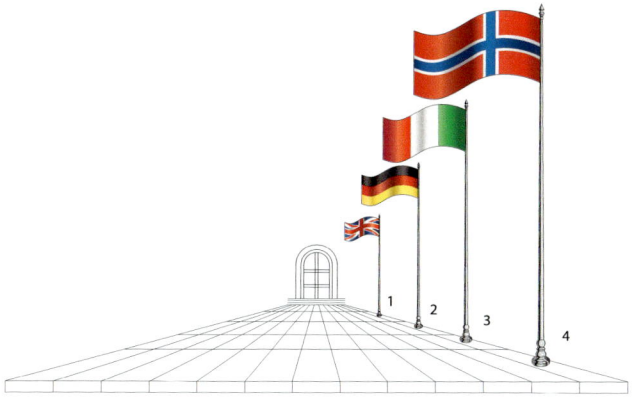

As seen from the street

Flying two or more flags on the right side of the forecourt of a building at an angle to the main entrance

If only one flag is to be flown and there are two flagpoles, it should be flown on the left-hand flagpole as seen from the street. If there are more than two flagpoles, it should be flown as near as possible to the centre. This only applies when the other flagpoles remain empty.

If one flagpole is higher than the rest, the national flag can fly from that flagpole but no other national flags can be flown on the other flagpoles. These can still be used for lower level flags such as county and city flags. Alternatively the higher flagpole can be left empty and the remaining flagpoles used as if it did not exist. In general when siting flagpoles it is a good idea to keep them all at the same level to avoid these protocol problems.

Flags in a semicircle

When multiple foreign flags are presented in a semicircle, the national flag must be flown in the centre. From the street point of view, the remaining flags should be placed with the next most important flag (or first in alphabetical order if all the flags are of equal importance) on the left of the central flag, the next on the right of the central flag, the next on the second left from the central flag and continuing to alternate left and right.

As seen from the street

Flags in a semicircle

Flags in a full circle

When flying flags in a full circle, such as around a stadium, the national flag is flown from the flagpole directly across from the main entrance or above the royal/VIP box if there is no main entrance. The other countries' flags then follow in order of protocol as described with the semicircle. Alternatively, they can be arranged alphabetically going clockwise.

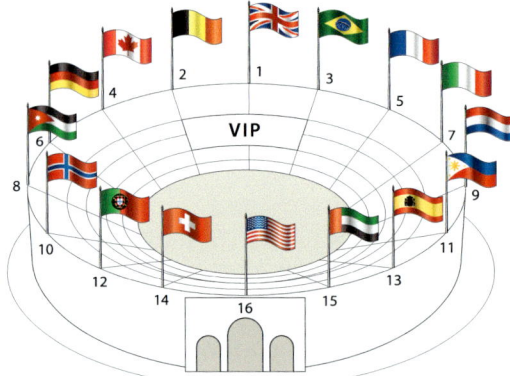

As seen from the street

Flags in a full circle

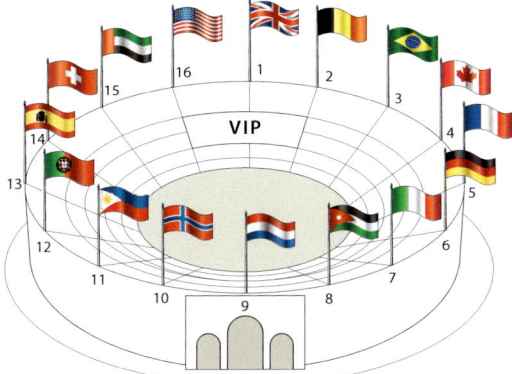

Alphabetically clockwise as seen from the street

Flags in a full circle, clockwise

Flags in a procession or parade

The most important flag is placed as the first in the procession, and the other flags follow in order of protocol. In the case of many flags being presented, and the flag carriers walking side by side, the most important is placed on the outermost right side in the procession. In the case of a flag parade undertaken by a head of state or another person of high authority, the flag is passed horizontally in front of this authority and the other honoured person, before returning to its normal position. At the opening of the Olympic Games, the flag carriers in the parade lead their national Olympic delegation in the alphabetical order of the language of the host country. Traditionally, the parade is always opened by Greece and closed by the host country.

Flags placed vertically against a wall

The flag can be hung vertically against a wall. For example, the red of the Dutch flag, seen from the room, should be on the left side and the blue on the right. As for the flag of the United States: 'The union should be uppermost and to the flag's own right, that is, to the observer's left.' The union is the canton with the stars.

American flag vertically against a wall

For the flag of the United Kingdom: 'The Union Jack if hung horizontally or vertically, the uppermost broad white diagonal should be on the left. In the case of other Commonwealth flags, like the flag of Australia, the Union Jack canton is shown in the upper left corner.'

Union Jack vertically against a wall

The flag of Saudi Arabia, must be displayed vertically on a wall with the sword pointing down due to the religious nature of the Arabic text on the flag. The flag of Saudi Arabia displays the *Shahada*: 'There is no God but Allah, and Mohammed is his messenger.'

Flags on a podium, speaker's platform

In the case of multiple flags being displayed from a staff on a podium next to a speaker, the national flag should be placed on the right-hand side of the speaker, or to the left from the point of view of the audience. The second flag can be placed on the left-hand side of the speaker or to the left of the first flag to the right of the speaker. In this way, the audience sees the national flag to the left and the second flag to the right of it. With three flags, the national flag can be placed to the right of the speaker and the two other flags to the left, or all the flags can be placed in the middle behind the speaker. The three flags can be presented in two different ways. First, the national flag can be placed in the middle, the second to the right (left from the audience), and the third flag to the left (right from the audience), or it is possible to display the flags as is done in the United States and the United Kingdom, where the national flag is placed to the right (left from the audience), and the other two flags follow in order of protocol to the left of the national flag (to the right from the audience).

As seen from the audience

Flags on a podium, speaker's platform, example 1

As seen from the audience

Flags on a podium, speaker's platform, example 2

Double-flagging

Sometimes it might occur that only one flagpole is available. If the two flags are from one nation, it is possible to display two flags on one pole. The national flag should fly at the top, with a gap of 30 cm, and the second flag then follows it, e.g. the federal state or city flag.

Displaying flags on a coffin or at a ceremony

During a funeral ceremony or state mourning, coffins are often covered with the national flag. In the United Kingdom and the United States, the protocol is for the flag to be placed with the upper-left corner on the side of the left shoulder of the deceased. This practice deviates from the principles of hanging the flags vertically against the wall. In the Netherlands however, it is protocol for the flag to be placed with the red stripe over the right shoulder of the deceased, the white stripe above the chest, and the blue stripe over the left shoulder. In this way, it follows the practice used for hanging the flag on a wall, where red is also on the left side, seen from the viewer.

The flag should always be removed from the coffin and immediately folded up in the proper way at the end of the mourning ceremony, cremation, or burial. In the United States, the flag is then handed to the loved ones of the deceased.

Flags or standards on a car, bus, or aircraft

We will now explain how royal, presidential and national flags, or standards are displayed on automobiles, airplanes, and busses. On a car, these are always placed on the side where the important person or honoured guest is sitting: on the right side where traffic is on the right and on the left side where traffic is on the left. In the case of two heads of state being seated in the car, the flag of the guest is always placed on their side, the place of honour. The flag of the host is on the other side – the left side when traffic is on the right. Exceptions to this rule are the flag of the United States and the flag of the Russian Federation. These are always placed on the right side of the car.

When the president of the United States travels alone, the flag of the United States is placed on the right side of the car and the Presidential Standard is placed on the left.

In the United Kingdom, the flag holder is generally placed in the middle of the front of the roof.

FLAG PROTOCOL

Vehicle of the president of the United States of America with U.S. flag and personal flag of the president

Vehicle of HM Queen Elizabeth II with Royal Standard on top

Travelling in a bus with two heads of state, the personal flag or standard of the guest will fly on the right front side of the bus and the flag of the host on the left side. In the case of more than two heads of state traveling in the bus, no standards are carried.

In the case heads of state arrive by aircraft, their personal flag or standard is placed after landing visibly on the left side of the cockpit, on the side where passengers disembark.

Royal Standard of HM Queen Elizabeth II flying outside a cockpit

The US president's personal aircraft Air Force One displays the US national flag on the left side of its tail, which is mirrored on the other side. This is also the case on Marine One, the presidential helicopter.

Flying flags half mast

A national flag is said to be at half mast when it is flown not from the top of the flagpole but instead approximately between halfway to two thirds up the flagpole. This is a sign of mourning. Symbolically, the invisible flag of the dead is flown above the national flag. A royal standard cannot be flown half mast. In the Netherlands, a black pennant is flown with the standard to show mourning.

Royal Standard of former Queen Beatrix of the Netherlands with black pennant

After the death of Diana, Princess of Wales in 1997, this practice created a debate in the United Kingdom. Queen Elizabeth II maintained the tradition of not flying the Royal Standard at half mast, but many in the United Kingdom criticized this decision. Since the Queen resided at Balmoral Castle in Scotland, there was no flag at Buckingham Palace, so no sign of mourning whatsoever. The Royal Standard flew at full mast at Balmoral Castle, but as a compromise, due to protests of the British population and the (international) media and after consultation with the government, the Union Jack was ultimately flown at half mast at Buckingham Palace until the funeral service.

A Royal Standard is never half masted. Nor would it be appropriate to half mast any 'personal' heraldic banner or flag. In accordance with the law of arms, the arms granted to a private individual normally pass on to the heir by right on the death of the bearer of the arms. Thus, the arms and their representation as shown on a flag, banner, or standard, immediately pass on to the deceased person's heir.

Special rules also exist for flying the flags of international organisations at half mast. Generally, only organisational flags are flown at half mast, while the other flags around it are taken down. At the United Nations, for example, in the event of the death of a head of state, the UN flag is flown at half mast from sunrise to sunset while all the national flags are removed for the duration of one day. In the situation of the flags already being displayed, this procedure will be followed the next day.

Under extreme circumstances, such as extremely strong weather or natural disasters, one could also choose for the day of the funeral or the entombment.

The flag of Saudi Arabia must never be flown at half mast as a sign of mourning, due to the religious nature of the symbols on the flag.

At a joint memorial, all flags of the participating countries can be flown at half mast.

Flying national flags at half mast should officially follow the following rules:
- The flag should first be raised to the top, and then lowered approximately between halfway to two thirds of the way up the flagpole. The flag should then be fastened.
- When lowering the flag, it should first be raised to the top and then lowered.

In the Netherlands, the national tricolour should be flown at half mast:
- In the event of a death in the royal family between the death and the funeral, except on Sundays.
- On national days of remembrance such as 4 May (National Memorial Day, the day that the victims of war and of peace missions are commemorated). There are special rules concerning the times when the flag should be at half mast on these days. On National Memorial Day, the flag may be flown at half mast until sundown (usually at 21:10 on 4 May). On National Memorial Day, the flag should be flown outside after 18:00.
- If the prime minister gives an instruction on a special day (such as a national day of mourning).

Trivia

It is interesting to note that:
- The flag of Denmark is the oldest national flag still in use. The design of the Dannebrog is recorded on a seal from 1397. According to legend, the flag came into Danish possession during the battle of Lyndanisse in 1219. The Danes were on a failing crusade in Estonia, but after praying to God, a flag fell from the sky. After this event, Danish King Valdemar II went on to defeat the Estonians. The first recorded use of the flag appeared a hundred years later.
The cross design, which represents Christianity, was subsequently adopted by the other Nordic countries.
- In Hungary, on days of national mourning, a black flag is raised on public buildings next to the national flag that is flown at half mast.
- The tallest flagpole in the world, which stands at 171 meters, is in Jeddah in Saudi Arabia.
- The largest flag in the world, with an area of 101,000 square meters, was unfurled in Qatar on 18 December 2013 on the emirate's national day. The purple-brown and white flag was revealed in Loussail, an industrial area north of Doha.
- Until that date, the largest flag in the world was a Brazilian flag in Brasilia with an area of 3,380 square meters. The flag has been flying permanently since 1960.
- Since the 1970s, a new tradition in the Netherlands has been to fly the national flag together with a backpack outside a home to signify that a child has successfully completed secondary school–they have passed their final exams and the next stage in study or work can begin. This clearly shows the neighbourhood who has passed their exams, and invites neighbours to come by to congratulate the family. The Dutch saying 'to finish school with a flag and a pennant' comes from this tradition.

Flag of the Netherlands with backpack

Mr François Brunagel, former Head of Protocol of the European Parliament

François Joseph Brunagel, born in Strasbourg, France, is ambassador, representative of the Sovereign Order of Malta with the Council of Europe. He started working as a European official in 1972 in the Economic and Social Committee as deputy to the head of cabinet of the secretary-general. Having been the secretary of the group of various interests, he was appointed spokesman of the Speaker of the European Parliament, Pierre Pflimlin, in 1984. Became the advisor to Lord Plumb, Speaker of the European Parliament in 1987 and in 1989 head of the unit of Publications and Events. In 2001 appointed director of cabinet of Mrs Nicole Fontaine, Speaker of the European Parliament, followed by his assignment in 2004 to head of protocol, a position he held until his retirement in 2014. He has been the recipient of the following state honours; *Chevalier de la Légion d'Honneur, Officier de l'Ordre National du Mérite*, Gold Medal of the Foundation of the European Merit (Luxemburg) and Commander of the Order of Saint-Gregory the Great.

A genuine experience, protocol in an international institution, the European Parliament by Mr François Brunagel

Like all public institutions, the European Union has a protocol that has evolved over the years. New institutions have been created, their respective competences and status have changed, and the overall place of the EU in the world has become of major importance.

I joined the European Economic Community, forefather of the European Union, in late 1972, when it counted only six member states, the so-called 'original six.' At that time, the only institution with some prestige was the Commission, a kind of prefiguration of a government. The other institutions were less established, the Council bringing together ministers of the member states and the Assembly, not yet called 'Parliament', gathering members deputised from the national parliaments.

When I left forty-three years later, at the end of 2014, the European Union had twenty-eight member states, and several new institutions have been created, like the Court of Auditors (1977), the European Central Bank (1998), and the European Council (meeting of heads of state and government), (2009). Above all, the European Parliament, directly elected since 1979, has won its competences at all levels, legislative and budgetary – shared with the Council of the Union – and the control of the executive. Since 2014, the *Spitzenkandidat* of the party that wins the European elections becomes elected by the Parliament as the president of the Commission. The European Parliament has become a major player in European politics and a key actor amongst the institutions.

I had the privilege of experiencing this fascinating period over the last four decades, especially during the last thirty years as an official of the European Parliament. I have in fact never been very far from protocol since I often served in cabinets or as a responsible for communication, all jobs linked with the welcoming of personalities or organising ceremonies and events. As a member of the cabinet of the secretary-general, I had, for example, been in charge of organising the fifteenth anniversary of the creation of the Economic and Social Committee in 1973. In the cabinet of former French Prime Minister Pierre Pflimlin, who became president of the European Parliament, I was involved in 1985 in the official visit of the President of the USA, Ronald Reagan, and many other heads of states. On top came the official visit of Pope John Paul II to the European Parliament in 1988, in Strasbourg. Being the only Frenchman and the only Roman Catholic in the cabinet of Lord Plumb, I was in charge of the preparation of that visit in liaison with the French authorities as well as the local Catholic Church. I have excellent memories of that very challenging task.

Once you successfully carry out one difficult task, you are often given other challenges. That was the case with the visit of Yasser Arafat, the Palestinian leader who in the 1980s was considered a dangerous terrorist. He had been invited by the Socialist Group of the European Parliament to come to Strasbourg. I again was appointed, on behalf of the cabinet of the president, as the liaison officer with the French authorities, who had to set up huge security measures. Many years later, when I headed the cabinet of Mrs Nicole Fontaine, a French President of the European Parliament, we welcomed President Yasser Arafat in his capacity as the

President of the Palestinian Authority with the honours reserved to heads of states... The relativity of things in politics!

These many experiences may be at the origin of my appointment as the head of protocol of the European Parliament in 2004. To start formally in this new post I had my 'baptism by fire' – the organisation of the welcome ceremony for the ten new member states from Eastern and Central Europe in May 2004. Rarely had so many VIPs been present together at the European Parliament in Strasbourg: Speakers of national parliaments, ministers, presidents of the European institutions. Thank God the weather was excellent and the ceremony could be held on the esplanade in front of the main building of the Parliament. The high point of the ceremony was when the ten flags of the incoming member states were carried at arms by soldiers of Eurocorps walking in procession around the flags of the other member states before being raised together with the European flag while a choir sang the European anthem.

The protocol service was staffed in 2004 with one administrator and half a dozen assistants; all of them were experienced colleagues. When I left, my team counted twenty people. The tasks of the protocol service were rather vast, including the preparation and execution of visits of guests deserving protocol treatment, the preparation and execution of formal visits of heads of state invited to address the plenary of the Parliament, the preparation and execution of visits of inter-parliamentary delegations, the management of gifts, organisation of ceremonies and commemorations, the preparation and accompanying of visits done by the president of the Parliament abroad, and so on.

The protocol of the European Parliament is based on customs and a few rules. From its beginning it has been based on protocol customs of the member states and especially of their parliaments. Among the original six, three were kingdoms (Belgium, Luxemburg, and the Netherlands) and three were republics (France, Germany, and Italy). All of them had strong protocol traditions, which could be defined as imperial and Latin. Great parts of their decorum have been taken over like, for example, the ushers wearing the tailcoat with the silver or gold chain and the white gloves. Others had to be abandoned, like for instance the entry procession of the speaker into the chamber with presentation of military honours, because the EU doesn't have any military guards!

Internally, the rules applied for precedence stem mostly from elections. For example, the ranking of the fourteen vice-presidents depends on the number of votes they get in the election, the advantage being given to the most senior in age in case of an equal number of votes. Contrary to many national parliaments, in the European Parliament seniority in the function doesn't give any advantage, each period of mandate being considered as a new start of the parliament.

A major issue is of course the protocol in inter-institutional relations. What is precedence between the presidents of the Parliament, of the European Council, and of the Commission? In any country, the head of state ranks first, followed by either the Speaker of the parliament or the prime minister, depending on the national rules. At EU level it was agreed that the legal basis for the determination of precedence is the enumeration of the institutions in the Treaties (Art. 9 of the Treaty of Lisbon): the European Parliament, the European Council, the Council of the Union, the European Commission, the Court of Justice of the European Union, the European Central Bank, the Court of Auditors. Nobody will pretend that it is easy in practice because all these prominent people are representing institutions that consider themselves as the most important. The funny thing is that in international protocol the difference of customs may be very helpful. Let's take the case of an event bringing together two strong personalities whose entourages think that their boss should be given priority. In Anglo-German protocol, the most important person will be given the floor first; it is the opposite in the Latin Roman tradition where the most important person speaks last. It happened that I had the good fortune to accommodate everyone by combining the two protocols, each one of the speakers having the feeling of his importance, one because he spoke first and the other for exactly the opposite reason!

The notable thing is that this order of precedence is valuable only 'inside' the EU, because for the 'outside' representation, in non-EU member states, the treaty gives priority to the president of the European Council and for certain competences to the president of the Commission. One of the first occasions on which the three presidents of the European Parliament, the European Council, and the Commission were present and where the protocol made use of this was the ceremony of the awarding of the Nobel Peace Prize on 10 December 2012 in Oslo. All three presidents were standing on the stage, they were addressed by the president of the Norwegian Nobel Committee collectively as 'Honourable Presidents of the European Union', but only the presidents of the European Council and the Commission took the floor to reply to the speech on behalf of the EU. *Dura lex sed lex*, the president of the European Parliament accepted the rule of the game.

Over time it has become accepted at the international level that the EU may on major occasions be represented 'outside' by that kind of 'trinity'.

That was the case at the papal inauguration of Pope Francis in the Vatican on 19 March 2013, where the EU got three seats.

It is apparent that the Lisbon Treaty provided useful clarification which allowed us – my colleagues from the Council and the Commission and myself – to manage these extraordinary occasions with great serenity and ... to become friends.

The protocol of the European Parliament had to demonstrate its professionalism and quality. Many colleagues from protocol services of the executives had doubts: a parliament is often unpredictable and, if in addition it is European…, they could expect the worse! Visit after visit of heads of state or heads of government invited by the European Parliament, we demonstrated our ability to run a professional protocol. Generally, the visit of the advance team was sufficient to give all necessary assurance and confidence.

Indeed, to prepare and manage the visits of heads of state invited to address the plenary of the European Parliament in a formal sitting is one of the most exciting tasks of the protocol service of the European Parliament. I was given the privilege of welcoming nearly all the heads of state of the EU member states who usually pay a formal visit to the parliament during the presidency in turn of the EU by their country. But the European Parliament is also regularly chosen by heads of state of non-EU states to deliver a message to Europe through its elected representatives. The European Parliament is very proud of this and gives a major protocol importance to those visits: official welcome at the airport, motorcade to the Parliament premises, police escort, welcome ceremony with flags and national anthem, bilateral meeting with the president, formal session and public address in the chamber, press conference, formal lunch... In ten years as the head of the protocol service, I welcomed some fifty-five heads of state, including HM Queen Beatrix, HH Cheikh Hamad Bin Khalifa Al-Thani, the Emir of Qatar, HE UN Secretary-General Ban Ki-moon, the President of China, HE Mr Xi Jinping, and finally, in November 2014, HH Pope Francis. I have also greeted and accompanied numerous heads of government like Mrs Angela Merkel, or other VIPs such as HRH Prince Charles and Mrs Hillary Clinton. On every occasion protocol had to be adapted and to offer the highest level of quality and respect in order to serve the image of the institution; the image of the European Union.

On the European level, more perhaps than on a national level, protocol is in certain respects still under construction. But like all protocol services, it has to combine high traditions of courtesy and etiquette with modernity, rapidity, and frequency of international relations, seeking both effectiveness and quality. It also has to cope with major players of growing importance in public events, namely the security services and press. More than ever, there is a need for both professional skill and creativity.

In that sense I am convinced that protocol is not an ordinary job; it is an art.

Composition of invitations

5. Invitations and dress codes

History and introduction

According to Dr Carbone's article about the history of the social invitation (2004), there is a long history to the evolution of the invitation as we know it today.

> *Invitations to social events were used by the aristocracy in England and France probably beginning in the 18th century. It may be possible to go back another hundred or two hundred years to find the foundations which began the tradition of the invitation. The Kings, Queens, Lords, Ladies, Dukes, Duchesses, or in today's vernacular, 'High Society' would invite their peers to their social events with hand written announcements of the event. These were written by the wife, butler, or secretary. Writing was a mark of education. Even after the printing press, the aristocracy hand wrote invitations since 'mass production' would be in bad taste.*
>
> *Even though the printing press appeared in Europe in the mid-13th century, the printing of social invitations did not begin until the start of the 20th century. Some of the elite, fascinated with industrialization, began using 'mass produced' invitations probably as either a novelty or simply as another expression of wealth.*
>
> *The real beginning of the commercially printed invitation began in the United States probably after World War II. One of the great features of the combination of democracy with industrialization is to give the common man the ability to mimic the lifestyles and materialism of society's elite. About the same time, Amy Vanderbilt and Emily Post appear on the scene to help correct the fumblings of society. The first appearance of the printed invitation was probably for large events hosted by wealthy industrialists wishing to exploit 'new technology'.*
>
> *If you and I could afford ordinary printed invitations, then the socially elite needed to distance themselves from such an abomination. They then elected to have their invitations 'engraved'. This served a second purpose. It permitted the printed invitation to emulate handwriting since engraved copper plates were made by hand. Engraving, as the name implies, requires an artisan to 'hand write' in reverse into a metal plate using a carving tool. To this day, the finest invitations are engraved.*

Engraved invitations are indeed still used for formal and official occasions, but a wide range of other formats are very common nowadays as well, ranging from colourful multi-folded cards to well-designed electronic invitations. However, some basic elements should still be taken into consideration, no matter what layout will be used. In this chapter, useful guidelines and tips will be provided concerning the necessary content and wording of official invitations, as well as common practices related to sending out invitations and the proper prescriptions of relevant dress codes. Further information regarding guest lists will be provided in Chapter 9.

The timing of sending out invitations depends to a great extent upon the country, the city, the social activity, and the kind of guests involved. In the diplomatic community around the world, invitations for receptions are normally sent out two or three weeks in advance. If the function is larger, three or four weeks may be more suitable. In Western Europe and, for example, Australia and New Zealand, invitations to formal events should ideally be sent four to six weeks prior to the event, otherwise it is likely that few people could accept, having made other engagements earlier. In the Middle East it can be quite appropriate to send invitations less than a week prior to an event. Invitations with the qualification 'p.m.' (*pour mémoire*) or 'To Remind' may still be sent out at a relatively late stage, since in these cases, the invitees will already have been notified of the upcoming event via telephone or some other channel and have accepted. On these invitations, one could draw through the 'RSVP' (*répondez s'il vous plaît*) and telephone number, and write the words 'To Remind' underneath, or have the words 'To Remind' printed on the invitation where the RSVP would normally be written. In some cases it could be wise to send a preliminary announcement that can be sent as soon as an event date and time are fixed and in order to make sure that the guests know well in advance that the event is upcoming. This announcement could be sent as an informal letter, a card, or an email. Not all the details of the event need to be indicated yet, since a real invitation should be sent afterwards as well. One could, for example, indicate in the announcement that 'An official invitation will be sent in good time.'

Responding to an invitation should be done generally by phone, email, or reply card, within two or three days of receiving the invitation. Often, a deadline for responding is indicated on the invitation as well. Be sure to observe the request on the invitation. 'Regrets only' means to inform only if you will not attend, and 'RSVP' means to respond whether you will or will not attend. A formal invitation may request that the reply be addressed to a protocol officer or social secretary. If this is not indicated under the RSVP on the invitation, the reply could be addressed to the host and hostess.

INVITATIONS AND DRESS CODES

An invitation is a document that should give an invitee the most essential details of the event. Every invitation should actually include an answer to the following 8 Ws:
Who is inviting?
Why is he/she inviting?
What kind of function is it?
Where is the event taking place?
When is the event taking place?
Which dress code applies?
Whom to contact for a reply?
Whatever information is also relevant to know?

General guidelines for composing an invitation

- Formal invitations are always in the third person (it is appropriate to respond in the third person as well).
- Invitations to official functions should give the host by his or her office and/or name with full title and rank, but prefixes such as His Grace, His Excellency, His Worship, the Honourable and the suffix Esquire are hardly ever used.
- In the case of an invitation to an official function, the inviting party is regularly only identified by his/her position – without including the individual's name. This is due to the fact that such positions are often unique, meaning that there can be no misunderstanding as to who is sending the invitation.
- 'Request the pleasure of the company of' and 'Request the honour of the company of' are used most frequently and are the most appropriate on invitations issued by and to ambassadors and other high-ranking officials.
- In the case of pre-printed invitations from the diplomatic corps, one often finds a strip fixed along the top of the card specifying the occasion.
- Timings can be indicated as follows:
    - at six o'clock
    - at 6 p.m.
    - at 18.00 hours
- Please make sure to verify if the local concept of social time is similar to yours. In some countries, an invitation for 6 p.m. means you should arrive at precisely 6 p.m. In some other countries, it means you should

- arrive no earlier than 7.30 p.m. To avoid awkward situations, ask an insider before attending social events in another country.
- Invitations for a reception held during the day (for example, a festive lunch, high tea, or cocktail event) often specify both the start and end times for the occasion.
- Formal invitations are commonly printed in landscape format on an A5-size invitation card. Invitations for embassy receptions in celebration of a national day are often printed on a slightly smaller format.
- Vertically-oriented folded A4-size invitations that visualise the upcoming event by means of photographs or other images are becoming increasingly common, within both the public and private sectors.
- In the case of folded invitations, the most important text should be found on the right-hand side of the opened invitation: in other words, the invitation text is printed on the right-hand inside page. Further details of the occasion, including possible programme information, may be printed on the left-hand side. Logos, emblems, and similar elements (including the logos of possible sponsors) may be included on the rear of the invitation.
- If the invitation is printed in two languages, the main language of the occasion is printed on the right, with the second language on the left.
- On most invitations in the English language, one will mention the location of the event first, followed by the date and time. The United Nations uses this principle of PDT (place, date, time) as well and uses British spelling in English.
- Common French abbreviations used on invitations on either the lower left or lower right side (also if the invitation is written in other languages):

    | p.c. | *pour condoler* (to express sympathy) |
    | p.f. | *pour féliciter* (to extend congratulations) |
    | p.m. | *pour mémoire* (to remind) |
    | p.p. | *pour présenter* (to introduce) |
    | p.p.c. | *pour prendre congé* (to say goodbye) |
    | p.r. | *pour remercier* (to express thanks) |
    | r.s.v.p. | *répondez s'il vous plaît* (request for response) |

- Examples of possible remarks at the bottom of an invitation (answers on *Whom to contact for a reply?*):
    - Your confirmation of attendance could be sent before (date) to (email address).
    - Please let us know if you will be attending before (date).
    - You can register via (website url) by entering the following unique code: ...

- RSVP by (date) by means of the enclosed reply card and envelope or via email.
- Regrets only
- To Remind
- If you wish to be present on this occasion, please complete and return the reply card before (date). An entrance card will be sent to you in good time.
- You will receive a confirmation with further details on the evening's events one week in advance.

– Examples of possible remarks at the bottom of an invitation (answers on *Whatever information is also relevant to know?*):
- Please present this invitation at the entrance.
- You are kindly requested to show this invitation upon arrival.
- This invitation admits one person.
- This invitation is valid for two persons within your organisation.
- This invitation is also your admission card. Please do not forget to bring it with you.
- This invitation is personal and not transferable.
- Please hold on to this invitation card. Once you have formally accepted the invitation, this strictly personal card will give you admission to the event in combination with a valid proof of identity.
- You may be required to present proof of identity.
- The performance will start at 20.00 hours. For security reasons the doors will be open from 19.00 hours.
- Guests are asked to be seated by (time).
- The concert will be followed by a reception.
- In connection with the holy month of Ramadan, Iftar will commence at 21.30 hours.
- In case of dietary restrictions, please advise.
- A simultaneous French translation of the ceremony will be provided.
- For further information or enquiries, please contact the protocol department on (telephone number).

– Examples of possible forms of dress code at the bottom of an invitation are provided at the end of this chapter.

Diplomacy has witnessed a growing informality throughout the twentieth century, and because protocol does not operate in a vacuum, it has adapted to mirror broader societal norms. Digital diplomacy via email is one example where technological innovations have helped facilitate speedier communication and provide reliability in communication. Invitations, therefore, may nowadays be sent via email as well, even though a printed invitation remains more stylish and professional. Invitations should not be sent, however, via SMS, Facebook, Twitter, or any other kind of social media. Digital invitations should continue to follow the guidelines and discourse of hard copy invitations despite their more informal nature. Make sure as well that, for privacy reasons, digital invitations are not sent as one bulk with all the email addresses in the 'To' line, but place all the addresses in the 'Bcc' line instead.

Forms of address

There are certain universal conventions governing forms of address, but all countries have their particular style. Generally, the style of addressing a person is determined by his or her status as well as the relationship between that person and the speaker or writer. Many books and manuals have been written on this subject, and it is not the intention of the authors to repeat all the different styles in this guide. Therefore, the following book is recommended and constitute points of reference for the various forms of address for heads of state and government, as well as other religious, legal, diplomatic, royal, and political officials from around the world:

Honor & Respect, The Official Guide to Names, Titles, & Forms of Address by Robert Hickey.

In the foreword of Hickey's book, Pamela Eyring, as owner and director of the Protocol School of Washington, highlights the importance of the correct usage of names, titles, and forms of address:

> *These topics are complicated but must be mastered by professionals planning high-level events. All officials and event participants appreciate receiving the honors of their rank and the courtesies of their office. When distinghuised visitors see their names presented in the proper way, they feel they are personally and warmly welcomed.*

A useful point of reference for official diplomatic correspondence in the French language is:

Manuel Pratique de Protocole, Nouvelle Édition by Jean Serres.

Finally, the UN Correspondence Manual ('*www.archive.unu.edu/hq/library/resource/UN-correspondence-manual.pdf*') gives instructions regarding composing formal and informal letters, notes verbales, and other official means of communication.

When unsure of an official or person's title or position, one can consult the protocol department of the respective country to confirm.

Be aware, that personal preferences can differ from the formal applicable forms of address. Due to developments in emancipation in a.o. Scandinavia and Western Europe, for example, quite some women in related countries who are career oriented tend to use their own surname more often than in the past, even though they formally adopted the surname of their husband.

Examples of invitation texts

Reception on the occasion of Presentation of Credentials

> (NAME OF HOST)
> ambassador of (COUNTRY NAME)
> requests the pleasure of the company of
> (NAME OF GUEST)
> at a v in d'honneur
> on wednesday 1 july from 13.00 – 14.30 hrs

With a separate strip in the top left-hand corner:
On the occasion of Presentation of Credentials

Farewell reception for ambassador

> the ambassador of (COUNTRY NAME) and mrs ...
> request the pleasure of the company of
> (NAME OF GUEST)
> at a reception to bid farewell
> on wednesday, 1 July 2015 from 17.00 – 19.00 hours

Reception in celebration of a national day

> on the occasion of the national day of (COUNTRY NAME),
> ambassador of (COUNTRY NAME)
> requests the pleasure of the company of
> (NAME OF GUEST)
> at a reception
> on wednesday 1 july 2015 from 12.30 to 14.30 hrs.

Reception on the occasion of ... within the hosting organisation

(NAME AND POSITION OF HOST) requests (NAME OF GUEST) to do him the honour of joining members of the (NAME OF ORGANISATION) at a reception to be held on wednesday 1 july 2015 from 5 p.m. to 7 p.m. in order to mark (OCCASION OF THE EVENT)

Lunch during a bilateral visit (United States)

in honor of
their majesties king juan carlos I of spain and queen sofia
the secretary of state requests the pleasure of your company at luncheon
on wednesday, the twenty-third of february two thousand at twelve-thirty o'clock

American invitation (dating from 2010) for a reception hosted by President Obama

INVITATIONS AND DRESS CODES

Formal dinner during a bilateral visit (United States)

the president and mrs. clinton
request the pleasure of the company of
the chief of protocol
at a dinner to be held at the white house on wednesday, february 23, 2000 at seven-thirty o'clock

black tie

On first enclosure card:
on the occasion of the visit of
their majesties king juan carlos I of spain and queen sofia

On second enclosure card:
please respond to the social secretary
the white house
at your earliest convenience giving name, date of birth and social security number of your guest

Formal dinner during a bilateral visit (New Zealand)

on the occasion of the visit of their royal highnesses prince ... and princess ...
their excellencies the governor-general of new zealand the hon ... and (*NAME OF SPOUSE*)
have pleasure in inviting
(*NAME OF GUEST*)
to a dinner
at government house, wellington
at 7.30 pm on (*DATE*)

State dinner at Noordeinde Palace (the Netherlands)

on the occasion of the state visit of
his excellency mr (NAME),
president of (COUNTRY NAME)
and mrs (NAME OF SPOUSE)
the grand master of the royal household has the honour,
by order of their majesties the king and queen,
of inviting (NAME OF GUEST) to the state dinner held on
(DAY AND DATE) at noordeinde palace.
invitees are requested to arrive no later than 19.30 hours.

State dinner (United Kingdom)

the lord steward
has received her majesty's command to invite (NAME OF GUEST)
to a state banquet to be given at buckingham palace by
the queen and the duke of edinburgh
in honour of
the president of (COUNTRY NAME) and mrs (NAME OF PARTNER)
on (DAY), (DATE), (YEAR) at 8.30 pm.

evening dress (white tie),
decorations,
full ceremonial evening dress for serving officers,
or national dress

Lunch at Buckingham Palace (United Kingdom)

the master of the household
has received her majesty's command to invite
(NAME OF GUEST)
to a luncheon to be given at buckingham palace
by the queen and the duke of edinburgh
on (DATE)
at 12.50 pm. for 1.00 pm.

INVITATIONS AND DRESS CODES

Lunch at the Royal Palace of Stockholm (Sweden)

the first marshal of the court
is commanded by his majesty the king
to invite
(NAME OF GUEST)
to a luncheon
to be given by
their majesties the king and queen of sweden
at the royal palace (eastern wing)
on (DAY AND DATE) at 1.00 pm.

Head of state lunch at the United Nations headquarters in New York (United States)

the secretary-general of the united nations
requests the pleasure of the company of
(NAME OF GUEST)
at a luncheon
in honour of heads of state and government
attending the (NUMBER) session of the general assembly
on (DAY AND DATE), at 1.15 p.m.
at the north delegates' lounge of the united nations

Reception on the occasion of an assembly of an international association, organised by the mayor of the host city (Czech Republic)

mayor of the city of prague
tomas hudecek
requests the pleasure of your company
at a reception on the occasion of the meeting of
the policy committee of c.e.m.r. member associations
to be held in the mayor's residence, marianske nam. 1, praha 1,
on monday 2 december 2013 at 7 pm

Reception on the occasion of a welcome reception for a new international organisation in The Hague (the Netherlands)

> the mayor of the hague
> has the honour to invite you
> to a reception on the occasion of
> the launch of the branch office in the hague of
> the international development law organization
> in the atrium of the city hall of the hague
> on tuesday, 1 april 2014 from 5.30 pm till 7 pm.

Event held on the occasion of an international day at the Peace Palace in The Hague (the Netherlands)

> the international day of peace, as of 2002, 21 september was declared a day of global ceasefire and non-violence, and commemorates and strengthens the ideals of peace.

> to mark this occasion
> the mayor and aldermen of the hague
> cordially invite you to
> a brunch and the launch of the peace run
> at the peace palace on saturday 21 september 2013 at 10.30 am.

Network event for a select, high-profile audience (the Netherlands)

> the mayor of (NAME OF CITY)
> has pleasure in inviting (NAME OF GUEST)
> to the (NAME OF NETWORK EVENT) at (NAME OF VENUE)
> on wednesday 1 july 2015 from 6 pm till 8 pm.

> leading members of the national and local government will be meeting the top representatives from the international institutions, the business world and the cultural sector.

INVITATIONS AND DRESS CODES

Reception organised for the purpose of thanking invitees for their contribution to a major international conference (the Netherlands)

> to express gratitude for the great cooperation of your
> institution in realising the nuclear security summit
> the mayor of the hague has the pleasure to invite you
> to a reception in the gemeentemuseum
> on tuesday 29 april 2 014 from 5.30 until 7 .30 pm.

The Lord Chamberlain is
commanded by Her Majesty to invite

Mr.

and

to a Garden Party
at Buckingham Palace
on Tuesday, 3rd June 2014 from 4 to 6 pm

This card does not admit

British invitation (dating from 2014) for a garden party hosted by Queen Elizabeth II

Der Bundespräsident und Frau Daniela Schadt
bitten
Herrn Georg Wild
und Begleitung
zu einem Bürgerfest in den Park von Schloss Bellevue
am Samstag, dem 8. September 2012, um 17.00 Uhr.

German invitation (dating from 2012) for a garden party hosted by Federal President and Mrs Schadt

Reception on the occasion of the twentieth anniversary of an international organisation (the Netherlands)

> ambassador (NAME),
> the osce high commissioner on national minorities,
> has the honour to invite you
> to a reception marking the occasion of
> the 20th anniversary of the osce high commissioner on national minorities.
>
> the ceremony will take place on 7 march 2013 at 15.30
> at sociëteit de witte, plein 24, the hague.

Celebration of Leiden University's Dies Natalis (the Netherlands)

> the executive board of leiden university
> is pleased to invite you to the celebration of
> the dies natalis is (YEAR) on (DAY AND DATE) at 15:00 hrs.
>
> the ceremony will take place in the pieterskerk,
> pieterskerkhof 1a in leiden.

French invitation (dating from 2014) for a reception hosted by President Hollande

INVITATIONS AND DRESS CODES   139

The Lord Chamberlain is commanded by
The Queen to invite

....

....

to the Marriage of
His Royal Highness Prince William of Wales, K.G.
with
Miss Catherine Middleton
at Westminster Abbey
on Friday, 29th April, 2011 at 11.00 a.m.

A reply is requested to:
State Invitations Secretary, Lord Chamberlain's Office,   *Dress: Uniform, Morning Coat*
Buckingham Palace, London SW1A 1AA   *or Lounge Suit*

British invitation (dating from 2011) for the marriage of HRH Prince William of Wales with Miss Catherine Middleton

Gala concert hosted by a multinational (the Netherlands)

the executive board of (NAME OF COMPANY)
has the honour to invite

........................(NAME OF GUEST)................................

and partner to the (NAME OF COMPANY) gala concert.
the concert takes place on wednesday 16 december 2015
in the nieuwe kerk, spui 175, the hague.

welcome between 19.15 and 20.00 hours.
festive reception following the concert
between 21.45 and 00.00 hours.

black tie

(DETAILS OF ORCHESTRA AND CONCERT PROGRAMME ARE INDICATED ON THE
LEFT SIDE OF THE FOLDED INVITATION CARD)

Reply card and admission card

REPLY CARD
i / we shall be able / unable to attend
name: ...
address: ....
tel. no.: ....
kindly contact or forward to
(name and address of organisation)
(tel – fax – email)

ADMISSION CARD
for
(NAME OF GUEST)
to a dinner banquet held in honour of
the president and the first lady of (COUNTRY NAME)
he mr (NAME) and mrs (NAME OF PARTNER)
kindly present this card and identification document upon
request at the (NAME OF VENUE, CITY)
on (DAY AND DATE, YEAR)

Dress codes

Throughout history, clothing has influenced people's way of life. It is commonly known that first impressions are formed within the first twenty seconds of meeting someone, and the main element of that impression is appearance. Keep in mind that local customs can impose many modifications to the guidelines below, but in general these are common instructions for the kinds of dress code one might find on an invitation. Women should be particularly mindful in many countries when conservative dress rules are applied such as skirt length, low necklines, and having one's arms covered. If one remains unsure of the terminology used, it is always appropriate to clarify before the event. This might count for, for example, the terms Traditional Dress or National Dress. Every country has its own interpretation of these.

The main terms that apply to dress codes are listed on the following pages.

Formal, White Tie, Cravate Blanche, Full Evening Dress, Tails, Frack

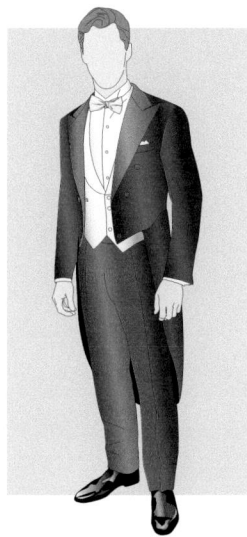

White tie is the most formal evening dress that exists for civilians today.

Possible components:
– Black tailcoat with silk facings, sharply cut-away at the front and always single breasted.
– Black trousers with double black braids (in the United States a single black braid) without turn-ups.
– White stiff-fronted wing collar in cotton piqué with shirt studs in silver and mother-of-pearl and single cuffs fastening with cuff links.
– White bow tie in cotton piqué.
– White low-cut waistcoat in cotton piqué with inlaid or mother-of-pearl buttons (in Southern Europe and Latin America the waistcoat could be black as well).
– Black socks mid-calf length (no skin should be visible when seated).
– Black patent leather pumps or shoes.
– Full decorations if appropriate for the occasion (plaques et cordon), sash under the waistcoat. In the presence of a member of the royal family over the waistcoat.
– No wristwatch.
– Not to be worn before 6 p.m.

Ball Gown

A ball gown is the most formal female attire for social occasions. According to rules of etiquette, a ball gown must be worn where 'white tie' or 'long evening dress' is specified on the invitation. It is traditionally a full-skirted gown reaching at least to the ankles, made of luxurious fabric. Most versions are cut off the shoulder with décolleté necklines. Such gowns are typically worn with a stole or cape, jewellery, and opera-length gloves. Where 'state decorations' are to be worn, they are on a bow pinned to the chest, and members of royal families might wear a tiara.

Possible components:
- Ball gown – ballerina (to the ankle) or full-length to the floor.
- Appropriate pair of tights.
- Dancing shoes – formal pumps, high-heel shoes.
- Jewellery – earrings, necklace, rings, and bracelets. A watch is not considered appropriate except for jewelled versions.
- Gloves – above-elbow gloves are optional with a sleeveless evening gown, and short gloves may be worn with a long-sleeved gown. If worn, gloves need not be removed for a receiving line or dancing, but are removed prior to eating or drinking.
- Stole, cape or cloak, or an opera coat.
- Handbag – clutch style, small evening purse.

Semi-Formal, Black Tie, Cravate Noir, Tuxedo, Dinner Jacket, Evening Dress

Possible components:
- Short or medium black jacket that may have gross grain- or satin-faced lapels, either single-breasted (with one button) or double-breasted, a white handkerchief in the left pocket is optional.
- Black trousers with a single black silk braid (in the United States sometimes without a black braid) matching the lapels, without turn-ups.
- Long-sleeved cotton or silk white dress shirt with either a Marcella or a pleated front and a normal collar, often closed by nice shirt studs and French cuffs. A wing collar shirt has become appropriate.
- Black silk bow tie (for less formal occasions, coloured bow ties can also be appropriate).
- Black low-cut waistcoat or black cummerbund – *optional* (coloured for less formal occasions).
- Black socks mid-calf length (no skin should be visible when seated).
- Black patent leather pumps or shoes.
- Decorations might be worn.
- No wristwatch.
- Not to be worn before 6 p.m.

Some local varieties:
- A white tuxedo could be worn at open-air evening parties, on cruises, and in tropical countries for certain official occasions. It is either

genuinely white or light beige. The trousers worn with a white tuxedo are black.
- 'Red Sea Rig' or 'Gulf Rig' means a tuxedo minus the jacket.

Long Evening Dress

Long Evening Dress can be either an evening gown or silk or other high-quality fabric skirt – ballerina (to the ankle) or full-length (to the floor) – with a luxury fabric blouse.

Possible components of a long evening dress:
- A formal ballerina to the ankle or full-length to the floor gown or long skirt with blouse.
- Appropriate pair of tights.
- Dancing shoes – formal pumps, high-heel shoes.
- Jewellery – earrings, necklace, rings and bracelets. A watch is not considered appropriate except for jewelled versions.
- Colours may vary as long as they are appropriate.
- Clutch style small evening purse.

Short Evening Dress

The short evening dress is currently often used instead of the long evening dress at black tie events.

Possible components:
- A formal knee-length dress or skirt with blouse.
- Appropriate shoes for the occasion, high-heel shoes, formal pumps.
- Appropriate pair of tights.
- Jewellery – earrings, necklace, rings and bracelets. A watch is not considered appropriate except for jewelled versions.
- Colours may vary as long as they are appropriate.
- Small evening purse.

Protocol tip:
- If an invitation indicates just 'Black Tie', the dress for the ladies can be either Long Evening Dress or Short Evening Dress. In case the host prefers Long Evening Dress, it will be mentioned on the invitation.

Morning Dress, Morning Coat, Jacquet, Cut-away

Morning dress is the daytime form of men's formal dress and can be appropriate to wear during formal events such as weddings, funerals, presentations of credentials, and e.g. Royal Ascot. Despite its name, morning dress may be worn to afternoon official or social events before 6 p.m.

Possible components:
- A black morning coat / cutaway and the skirt of knee length (often light grey coat at Royal Ascot) and always single-breasted.

- Black (more formal) or grey double-breasted or single-breasted waistcoat and the lowest button always open with single-breasted.
- A white double-cuffed shirt (French cuffed).
- Formal grey / black striped trousers without turn-ups.
- Formal grey or black tie (a cravat with winged collar at weddings, or Royal Ascot could be appropriate). Decent coloured ties may be worn if the occasion allows.
- Dark grey socks mid-calf length.
- Black formal leather shoes.
- Formal grey or black gloves and top hat (*optional*).

Formal Day Wear, Morning Dress, Afternoon Dress

This form of clothing is worn during the daytime at weddings, the Royal Ascot, and other formal day functions.

Possible components of women's morning dress:
- Luxury dress or 'deux pièces.'
- Shoulders covered.
- Medium-heel shoes.
- Appropriate pair of tights.
- Colours and fabric suitable for the occasion.
- Jewellery – earrings, necklace and rings; bracelets – *optional*.

- For formal events and Royal Ascot it is recommended to wear a hat and gloves.
- A veil, usually made of thin white silk – *optional.*
- Little handbag.

Informal, Dark Suit, Business Suit, Lounge Suit, Tenue de Ville

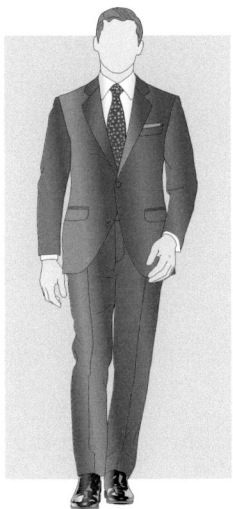

Double-breasted suit coats are almost always kept buttoned. When there is more than one button to fasten (as in a traditional six-to-two arrangement), only the top one need be fastened. However, it all depends on the cut of the jacket.

In two-button suits the bottom button is generally left unfastened. The current fashion trend for three-button suits is to leave the bottom and upper button unfastened.

Possible components:
- Jacket and trousers in same fabric, preferably dark blue or dark grey with or without stripes. Most suits have two or three front buttons.
- Good quality (silk) tie, no tiepin.
- Long-sleeved dress shirt (*preferably French-cuffed*) even in summer and at least a half inch (1 cm) of the cuff will show from under the jacket.
- Waistcoat – *optional.*
- Dark socks (mid-calf length).
- Black or dark brown leather shoes (lace-up or slip-on).
- Belt (*optional*) to match the shoes.

Cocktail Dress, Long Skirt

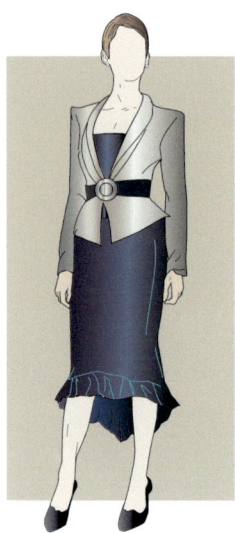

A cocktail dress can be worn at cocktail parties and other semi-formal occasions in the afternoon.

Possible components:
- A formal dress that varies in length depending on fashion and local custom. It ranges from just above or below the knee.
- A wide variety of materials, styles, and accessories is acceptable: silk, satin and chiffon are always popular choices.
- Colours may vary as long as they are appropriate.
- Medium- or high-heel shoes.
- Appropriate pair of tights.
- Jewellery – earrings, necklace and rings; bracelets- *optional.*
- Little handbag.

Ladies Business Suit

In the 1970s, women who wanted to reach the executive level created the concept of 'dress for success' which meant dress similarly to male counterparts if they wanted to succeed in the business world. A business suit for ladies can be worn in the office but would be appropriate for official and social functions throughout the day as well.

Possible components:
– Two pieces of matched suit trousers/skirt (colours usually are navy, dark grey, dark brown and black).
– Tailored pantsuits are appropriate.
– Skirts should cover thighs when seated.
– Appropriate pair of tights.
– Appropriate choice of jewellery.
– Shoes should be leather, fabric, or microfibre and closed at the front so that no toes are visible.
– Purse or bag should be small and simple, matching the type of clothing worn.

Business Casual, Smart Casual

Business/smart casual is probably one of the least understood descriptions of appropriate attire. This common label is subject to a wide spectrum of interpretation and is dependent on the character of the occasion.

Possible components:
– Blazer or sports jacket and/or fashionable sweater.
– Polo shirt, collar shirt.
– Shirt with a tie optional.
– Decent shoes (no trainers or colourful sneakers, but loafers will do).
– Cotton or corduroy trousers grey or khakis or other appropriate colour (smart or fashionable jeans in good condition might also be accepted in certain cases).

Protocol tips:
– Please note that there is a dress code known as 'Informal' which although it sounds casual, traditionally means 'Business Suit.' Ladies should dress accordingly.
– Casual or leisure clothes should be avoided at any time.
– An invitation for a 'casual' dinner still means wearing smart casual!

Some local varieties:
- 'Bush shirt' is a long- or short-sleeved shirt with a finished bottom edge worn outside rather than tucked into the slacks, or a long- or short-sleeved embroidered man's shirt.
- 'Batik shirt' is worn in a.o. India, Indonesia, Malaysia, the Philippines, Singapore, and Sri Lanka. There are diverse patterns and colours influenced by a variety of cultures.
- 'Island casual' means a Hawaiian shirt and casual (usually khaki) slacks.
- 'Territory Rig' means casual in the Northern Territory of Australia.

Ladies Business Casual, Smart Casual

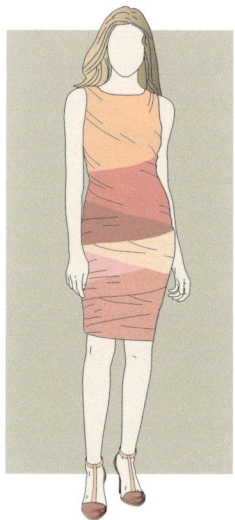

The smart casual wardrobe has to have a sporty look, but one should not wear gym shoes or sweatshirts.

Possible components:
- Sporty dress.
- Blazer type of jacket.
- Skirts or trousers.
- Shirt, roll-neck pullover, or sweater.
- Appropriate choice of accessories.
- Low-heel or flat shoes or fashionable boots.

Professor Olivier Arifon, former Professor at the Université libre de Bruxelles in charge of the chair in communication

Olivier Arifon, born in Paris, was Professor at the Université libre de Bruxelles in charge of the chair in Communication. He taught Influence, Lobbying and Communication, Competitive Intelligence and Public Diplomacy with a European perspective, introducing experts and case studies as well as theoretical elements. From 1997 to 2011, he was an associate professor at the University of Strasbourg (France) on the same topics. Besides academic activities, he led a communication company for five years, was an expert in training of diplomats and managers in Poland, Croatia, France, and Singapore, and fulfilled the position of high education attaché for the French ministry of Foreign Affairs in Germany for two years. In his research, he examines how companies and civil society are developing successful strategies, considering Brussels' activities as a model. In a comparative perspective between Europe and Asia (India), he identifies methodological approaches and communication policy for European or Indian protagonists of civil society. He is the author of more than fifty papers, book chapters, and articles in mostly academic journals.

Diplomatic language and formal language: a code with a double meaning by Professor Olivier Arifon

In France and, by extension, in other chancelleries until the beginning of the twentieth century, the language used in diplomacy had its roots in the language of the court, more specifically that of the court of Louis XIV, which explains the place of French as the language of diplomacy (Fumaroli, 2003). The present article attempts to provide a historical and anthropological perspective on the forms of expression used by diplomats. I shall address why diplomatic language is both formal and necessary, characteristics that bring it closer to doublespeak (Delporte,

2009). The notions of ambiguity, context, emotion, and values shall be dealt with. I shall also try to show why decoding techniques are necessary to shed light on hidden meanings, the stakes and strategies involved. Indeed, diplomacy is based to a large extent on language and the received and perceived meanings of the phrases and arguments put forward. The language of diplomacy has both an internal – among diplomats – and external – for the public and the media – dimension. The present work draws upon my experience as attaché for university cooperation with the ministry of External Affairs, trainer of French and foreign diplomats in Singapore, and discussions with foreign diplomats. Finally, it is focused on the French language for two reasons: first, because it is the 'historical' language of diplomacy and second, because it is my mother tongue. We may argue here that in other languages too speech acts are subject to similar constraints and formality, even if accounts suggest that English and the Anglo-Saxon relational style make for simpler and more direct relations.

Diplomacy and representations

The general public tends to view diplomacy as the art of dissembling through the use of speech and a coded or formal language along with the cultivation of secrecy for the benefit of those in power. From an academic perspective, the search for invariants in diplomatic practices leads us to define the notions of borders, immunity, permanence of relations, reciprocity of treatment, the place and code of information, and finally secrecy. A perusal of studies on diplomacy, especially international relations, shows the absence of a specific category for the forms diplomatic language takes and, more importantly, the absence of case studies. In other words, little has been said about the language used in diplomacy other than viewing it as a variant of political language, which it no doubt is, as we shall see later on. More often than not, the studies identified deal with negotiating procedures, strategy or on-the-ground experience as elements for the understanding of foreign policy. In the only French work listed on the subject (Villar, 2006), a linguistic analysis is confronted with the theories of international action. The author proposes a semiotic approach around four aspects of diplomatic discourse:

Sincerity	versus	duplicity
Truthful speech	versus	lies
Truth	versus	falsehood
Transparency	versus	secrecy

On the basis of these aspects, it is possible to consider, in concurrence with discourse analysis studies, that the language used in diplomacy is an ordinary language and not a technical discourse (except in some rare cases, such as the negotiations leading to the Iran nuclear deal of 2015).

Doublespeak as defined in our research is conceived as a set language consisting of stereotype phrases and related to political discourse. In everyday language, the term refers to a constrained manner of expression, generally thought to be pejorative.

Studies on doublespeak highlight the absence of a precise message, which invades space to prevent any sensitive discourse, characterised by sincerity. As discourse appears to be powerless to change the world, the speaker uses language – or rather doublespeak – to articulate the world in accordance with a given order of power. Accordingly, language is constrained and its value becomes a substitute for meaning. A distortion between deeds and words comes into play, as Thomas Legrand observes: « [...], c'est plutôt une mauvaise appréciation de la puissance de son discours ou de la puissance de la réalité face à sa propre volonté ! » (It is rather a poor appraisal of the power of one's discourse or the power of reality in the face of one's own desire) (Legrand, 2010: 27). Finally, doublespeak is different from administrative jargon; the former aims to convince, the latter incites one to act in a given sphere.

In the case of the language of a totalitarian regime, an idiom pushed to the extreme, the subjugation of language serves to reduce the critical faculties of the listener. Victor Klemperer, a philologist under pressure during the Nazi regime, wrote in his analysis of the language used by it: '... the listener's emotions (and Goebbels's audience always comprises listeners, even if it only reads the doctor's essays in the newspaper) never come to reset, they are constantly attracted and rebuffed, attracted and rebuffed, and there is no time for critical reasoning to catch its breath' (Klemperer, 1996: 327). From a tool for reasoning, language becomes an emotion centric discourse. In his book *1984*, George Orwell invented Newspeak using single word concepts with a very restricted meaning.

The language of diplomatic exchanges and writings is far removed from such extreme approaches. In place of a set language or emotional logic, we suggest fuzzy logic in a formal framework. Thus, paradoxically, a positive language embodying the specificities of diplomacy becomes a part of political discourse and constitutes the art of persuasion in the uncertain and ephemeral context of diplomatic negotiation. The aim of course is to enunciate enduring convictions. But as diplomatic language has political overtones, it shares some of the features of political discourse such as avoidance, ambiguity (of meaning), understanding (of position) or even dissimulation. In the eyes of the public and observers of international relations, it is these aspects that give rise to the perception that diplomatic language is merely doublespeak.

The art of worldly wisdom and language

When diplomacy as a profession began to expand and become organised in the European courts during the modern era, some diplomats wrote about the necessary attributes of a good diplomat of which evidently mastery of language was a part. Under the strong influence of relations among the European monarchies of the seventeenth and eighteenth centuries, these attributes were first and foremost signs of good breeding.

One of the oldest works entitled «De la charge et dignité de l'ambassadeur» by Jean Hotman de Villiers was written in 1604. It is a pragmatic work in which the author attempts to define the qualities of a diplomat. Knowledge of history and culture and the ability to express oneself promote *'le contact avec les autres, une communauté d'apprentissage, alliant les pratiques et les théories, le passé et le présent, l'expérience, la découverte et l'application personnelles, aussi bien que les cours formalisés, l'étude et la réflexion.'* (Contact with others, a community of learning, combining practice and theory, past and present, experience, personal discovery and application, as well as formal classes, study and reflection.) (Hotman de Villiers, 2003: 20).

In a similar vein, the Spanish Jesuit Baltasar Gracian published in 1647 *The Art of Worldly Wisdom*. The book portrays a man who from a courtier became a diplomat. A short essay by Baron d'Holbach gives a caustic description of the courtier in the presence of the monarch: 'Under the cover of friendship he knows how to lull his enemies, show an open, affectionate face to those he most detests, embrace with tenderness the enemy he'd like to suffocate. Finally, the most impudent lies mustn't produce any alteration in his face' (D'Holbach, 2010: 18).

Closer to our times, the works of Norbert Elias incorporate these qualities of the court system into the mechanisms of self-control and strategic relations (Elias, 1985). Norbert Elias combines etiquette with the essential motivation of members of the court, namely prestige and recognition. Thus, *'par l'étiquette, la société de cour procède à son autoreprésentation, chacun se distinguant de l'autre, tous ensemble se distinguant des personnes étrangères au groupe, chacun et tous ensemble s'administrant la preuve de la valeur absolue de leur existence.'* (As a matter of etiquette, the court society proceeds to its self-representation, each one distinguishing himself from the other, collectively distinguishing themselves from those outside the group and individually and collectively administering to themselves the absolute value of their existence.) (Elias, 1985: 97). When all is said and done, a good ambassador of the classical era was one who possessed a sense of tradition and had inherited or acquired natural social skills in osmosis with the great courts of Europe. He was someone who cultivated style and eloquence, conscious of his values and of pleasing and civil manners.

In fact, the memoirs of ambassadors often emphasised these social skills and ways of conducting oneself, akin to good breeding. Little is said about language; instead the stress is on physical behaviour and the degree of individual freedom a serving diplomat enjoys. This shows the extent to which the context, the forms, and the structures of the profession condition the modalities of expression, both verbal and non-verbal, as pointed out by Martine Kingston de Leusse (1998: 86): 'À partir de son entrée en accréditation, l'ambassadeur se trouve dans un milieu fermé où les actes, les vêtements, les gestes, les formes de sociabilité revêtent une spécificité qui permet d'en faire le support institutionnalisé de l'échange diplomatique courtois et pacifique.' (From the moment of his accreditation, an ambassador finds himself in a closed milieu where actions, clothes, gestures and forms of sociability take on a specificity which allow them to become the institutionalised support of courteous and peaceful diplomatic exchange.) The ambassador effaces himself as a subjective individual; he marshals his arguments and chooses his words with care, a reflection of his social skills and the political position of his country.

A scene from Nicolas Ray's film *55 Days at Peking* illustrates this clearly. The British ambassador is talking with his wife when his secretary opens the door and announces a visitor: 'Commander Lewis' (an officer in the American army).

The ambassador replies: 'Keep him waiting for a moment.'

He turns to his wife and says, 'Excuse me. I have to put on my official face.'

The wife leaves the room immediately, and the ambassador nonchalantly examines a set of papers and documents on his desk. Finally, he composes himself and says, 'Show him in.'

In the courts of Europe and later in international organisations, control of gestures and attitudes is paramount. Kings and emperors, high-ranking officials, mandarins and diplomats are supposed to remain in control of their emotions and bodies, regardless of whether this is actually the case or imposed by social frameworks and cultural codes. As the diplomat moves in circles that overinterpret signs, he must take into account the effect of his control (or lack of control) over his words and emotions to describe a situation or the terms of an exchange. The choice of words is of the essence. And beyond the mastery of speech, the manner in which he expresses his emotions in an exchange serves, in turn, to arouse the same feelings in the person he is addressing, in other words we are dealing with the register of persuasive charm. Though this could be dangerous, for an expressive man runs the risk of revealing himself: 'In order to live at court one must have complete control over the muscles of one's face in order to experience disgust without flinching. A pouter, a man of moods or susceptibility cannot succeed' (D'Holbach, 2010: 17).

The expression of ideas and emotions is also limited by the incompleteness of language, a dimension revealed by linguists (Goldschmidt, 2009) and ethno methodologists (Lecerf & Parker, 1987). These scholars have shown, often convergently, how language does not allow for complete expression of ideas and emotions. Indeed, when the individual who speaks its appropriate language, there can always be misunderstandings, errors, and shifts in meaning, blanks and gaps. This creates a distance between the two speakers, a median space constituting the relationship between the two.

The essence of diplomacy is to use everyday vocabulary and combine it with a specific code, namely the code of relations among states and the individuals entrusted with the task of negotiating with each other. Beyond this code, and as recommended in the principles of negotiation (Dupont, 1992), the attempt should be to understate words and emotions.

There are a number of reasons for this:
- One should maintain one's rank and show self-control; expressing disagreement while keeping a smiling face is the perfect illustration of this.
- One should also not offend one's interlocutor, for getting angry can interrupt or even break the dialogue and thereby the negotiation.
- Caution is the keyword of diplomacy, and this for two reasons. Both sides must avoid offending each other or saying too much about their positions; speaking too much can also hamper the smooth progress of negotiations.
- Finally, one should avoid showing one's weaknesses, which may be divided into two categories: insufficient mastery of subject in case of technical matters, or the desire to stand on prestige and symbolic

power (here, any sign of weakness on the part of the other may be interpreted as a factor favourable to one's interests).

In conclusion, the forms of expression used in diplomacy reflect the respect given to the representative of a state. The types of expressions and emotions help in perpetuating relationships, both human and political.

Discourse and rhetoric, the context of language

A diplomat's experience is directly related to his practice and the extent of his resources: similarities with other situations, quality of his information, training, and culture. Such experience helps him adapt to different contexts while remaining effective, for deciphering and adapting to changing situations is what the profession is all about. The trick is to have the cognitive, cultural, and communicational resources to apply them on the one hand and on the other, accept a certain amount of incomprehension and uncertainty in the situation as well as the social, political, and communicational elements that make up diplomacy. We are of the view that these frameworks of experience (Goffmann, 1996) constrain the diplomat and his language. And in the public mind, this is no different than doublespeak.

Diplomatic language is a subset of political language that thus relies on the same categories such as rhetoric, persuasion and manipulation, attention to the signifier and the signified. Historically, the West developed early on the art of oratory. Rhetoric, born in Greece at the beginning of the fifth century B.C., is part and parcel of democratic, legal, and commercial systems. Even today, this discipline is considered the art of acting through speech on opinions, emotions, and decisions.

One of the attributes of a diplomat is the ability to interpret vague and ambiguous elements to give him some leeway to manoeuvre. This vagueness is embodied in the words and forms of the discourse and has several names. It may be perceived as or called a euphemism. In the same vein, the French language uses the litote, a figure of speech that, by attenuating the expression of one's thought, lets one suggest more than what it actually said.

One little-discussed aspect of diplomatic discourse, namely ambiguity, needs to be stressed here. There is a distinction between semantic ambiguity (a single statement with several meanings) and strategic ambiguity, a voluntary act between statement, speaker, and recipient. For the analysis of acts of communication of diplomacy, the notion of ambiguity is essential, as it allows one to decipher the roles and behaviour of the actors. The French language is replete with synonyms and expressions which bring out the depth of this notion: *ambages, allusions, demi-mots, contenus latents, sens cachés, sous-entendus, arrière-pensées* (beat about the bush, allusions, hints, hidden agendas, hidden meanings, innuendos, ulterior motives.) The processes of language, the ways they are understood, in a word, the analysis of the situations of discourse, silences, and assertions is an ability every diplomat must possess. Indeed, there is frequent uncertainty between cultural systems and value systems among diplomats. This is fully reflected in the strategies and skills of negotiators. '*La stratégie de communication ambiguë permet en effet de maintenir le doute chez l'interlocuteur. Certes, la communication est parfois rendue plus claire en cas de réaction favorable, mais bien souvent elle est laissée en l'état pour maintenir l'autre dans le doute. Elle permet aussi d'influencer l'impact final des signaux afin de gagner un plus grand contrôle sur les images que d'autres ont de l'émetteur.*' (The strategy of ambiguous communication helps keep one's interlocutor in doubt. Certainly, at times communication is made clearer in case of a favourable reaction, but very often it is left in such a state as to keep the other in doubt. It also helps in influencing the final impact of the signals in order to win greater control of the images others have of the speaker.) (Villar, 2006: 175).

However, it is not always a question of sidetracking or impressing one's interlocutor. Formal language has its usefulness in diplomacy: words help neutralise or soften what they describe. Examples of such words are enlightening. Thus, when a diplomat is 'surprised' at something, he is in point of fact expressing his dissatisfaction or disagreement about the ongoing situation. When he 'denounces', it means things are going badly. When he 'condemns', the situation is thought to be very serious.[9]

Similarly, when he 'regrets not being able to respond favourably to the request', it is an elegant (and classic) way of indicating refusal to one's interlocutor.

'The negotiations were frank and must be pursued further' indicates nothing substantial was achieved but that the partners decide to continue meeting each other so as not break the contact.

In this regard, one of my interlocutors told us of an interesting case. On 1 April 2000, the secretary-general of the French ministry of Foreign Affairs, the second in command after the minister, wrote a diplomatic

---

9   Drafting modalities encountered during our experience as high education attaché for university cooperation in Munich.

telegram. This contained all the forms and rituals of language a diplomat normally uses, the author delighting in playing on the ambiguities allowed on account of it being April Fool's Day in France. Sadly, I was unable to obtain a copy of it.

Finally, Marcel Proust expresses the same thing in his inimitable style while referring to the Marquis de Norpois, a diplomat: 'Miserly in the use of words, not only from a professional scruple of prudence and reserve, but because words themselves have more value, present more subtleties of definition to men whose efforts protracted over a decade, to bring two countries to an understanding, are condensed, translated – in a speech or in a protocol – into a single adjective, colourless in all appearance, but to them pregnant with a world of meaning.' (Proust, 1993: 91).

This brings us to the heart of diplomacy. As the custodian of good manners and a negotiator conscious of the historical ties with his partners, the diplomat is at times obliged to remain vague. In fact, the essence of political discourse is to create spaces, usable at any moment and in multiple forms, to maintain the relationship, the negotiation, and in the end, power. These spaces form the median space between two individuals, allowing for the construction of a dialogue, the very core of the interaction and mediation process.

A language both internal and external

These variances and representations only strengthen the public view of diplomacy as a distant and set profession, the very criteria attributed to doublespeak. Indeed, an ambassador always functions within an official framework. While working together, a diplomat made the following remark: '*Ce collègue (d'un autre pays) est un vrai ami. Je peux parler de tout avec lui.*' (This colleague (from another country) is a true friend. I can talk to him about everything), implying that he could drop his diplomatic discourse and that representation was a constitutive dimension of diplomacy.

We would like to conclude with the work of Charles Cogan (2003) on the French style. The ambassador identified six strategic and communication characteristics of a French diplomat: deductive approach, logic of arguments (built on the belief in Reason), care given to clarity of expression in order to convince, knowledge of history, Latin panache and the awareness of the need to stick tenaciously to one's position (based on Reason!). Thus, 'For the French, it is in the order of things to find a philosophical framework first, to establish a vision of things, before entering into practical matters' (Cogan, 2003: 44).

An interesting illustration of this is the famous speech by Dominique de Villepin, the then minister of foreign affairs, during a meeting of the UN Security Council on 7 March 2003. While presenting the French position in the face of the planned intervention of the United States and their allies in Iraq, the minister argued in favour of extending the mission of the UN inspectors. This is how the speech concluded: 'In a few days, we must solemnly fulfill our responsibility through a vote. We will be facing an essential choice: disarming Iraq through war or through peace. And this crucial choice implies others. It implies the international community's ability to resolve current or future crises. It implies a vision of the world, a concept of the role of the United Nations.'

At the end of the speech, those present in the room rose to give Dominique de Villepin a standing ovation, unprecedented in the history of the Council. It marked a break from normal practice in the Council. Clearly, such a demonstration in this polite, even regulated space was indeed unusual. A comparison of these elements with the tenor, style, and form of Dominique de Villepin's speech is enlightening, as Charles Cogan notes with finesse: 'Conceptions of honour are closely associated in France with the highly esteemed notion of glory (la gloire), which in turn is seen as a close companion to such French concepts as élan, panache and cran, all of which stand in contrast to the (nevertheless secretly admired) British phlegm' (Cogan, 2003: 45). He goes on to add: 'French negotiators pride themselves on their eloquence and their ability to present a logical, carefully ordered argument. The worst insult that can be laid at the foot of a French negotiator, according to several French interlocutors, is that of incoherence' (Cogan, *ibid*: 137).

The concern for precision and beauty of expression is typically French, though I lack the space here to expand on it any further. This leads some to say that French by its very structure is the language best suited to diplomacy. And so we come back to our starting point: the historical context, the political dimension, along with the common perception of the French abroad, the feeling of superiority and arrogance are the elements that make up the modalities of expression and communication of French diplomacy.

Conclusion

Diplomatic language must be viewed from two perspectives. The first is the paradox of a formal language, necessarily presenting ambiguities. As we have seen, this language with its specificities is at the service of diplomats to build relations and communication among themselves. It is thus for internal usage, and a diplomat's experience enables him not to be misled by his colleagues. However, the opaque meaning of words, associated with the classic image of diplomacy, makes the public discredit this language, as it lacks transparency and does not correspond to what 'true' communication should be. As such, the diplomat's discourse may be described as doublespeak on account of the formal framework in which it is delivered. However, diplomatic language also has a political dimension; it is addressed to citizens and the media and in a democracy everyone is keen to understand the meaning of what is being said, which gives it an external character. For this purpose, in a society of communication decoders, journalists and specialists are major and essential players whose work is to decipher the internal codes so that they become accessible to the public at large.

Bibliographical references

Chosson, Martine, *Parlez-vous la langue de bois?* Points, Paris, 2007.
Cogan, C., *French negotiating Behavior, Dealing with la Grande Nation*, Washington, Institute of Peace Press, 2003.
D'Holbach, *Essai sur l'art de ramper à l'usage des courtisans*, Paris, éditions Allia, 2010.
De Wilde d'Estmael, T. Liégeois, M. Delcorde, R. *La diplomatie au cœur des turbulences internationales*, Presses universitaires de Louvain, 2014.
Delporte, C., *Une histoire de la langue de bois*, Paris, Flammarion, 2009.
Dupont, Christophe, *La négociation*, Paris, Dalloz, 1992.
Elias, N., *La société de cour*, Paris, Champs Flammarion, 1985.
Fumaroli, M., *Quand l'Europe parlait français*, Paris, Poche no. 15418, 2003.
Goffman, E., *La mise en scène de la vie quotidienne*, Paris, Éditions de minuit, 1996.
Goldschläger, A., *Le discours du pouvoir*, Belin, Paris, 1983.
Goldschmidt, G.-A., *A l'insu de Babel*, Paris, CNRS éditions, 2009.
Hotman de Villiers, J., *De la charge et dignité de l'ambassadeur*, Paris Cergy, Essec Iréné, 2003.
Kingston de Leusse, M., *Diplomatie, une sociologie des ambassadeurs*, Paris, L'Harmattan, 1998.
Klemperer, V., *LTI, la langue du IIIe Reich: carnets d'un philologue*, Paris, Albin Michel, 1996.
La langue confisquée, Victor Klemperer et la LTI, exhibition catalogue, European Centre of Deported Resistance Members, Bibliothèque nationale et universitaire de Strasbourg, March 2009.
Lanzac, A., Blain, C., *Quai d'Orsay*, Dargaud, Paris 2 vol., 2010-2011 (Comic).
Lecerf, Y., & Parker, E., *Les dictatures d'intelligentsias*, Paris, PUF, 1987.
Legrand, Thomas, *Ce n'est rien qu'un président qui nous fait perdre notre temps*, Stock, Paris, 2010.
Lemaire, Jacques, *La langue de bois*, De Boeck, Brussels, 2001.
Proust, Marcel, *A l'ombre des jeunes filles en fleurs T1*, Flammarion, Paris, 1993, p. 91.
Tavernier B., *Quai d'Orsay*, 2013, (Movie).
Villar, C., *Le discours diplomatique*, Paris, L'Harmattan, 2006.

Composition of state decorations

6. Gifts and honours

Gifts

During official visits in the international diplomatic world, it is customary to exchange gifts between heads of state, heads of government, diplomats, authorities, delegations, and business partners as a form of respect and recognition. The size of the gifts is often dependent on the country the visit is taking place in and its local customs. In the Middle East, for example, countries give each other lavish gifts at state visits as a symbol of their generosity and respect for one another. In the West, this is much less customary, the meaning of a gift having more importance than its price.

It should also be noted that the exchange of gifts, while private, cannot always be considered as a personal exchange. The head of state concerned represents his or her country during a state visit. For this reason, the gifts received are seen as state property. In some countries, such as the Republic of Indonesia, for example, these gifts are kept at a special state museum. Institutions, ministries, and companies also have special rules and instructions for receiving gifts (e.g. they may cost up to a certain amount). These kinds of rules revolve around integrity in many cases, giving and receiving gifts is disallowed in order to avoid any kind of preferential treatment.

Protocol surrounding the exchange of gifts is different in each country and is often dependent on its respective culture, such as can be seen in Asia. The Japanese, for example, prefer to receive gifts in a small bag. Furthermore, the feelings associated with certain gifts in the culture concerned should be taken into account. For example, a wine decanter would not be an appropriate gift in the Middle East. In China, it is inappropriate to give a letter opener as a gift, as is giving a clock to an elderly person. White or yellow flowers should also not be given as gifts, as these are associated with death.

During the preparation of an official visit, it is recommended to go through the gift exchange ceremony with the receiving party beforehand. Focus should be given to the actual moment of giving the gift and the symbolic meaning of the gift. It must be clear that gifts from both sides are prepared with care and knowledge – alongside cultural considerations, personal aspects should be taken into account in the choice of gift, such as the hobbies or interests of the receiving party.

In most countries, an exchange of gifts between the heads of state and their spouses takes place on the first day of a state visit, and it is in many countries covered by the press. The gifts are then put on display on a table, together with the decorations and honours that have been exchanged. In other countries, the exchange takes place in a more private setting. In this case, a private photographer will sometimes be present.

During official visits, which are of a lower level than state visits, the exchange of gifts often does not take place in an official manner, but the gifts are instead placed in, for example, hotel rooms or guest residences. It might also occur that gifts for the heads of delegation are exchanged from protocol officer to protocol officer behind the scenes.

Art is generally a good gift, such as a sculpture, a picture, a painting, a gouache, a watercolour or a local form of art. An added advantage to art as a gift is that a contemporary artist, or a longstanding cultural form from the country giving the gift, becomes better known and popular in the rest of the world.

In the world of business, the exchange of gifts takes place at the beginning of a visit in some countries, and in some countries at the very end. At gift exchanges between delegates in many countries, it is important to remember the differences in function and rank between the members of the delegation, which should then be translated into the relative worth of the gifts being given. This is particularly important in Asian countries, where giving a gift to only the most important person in the presence of their subordinates should be avoided. In countries such as England and Spain, it is not customary to present a gift to a business partner, but the rules are flexible.

Gifts for Muslims are not given with pictures of people on them, as this is unacceptable in Islamic culture. This is also true for pictures of dogs and pigs, as these are seen as dirty animals. Furthermore, no alcohol or alcohol-related products, or products made from pig leather, should be given. The exchange of gifts always takes place with both hands or with the right hand. A compass, a fountain pen, or a business card holder are normally perfect gift ideas.

In Japan and China, white, black, or grey wrapping paper is, on principle, never used. Red and gold wrapping paper are preferred. Also, it is customary that gifts are refused three times before they are accepted, as a token of respect. The exchange of gifts generally takes place at the end of the visit.

Alongside the giving of gifts at official or trade visits, it is also possible to bring gifts when invited to dinner at someone's house. In most countries, bringing something personal, a delicacy, a book from your native country, or a bouquet of flowers is a good idea. In regard to flowers, it is always a good idea to keep colours in mind, as mentioned earlier, in some countries white or yellow flowers are associated with death. In some countries, the number of flowers in a bouquet is also culturally significant. In the Russian Federation one should avoid giving odd numbers of flowers, since this might cause a conflict in relationships. In Spain, bouquets should contain an odd number of flowers, but a bouquet of thirteen flowers should be avoided, as should dahlias, chrysanthemums, white lilies, and white roses. In France, the number of flowers should be uneven, and avoid the numbers seven and thirteen. The chrysanthemum pots available in French and Belgian shops in early November must absolutely not be used as gifts, as they are used on All Souls' Day as a memorial for the dead. All Souls' Day is the day in the Roman Catholic Church when the souls of the dead are remembered.

Honours

Before exploring the role of honours in international protocol, it is a good idea to give some consideration to what they mean. An honour is a sign for special merits in terms of the nation or business, or a symbolic recognition of personal, extraordinary deeds for society. Specific awards are often created for soldiers. These can be honours for long periods of faithful service, involvement in operational actions, participation in peacekeeping operations, and acts of bravery. The highest military honour is awarded for bravery and courage during special military operations. In the Netherlands, this honour is given under the Military William Order. This order was initiated by King William I on 30 April 1815. Moreover, non-Dutch citizens, such as members of the resistance during the Second World War, can receive this award. Similar awards are the Victoria Cross in the United Kingdom, the Medal of Honor in the United States, and the Gold Star in the Russian Federation.

Through the granting of an award, a person becomes distinguished from others. This distinction can take place in several different ways – in Belgium and the United Kingdom, the honour can elevate a person to the peerage or nobility, or give the person membership into a chivalric order or award a medal of honour. Honours are, in principle, meant for nationals, but can also be given to foreigners.

In some countries like the United Kingdom, many investiture ceremonies take place yearly. The official website of the British monarchy shows the following information:

> *An Investiture is a very special day when an individual who has been awarded an honour receives their award in person from The Queen, The Prince of Wales or occasionally The Duke of Cambridge or The Princess Royal. Investitures are also occasionally held overseas, during a State visit by The Queen or a foreign visit by another member of the Royal Family.*

> *Recipients can bring with them to the Investiture up to three friends or relations, who are invited to sit in the audience to witness the occasion. Around 25 Investitures are held each year. The majority happen in the Ballroom at Buckingham Palace, but others take place at the Palace of Holyroodhouse in Edinburgh and in the Waterloo Chamber at Windsor Castle.*

As mentioned earlier, an honour can include such things as an appointment to a knighthood. C. Baron van Heerdt, the Dutch author of *Nederlandse en Buitenlandse Ridderorden* writes the following about chivalric orders:

> *The word 'order' is derived from the Latin 'ordo', meaning 'row', referring to a row of sitting places in the theatre (seder in quattuordecim: sitting on the first fourteen rows, indicating knighthood), or, in military terminology, a rank or military unit. Moreover, it can mean the rank or position (hic ordo: this college / the senate; ordo equester: the knighthood). A chivalric order should therefore be an entity including persons given an award as a recognition of services recorded by the state, or rendered to a system under the control of the head of state.*

Most chivalric orders are divided into five or six grades or classes. In descending order: (Knight) Grand Cross, Grand Officer, Commander, Officer, and Knight or Member. This does not mean that these grades or classes are used in all orders. Sometimes, an order includes lesser grades or adds another class to an existing grade. Medals of honour are connected to many orders, which can be in gold, silver and bronze.

Some foreign orders include a grade above the Grand Cross: the Grand Collar or Collar (*'Grand Collier'* or *'Collier'* in French). This highest distinction is used in countries such as Denmark, Finland, Japan, Norway, Oman, Romania, Saudi Arabia, Spain, Sweden, United Arab Emirates, and the United Kingdom.

In the United Kingdom, the Order of the Garter is the highest order of chivalry and the third most prestigious honour after the Victoria Cross and George Cross. It was founded by Edward III in 1348. The insignia of this order includes a chain. The official website of the British monarchy writes the following:

> *The Order, consisting of the King and twenty-five knights, honours those who have held public office, who have contributed in a particular way to national life or who have served the Sovereign personally. The patron saint of the Order is St George (patron saint of soldiers and also of England) and the spiritual home of the Order is St George's Chapel, Windsor. Every knight is required to display a banner of his arms in the Chapel, together with a helmet, crest and sword and an enamelled stallplate. These 'achievements'*

are taken down on the knight's death and the insignia are returned to the Sovereign. The stallplates remain as a memorial and these now form one of the finest collections of heraldry in the world. The insignia of the Order have developed over the centuries, starting with a garter and badge depicting St George and the Dragon. A collar was added in the sixteenth century, and the star and broad riband in the seventeenth century.

Those who are to receive a knighthood (and who are therefore entitled to style themselves 'Sir'), kneel on an investiture stool before the queen. Her Majesty uses the sword that belonged to her father, King George VI, to dub the knight.

With regards to terminology, as used in many countries, honours are **awarded** or **granted**, but in case of grades within orders, such as the Commander of the Order of…., one is **awarded** or **appointed**. Medals and other distinctions are **awarded, granted, presented** or **given**.

What role do honours play in the international world? Besides individual recipients of foreign honours to civilians or soldiers for special merits to the country, in international protocol, the exchange of honours between heads of state is in many countries an integral part of state visits and is based on reciprocity between the two countries. Although this is not directly personal, the exchange of decorations can be seen as a form of respect and a confirmation of good relations between the two countries.

Exchange of honours between HM Queen Beatrix of the Netherlands and the late Sultan of Oman, HM Qaboos bin Said Al Said

Some countries, however, do not have honours at all or do not allow the exchange of honours at state visits.

The exchange not only includes heads of state and their spouses, it can extend to all members of the official entourage to a reasonable extent. Since many other officials are involved in state visits in the receiving country, such as the chairmen of parliament and the senate, hosts of visiting institutions, the mayor of the capital city, and the commander of the Guard of Honour, for example, it is internationally customary that the receiving country acquires two to three times the number of honours they give to the visiting country.

During preparations for the state visit, this aspect is discussed in detail with the responsible authorities such as chiefs of protocol and ministers of Foreign Affairs. The highest honours are exchanged between the heads of state. In the case of both heads of state already having exchanged the highest honours of their countries, there will be no exchange. Lower honours will never be exchanged. During a visit to a country that is unable, or where the policy is not to reciprocate honours, no exchange takes place. Examples of these countries include the United Kingdom and the United States.

For all other people who are recognised as recipients of honours, attention is given to their rank and status and whether they have received an honour on a previous visit. In this case, the person in question can be given a promotion to a higher grade of the same honour or can be appointed the same grade in another, higher honour. Generally, the time when the person in question received their honour for the first time is taken into account when considering the promotion. Generally, the promotion is not given if the first honour was given less than five years ago. An exception can be made if the person in question has been promoted to a higher rank or higher position. Another honour can obviously only be given if the other country has several honours that can be given to foreigners.

During deliberations on the awarding of honours, the number of people eligible for a high grade in a specific award is taken into account. In order to get a balanced distribution of honours, points are assigned to each grade in some countries – there is a large difference between the position of Grand Cross and that of Knight in a specific order. Lower-ranking functionaries are generally given medals of honour.

One should consider what grade should be granted to which person for every visit. A list for use at state visits when granting awards is presented on the next page. A few functionaries are included in each grade. The functionaries named and the grade connected to them are included as examples, and can differ from country to country.

(Knight) Grand Cross: Ministers, secretaries of state, ambassadors, chiefs of staff, high-ranking members of the royal household or of the presidential staff or equivalent.

Grand Officer: Secretaries general, directors general of ministries, officers of the rank lieutenant general and major general or equivalent in another military branch, mayors of the capital and other major cities, minister plenipotentiary of an embassy, directors of protocol, chairmen of the board of a multinational, attorneys general.

Commander: Diplomats with the rank of counselor, officers with the rank of brigadier general and colonel or equivalent in another military branch, directors of a ministry, a rector or president of the executive board of a university, mayors of large municipalities, and members of the board of directors in a multinational company.

Officer: Diplomats with the rank of first and second secretary, soldiers with the rank of lieutenant colonel or major or equivalent in another military branch, police commissioners, office heads in a ministry, mayors of smaller municipalities.

Knight: Diplomats with the rank of third secretary, officers with the rank of captain or equivalent in another military branch, police inspectors.

Member of the Order and Medal of Honour: All other officials at a lower rank than those mentioned above.

For the ranks of knight and member, their ornament is generally silver, while for the rest it is generally gold.

Preparation for the exchange of honours should be done with care and should always be based on reciprocity. Administrative preparations take a lot of time, as a royal or presidential decree grants the orders, and all the information about the person mentioned on the knightly diploma must be totally correct.

The distribution of the insignia of the honours to members of an entourage during a state visit takes place after the official exchange between heads of state. In some countries, this is coupled with a small ceremony, and in others the insignia are placed together with the gifts in the delegates' hotel rooms.

Dress code for wearing honours in white tie

The assigned honours can be worn on the first evening of a state visit during the state banquet, when the dress code is very often white tie. This dress code is described as 'white tie with full decorations' or *'cravate blanche avec plaques et cordon.*' Miniatures of honours granted earlier are worn on the left side of the jacket. For women, this means a long evening dress with decorations.

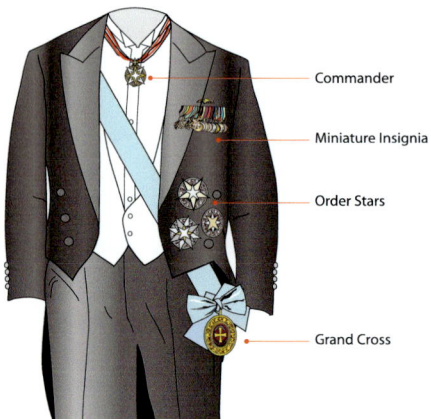

White tie with full decorations

Furthermore, it is possible that another dress code is standard in the receiving country, such as black tie or business suit. Under these circumstances, it is not customary to wear the full, ornate decorations. In some countries, they allow decorations and honours to be worn on a black tie, but these are often limited to miniature insignia or in some countries, like Sweden, to a buttonhole decoration.

Guidelines for wearing decorations with white tie are printed below.

Grand Collar

The collar is the highest grade in some distinguished honours and is worn around the two shoulders and on the dress jacket for men and on the long evening dress for women.

(Knight) Grand Cross

The Grand Cordon (the so called sash, ribbon, or cordon) associated with the Grand Cross and granted by the head of state of the receiving country or by the visiting head of state is primarily worn at the state banquet.

The corresponding order star (a plaque or a star) is to be placed on the left side of the dress jacket where the Grand Cordon goes under the dress jacket.

It is also possible that the dress code prescribes the order star to be worn on the right side. In France the *plaque* belonging to the *Légion d'Honneur* is worn on the right side of the dress jacket.

In the case of one wearing multiple order stars, a maximum of three or four should be worn on the left and / or right side of the dress jacket. One must be careful that one doesn't present oneself with an overabundance of awards. When wearing two, three, or four stars, the highest should be placed on top. When wearing three order stars, the second highest is placed on the left and the third on the right, from the perspective of an observer. The number four is always placed at the bottom.

A Grand Cordon should be worn **over the white waistcoat** when in the presence of a head of state, and **under the white waistcoat** when not.

Depending on the order, the Grand Cordon is worn from the right shoulder to the left hip, in such a manner that the ornamented bow is clearly visible. The Grand Cordon is usually 101mm wide. Some honours are worn from the left shoulder to the right hip, such as, for example, the Order of the Garter in the United Kingdom and the Order of the Elephant in Denmark. This designation can be found in the accompanying instructions on dress code upon receiving the honour.

For women, the Grand Cordon is worn over the long evening dress and is usually smaller, approximately 70 mm. Women wear the accompanying order star often at waist height and affixed to the ribbon.

Grand Officer and Commander

Grand officers and commanders often wear a neck cross and an order star. When wearing an order star, the same applies as above. Most of these awards will be worn on the left chest. For wearing the insignia of a grand officer, the rule is that multiple grand officer insignia can be worn, but it is recommended that only the honour received at a visit should be worn during a state banquet. Members of the military and officials in ceremonial dress with a high collar often wear multiple neck crosses under one another, limited, however, to a maximum of three.

The ribbon of the neck cross belonging to a grand officer or a commander must not be visible on the upright starched collar of the shirt. This must be worn under the white ribbon of the bowtie. In England, it is customary to wear the ornament on the neck cross two fingers below the top button.

Officers and Knights

Officer and knights' crosses are in general worn on the white tie as a miniature decoration. A miniature decoration is a smaller version of the grand model, often fitted with a rosette. These miniature decorations are supported on a clasp or chain on the left lapel. The officer or knights' cross that one has received on a state visit however can be worn during the state banquet as a model cross on the white tie on the side of the clasp or directly below it.

For female officers, the woman's decoration hangs from a bow made of the order ribbon. The bow is placed on a rosette.

For knights, members and a Medal of Honour, the ornament also hangs from a bow. Women wear the insignias on the left shoulder.

Hierarchy of the miniatures

The hierarchy of the miniatures in the clasp is generally as follows: national honours in hierarchy of the order of the class of the honour, followed by the foreign honours in alphabetical French language order according to the class of the grade. The highest and first honour is placed as close as possible to the heart.

Example of miniatures on white tie

During the general parts of a state visit programme, citizens wear the honour they have been given in the buttonhole of their jacket. The wearing of a buttonhole decoration is not only limited to official visits but is also allowed on a daily basis on a suit.

Buttonhole decoration, grade of officer

For every grade in an honour, a different buttonhole decoration exists. The decoration of a grand cross is recognisable by a rosette placed on a gold braid, a grand officer by a rosette placed on a half gold and half silver braid whereby the gold braid is placed on the side of the heart, and for a commander, the rosette is placed on a silver braid. The grade of officer is limited to just the decoration without a gold or silver braid.

Members of the military wear the honours on their daily uniforms or on a carrier pin on their uniform as batons, in the order according to protocol.

Example of batons on uniform

During ceremonial solemnities, honours are worn as model decoration, whereby the honours are laid out according to military specification on a carrier pin.

Mr José de Bouza Serrano, former Ambassador of the Portuguese Republic to the Netherlands

José de Bouza Serrano was the Portuguese ambassador to the Netherlands from 2012 to 2016. Currently he is Inspector-General of Diplomatic and Consular Affairs in Portugal. Prior to his posting in the Netherlands, he served as Portuguese chief of protocol, ambassador to Denmark, adviser to the prime minister and held numerous positions within the ministry of Foreign Affairs in Portugal as well as in Madrid, Brussels, and at The Holy See. He held high-ranking positions in other departments as well and was executive director for The Belem Cultural Centre during the Portuguese presidency of the European Communities. In 2011 his book *O Livro do Protocolo* was published. He graduated in Law from the University of Lisbon. He was awarded many high distinctions in recognition of his actions from countries around the world.

Protocol may be perceived as some sort of archaism,
which currently has no relevance. Just like the heritage
of ancient times, of lost civilizations.
Even if we do not waste much time reflecting upon it,
we do realise that it is quite the opposite.
People are courteous and courtesy
exists amidst the human groups and societies.
Rules change along with times. They react according to
mores, social events, or places. In a way, protocol
bears some of the courtesy between nations; a conventional language
which we can barely avoid since it exists under all latitudes
and because it has existed since all times and during all regimes.
– André de Fouquères

State visits by His Excellency Mr José de Bouza Serrano

The first state visit that I recall was the one made by Queen Elizabeth II to Portugal. In February 1957, I was six years old and went to Rossio with my cousin and tutor, Etelvina, to watch the Crown's carriage go by (which I knew from the Belém Museum), pulled by eight white horses and carrying President Craveiro Lopes and Her Majesty The Queen of England who waved at the Portuguese crowd which acclaimed her enthusiastically.

In the evening, my father took me to Fonte Luminosa where in a nearby shop window I watched – in the first TV testing broadcasts – the deferred delay of the arrival to the Colunas Dock, the royal barge, the carriages...

It was unquestionably the first and greatest media event I attended which really made an impression on me. Over days, the event was given full coverage by the national broadcasting radio and by the black and white photos in the newspapers, which I clipped to make a scrapbook.

Just like a Proustean reflex, all the intense emotions of those days came back to me when I ran across an old photograph, which, opportunely, rescues from oblivion the multiple images of state visits.

Though this designation may be used *lato sensu* to all officers of state serving the executive power, it must be applied and grasped in the context of the journeys undertaken by our heads of state to foreign countries, or to foreign heads of state in their visits to Portugal.

From a protocol perspective, state visits represent a moment of excellence in the relations between two countries at the highest institutional level. This implies that the entire agenda for the visit is thoroughly drawn up for the dignitary visitor and his crew in order to enable them to attend a series of ceremonies, which not only will meet the guest's preferences but will simultaneously convey the degree of importance granted by the host, as far as the priorities of Portuguese external policies are concerned.

Generally speaking, after the previous contacts made by respective embassies to set the dates (two or three days duration) and the past visits of preliminary missions, an official agenda is fully established and will have to be accepted by both heads of state.

Once it has met with official approval, the state protocol calls for a multidisciplinary plenary session, which usually coincides with the preliminary mission sent by the visiting country and includes the presence of the credited ambassador in Portugal.

The session is also attended by representatives of the diplomatic office, and of the Civil and Military Houses of the president of the republic, members of the Internal Security System (ISS), the Personal Security

Corps of PSP [Public Security Police] (PSC) and the INEM as well as the heads of airports (civilian and military) and, if needed, the heads of Customs (whenever there is need to import temporarily certain materials). The ISS follows the details of the visit and contacts the PSP (enforcement and traffic agents) and the GNR [National Republican Guard].

It is also customary for the members of the office of the prime minister and the minister of state and for the foreign affairs to attend the session since the respective agendas must be coordinated.

The office of the president of the republic assembly and its public relations are also briefed and participate in part of the agenda which usually takes place at the assembly chambers. The city hall also is represented whenever the agenda includes a visit to Paços do Concelho.

At this point, and for obvious reasons related to security and operations, the detailed content of the agenda is either Confidential or Secret according to the level of threat established considering the visiting head of state (e.g. the Holy Father).

After approval of the agenda by the chiefs of protocol of the visiting country and the host one, there are several aspects still to consider: details and coordination of gifts exchange (which may be in person or by the means of respective protocols), the banquet and lunches menus (taking into consideration the preferences and gastronomic intolerances of the visitors), the guest lists for the several events and the consequent follow-up and invitations mailing, menus, entry and marking table cards as well as presentation cards used to introduce the guest during the welcoming ceremony which paves the way to the banquet at Ajuda Palace (or at Queluz).

Likewise, the clothing standards for the gala banquet are previously set (monarchs' dress code consists of white tie with decorations, long gown and appropriate uniform) and the ladies may wear a hat or not in daytime ceremonies. For the spouses it is common to schedule a separate agenda in order to fill the moments when they do not accompany the heads of state.

Also, it is part of the tradition to scout the sites together with the preliminary mission (or the advanced mission that arrives one day before the visitors), accompanied by elements of the state protocol, to all monuments, palaces, airports, hotels (official residences with sorting of the rooms) and facilities that will be used throughout the stay until the day of departure of the visiting head of state and retinue.

Equally, car convoys are organised in order to estimate all the itineraries of the guest figures, their distribution by precedence, by cars and access areas. The itineraries are timed and, quite frequently, the retinues must split into several convoys in view of the agenda requirements.

In certain cases, some land, naval or air means of transportation are anticipated to travel across national territory in order to follow the agenda that provides the visitor the greatest comfort.

Members of the military house of the president of the republic work in agreement to set required previous courtesy rows, military honours, laying of flowers, the instrumental performance of both anthems, the Guard of Honour (on foot, motorcycle or on horseback) within the Portuguese tradition and following the Salute Regulation and Military Honours.

Abroad, the preliminary mission from Lisbon will have to prepare these details with the interlocutors of the visited countries.

In what concerns the exchange of decorations, from the moment it is accepted by both heads of state, it is agreed by their respective chiefs of protocol; the tradition usually observed is that the visiting country offers in double (or in certain cases, in triple) the decorations granted by the host nation to the dignitaries of his delegation as stated in the honorific orders stipulated in each state.

Finally, a pocket-sized official agenda is printed with all the useful information; in Portuguese for the visits abroad and bilingual for the visits made to Portugal.

Pierre de Fouquères (brother of the above mentioned and also a diplomat) characterises these diplomatic events as 'visits where – in an increasingly shorter lapse of time – we see the balance in profound sessions, political conversations, official banquets, meetings with the representatives of the economic means, parliamentary assemblies, deliberation guilds as well as press conferences and TV interviews.'

However, the protocol outline only offers the shape, choreography, and precise measure to the actual political content of the visit, which can be useful to revive the relations between the two countries, restate alliances, and draw international attention to the country or point out the permanent or renewed interests of the national external policy.

On this matter, it is fundamental for the head of state, as much as for the other members of the sovereign executive, to have the collaboration of the high administrative staff, the diplomatic attachés and the politicians, whenever they convey the accurate message, the one previously determined, to their interlocutors in their speeches, in the notes of bilateral meetings or in sessions at the highest level. To this message De Gaulle would give the name of 'the expression of the republic's order' or 'the nations savoir-vivre.'

For this purpose, the human factor is determinant since the personality of the heads of state and their personal prestige in the countries they visit, or in our country, will be decisive to the outcome of the visit and will influence the future relations, which do not diminish with presidential terms of office.

Along with the preparation aspects, which take place within the secrecy of the chancelleries or offices, the public and media dimension of these visits is unavoidable, especially in the virtual century we live in – a century where the media demand protocol be sacrificed for the sake of photographs and television footage, and where actions are remembered not because of what was said or signed and agreed, but rather because of the image that was captured and will remain silent (if that) in the archives.

During the visits abroad of our heads of state, I must absolutely mention the work carried out by the host countries' embassies and the Portuguese consulates not only in what concerns the hosting of the preliminary missions but also the agreement schedules of the details that will make possible the thorough preparation and the success of the visit until the day of return back to Lisbon.

When I held the office of secretary in Madrid, I lived that experience as I collaborated in the organisation of the official visit of President Mário Soares, on 12 September 1986, to decorate His Royal Highness, the count of Barcelona, in the presence of the king of Spain, other royal figures, and numerous guests of the Portuguese embassy.

The following year, December 14th was the date chosen by the president to travel back to Spain with a stunning crew; thus began a state visit that lasted several days.

Years later, in a position at the Portuguese permanent representation to the European Union in Brussels, I also had the opportunity to assist with the visit of President Jorge Sampaio to the European Community institutions on 15 January 1997.

The social and institutional modifications and the celerity of regular contacts between heads of state and information in general will eventually bear consequences and change the protocol rules. But they persist – even if the institutional structure changes – and they are the last things to disappear because protocol appears essentially associated with the practice of power, thus favouring stability within internal order and for nations to work in harmony with one another.

I wonder if someone had told that little six-year-old boy that fifty-eight years later he would already have been introduced to the sovereign in the carriage – still fortunately reigning – and that he would meet her several times throughout his life, that he would personally meet other members of her family; two Popes; numerous foreign heads of state; several kings and queens in power and exile; blood princes and princesses; and would be honoured to serve four presidents of the Portuguese Republic, would he have believed it? Even though he already loved fantasy!

Torchbearer arrives at Opening Ceremony Olympic Games London 1948

7. Ceremonies

Introduction

Ceremonies are an integral part of our lives. We make use of them every day, be it in our personal lives, such as at a wedding or a baptism, or in the professional sphere. Sometimes, ceremonies are used for one-off events, but they are more often used for recurring events as a part of government protocol, religious or cultural events, whereby the rituals connected with them often form the basis of ceremonies.

Many of these rituals are based on age-old traditions that have their origins in culture, religion, and the practices of ethnic groups and native populations who have played an important role in developing these cultures and religions.

In many cultures and belief systems, ceremonies take an important place as an expression of belief in a church, mosque, or temple where important personal events are marked by ceremonies, such as birth, marriage, death, and prayer. Religions often have ceremonies specific to their beliefs – in the Catholic Church, for example, specific ceremonies include baptism and confirmation, in Judaism, the bar mitzvah and bat mitzvah, and in Islam ceremonies are centred around belief and one's personal connection with God.

Besides religion, the armed forces have contributed to many kinds of ceremonies, still performed today, such as the change of command, military funerals, the laying of wreaths, arrival and departure ceremonies, and swearing-in, inauguration and decoration ceremonies.

A ceremony can be centred on one individual person and create an unforgettable moment, or become a fundamental part of national identity, such as the raising of a flag, the playing of the national anthem, a national remembrance day, the opening of parliament, the presentation of royal honours, etc.

Meaning of a Ceremony

When discussing ceremonies, it is common to associate the concept with solemn functions, commemorations, rituals, traditions and etiquette, which are often tied to memorable occasions and military protocol.

However, we need to define exactly what a ceremony is. One could say that a ceremony is an act, or series of acts, with a symbolic character, often prescribed by law, ritual, religion, custom, or authority, creating a memorable moment. The *Le Robert* dictionary describes ceremonies as follows: 'L'ensemble et l'ordre de succession des cérémonies tels qu'ils sont établis par l'usage ou réglés par une autorité pour célébrer une solennité.' [The assembly and the order of succession of ceremonies as established by usage or rules by an authority to mark a solemnity.]

The 2015 Wikipedia article for ceremonies gives the following definition: 'A ceremony is a solemnity that marks an important event. During a ceremony, ritual acts are performed, which are often strictly defined. Some ceremonies are one-off events, while other are performed regularly as tradition.'

We can therefore say that ceremonies are the externally expressed forms of solemnities, which, over continued use, can take on a set form, but can also be defined by a governing body. Examples of this include state visits, the laying of a wreath, or singular events such as the independence of a country or the presentation of credentials. A ceremonial solemnity can also be a part of a belief system or be a special part of a culture, such as a marriage ceremony, a procession, or a tea ceremony in countries like Japan and China.

A ceremony is often formed through a combination of rituals, symbols, traditions, military exercises, music, and protocol. In the area of protocol, special attention should be given to hierarchical order, seating, processions, flags, and the use of ribbons on wreaths.

Ceremonies are also to be found in the private sector – a celebratory launch of a new product, the celebration of a jubilee, or the distribution of awards, such as employee of the month.

Organising a Ceremony

When responsible for the organisation of a ceremony, the first question should be **why** the ceremony is being organised, and **how** this can be expressed in the presentation of the ceremony. Through an analysis of the project, the question of **who** will play a role in the ceremony should be answered, as well as who the stakeholders are, **what** the expectations of the ceremony are, and **where** and **when** it should take place.

In the organisation of a ceremony, it is therefore necessary to define exactly what the ceremony is commemorating and what its goal is – why is this ceremony being held? Is it an individual, one-off event such as a state visit, or is it geared towards fostering lasting goodwill, or achieving something specific, such as bringing an end to senseless violence? Is it intended to show specific aspects of a single culture, or is it intended to bring people from different countries together, such as in sporting events like the Olympic Games?

Once the purpose of the event is established, the rest of the ceremony can be worked out through a process of extrapolation.

First, the date, time and place should be considered. These will be affected by several factors.
- Date, time, and place are set in stone by the government, such as with an annual remembrance or national independence day;
- Date and place are determined by history or tradition;
- Date and time are determined by the availability of the chosen space;
- Date and time are determined by the availability of most important people attending the ceremony – the stakeholders.

Once date, time, and place are decided, the other details of the ceremony should be decided: What should people get out of the ceremony? What is its central goal? What funds are desired, and what is available? In which ways can these goals be expressed? Answering all these questions will eventually lead to a general plan, which will need to be further tailored by the organising team.

It is important that this information is shared with all parties concerned with the event. The delegation of responsibilities is essential – the military aspect of the event, for example, should be delegated to the military. Another important aspect is the composition of the guest list and the invitations to be sent out.

Components of a Ceremony

A ceremony is composed of five parts:
- The arrival of the invitees
- The signal that the ceremony has begun
- The ceremony
- The signal that the ceremony has ended
- The departure of the invitees

This organisation is used for all ceremonies whether it is a graduation ceremony, a wedding, the laying of a wreath, or the launching of a ship.

The launching of a ship is a ceremony in which a ship, after it is completed at the shipyard or dry dock, is launched into the water. Ship launches are often accompanied by traditions, some of which are centuries old. The naming is the most well-known. The signal that the ceremony has started is the arrival of the dignitaries and those responsible for the ship's naming. The actual moment of naming the ship is the ceremony. The departure of the officials is signalling that the ceremony has ended. The final component is the departure of the invitees.

State Ceremonies

State ceremonies have never been laid out in international law. They have either been governed by habits or were the products of happenstance. In order to reconcile the differences between the individual ceremonies of various countries, rules must be followed internationally. Reciprocity should take a place in these rules, as reciprocity has clearly been an important part of ceremonies in the past. In a text by a master of ceremonies from the time of the English Restoration, for example, it is written: 'The manner of reception in England is regulated partly by what is done to our ambassadors and envoys in other courts, partly by the latest precedents of what has been practiced here.'

State ceremony is the highest form of attention given to an event. A state ceremony can range in complexity from the inauguration of a head of state, a national day of remembrance, the opening of the parliamentary year, a royal wedding, or a state funeral.

A state ceremony can also be the presentation of credentials by foreign ambassadors as well as the ceremony surrounding state visits and welcoming foreign heads of state. This is the ultimate conveyance of respect, and it plays an integral part in fostering long-lasting bilateral relations between two countries. The ceremony connected to these visits varies depending on the kind of visit. The most formal form is that of a state visit, and the least formal form is that connected to a trade visit or courtesy visit.

Besides this, foreign heads of state can be invited to attend events such as one-off celebrations, memorials, and openings of foreign exhibitions. Visits like these are often called themed visits and do not have their own ceremonies. A themed visit can be described as a visit by a foreign head of state that comes about due to a theme in which both parties are mutually interested. A head of state can also visit a country after being invited by an organisation or business. These invitations should always be considered with the approval of the host country's own head of state, as any visiting head of state should be agreed upon by the host country's head of state. These kinds of visits are often simply called 'visits', and the head of state of the host country is not always present. Lastly, some visits are of a private nature. Private visits do not have any official protocol associated with them. Visitors can be offered accommodation by the host country's head of state, and these visits are sometimes carried out at a private meeting place.

As mentioned earlier, international state ceremonies are largely influenced by reciprocity, and are based on the acknowledgement and respect for a head of state, their representative, or an authority. This means that during state visits, the organisers of both parties need to work together. For arrival and departure ceremonies, the exchange of gifts, the laying of wreaths, dinners and state banquets, international gatherings and the presentation of credentials by ambassadors, cooperation is essential. Keeping in line with international norms and reciprocity, countries often use their own protocol connected with these events.

Jean Serres, a French diplomat and author of *Manuel Pratique de Protocol*, writes the following on this subject:

> *The importance of ceremony and protocol cannot be overstated. Ceremony creates the context and the atmosphere in which peaceful relations between sovereign states can be conducted. Ceremony and protocol impose the rules of courtesy that must govern relations between men of good faith. They also govern the negotiation, the settlement and the putting into effect of international acts. The ceremony that governs international events is, in fact, of the greatest importance. One is well aware of the care that governments give to the preparation of large international meetings and to what extent the pomp which accompanies them leads to success and if mismanaged, leads to their failure. The attention that nations pay to receiving a head of state or a minister, to the visit of a delegation, to the signing of a treaty, to the celebration of an event of common interest, all indicate the degree to which two governments wish to demonstrate the state of their relations, the direction in which they wish them to evolve and the improvements which they want to make to them. The solemnity of the ceremonies, generous hospitality, the drafting of speeches and liberality in the awarding of decorations which take place on such occasions indicate the degree to which both parties wish to make public their agreement, their friendship and their collaboration.*

It is clear that reciprocity has influenced a uniformity among state ceremonies, which has led to equal treatment and respect for each other's heads of state, ambassadors and authorities.

In the Netherlands, the military often plays an important role in ceremonies, such as during the joint assembly of both houses of the States-General (the upper and lower houses), where, every third Tuesday of September, on *Prinsjesdag*, the king gives a speech dubbed *de Troonrede* in the *Ridderzaal*. In other countries, the military also plays a large role in the opening of the parliamentary year, during state funerals, royal weddings, the laying of wreaths, crownings, inaugurations or steppings-down of heads of state, or the presentation of credentials to the head of state by a foreign ambassador.

We will now discuss in detail the several different forms of state ceremonies.

State Visits

In every country, the ceremony accompanying state visits is the highest form of respect that the host head of state can bestow upon a visiting head of state. It is an affirmation of outstanding equality and mutual respect between two states, politically, economically, and culturally. It is a misconception that a state visit is a visit from one country to another. Rather, state visits should be seen as a visit by one head of state to another, by virtue of their positions as heads of state and their legal standing as leaders of their respective countries. When examining the development of state visits from the 19th century to today, it becomes clear that four elements have been developed in terms of form and content:
- The change in the role of the head of state with regards to the development and implementation of national and foreign politics;
- The development of national foreign policy itself;
- The evolution of technology, namely in the area of the transmission of information and social media;
- The shift of values and norms as a result of social changes.

In the event that the head of state is also the head of government, the goal of the state visit will also be geared towards the realisation of concrete policy objectives between the two states. Political decisions can be discussed and taken bilaterally.

Elmer Plischke (1914 – 2005), former director of American state visits and political science professor from the University of Maryland, identified the following possible goals of a state visit:
- The promotion of goodwill and understanding by and for the countries in question;
- Personal or incidental reasons for a state visit;
- The promotion of economic factors;
- Consultation on common concerns over national security;
- The creation of a friendly climate for future negotiations on one of the two countries' important concerns;
- The elevation of the prestige of one of the two countries' heads of state – either internationally, in the host country, or in the head of state's native country;
- Attempting to foster friendship with the host country if it is a world power, with the goal of implementing national policies.

The Polish professor of international law and former judge at the International Court of Justice in The Hague, Manfred Lachs (1914-1993), describes in an article the importance of state visits in laying the foundations of personal contacts between the foremost personalities in the world. According to Lachs, this can be useful in thawing a climate of distrust and hostility between countries. Furthermore, according to Dean Rusk (1909-1994), the prominent secretary of state under President Kennedy, state visits are 'aimed at the exchange of courtesy and respect as a tangible expression of the goodwill of the American people.'

Every visiting head of state is accompanied by an official delegation as well as supporting staff that do not make up a part of the official entourage. The number of members in the official entourage can range from very few to very many. Nowadays, it is increasingly common for visiting heads of state to take an economic mission with them. The diplomatic representative, often the ambassador of the visiting country, is always part of the official entourage. Furthermore, the accredited ambassador in the host country will take part in the official visit. Host countries often impose limits on the number of people to make up an official entourage as accommodation, transportation, and attention in the official program for all the members must all be considered by the host country. In this situation, the visiting head of state will entrust his or her ambassador to the care of the rest of the general delegation. State visits only occur at the invitation of the host country, and, in principle, should occur only once in a head of state's reign. Exceptions to this are in neighbouring countries and friendly monarchies.

At the end of the state visit, the visiting monarch will in many cases invite the host head of state for a reciprocal state visit. According to hierarchy, the highest-ranking head of state should give the first invitation. For new heads of state, therefore, it might take a long time to be invited to nations they might wish to maintain relations with. The Dutch King Willem-Alexander, inaugurated in 2013, has found a way to circumvent this problem by taking the initiative in making courtesy visits. Making a courtesy visit to a longer-serving head of state is a way to show respect for the seniority of the host head of state without needing to wait for an official invitation or needing to complete the lengthy preparations associated with a state visit.

Generally a constitutional monarch will make a state visit around two or three times a year and will typically receive foreign heads of state at the same rate. If the head of state is also head of government, the number of state visits they make and receive will normally be higher. The length of a state visit varies from one to three days. In this hectic day and age, heads of state, and especially heads of government, will request shorter times for state visits, and they will often conduct state visits to multiple countries at a time.

Elements of a State Visit

Although there are differences between countries, the following elements often make up the schedules of state visits:
- Arrival and departure ceremonies (integral).
- Meeting with the most important national authorities (customary).
- Exchange of gifts (customary); this can take place at the same time as the exchange of decorations, or, as is common in some countries, just before the state dinner.
- Exchange of decorations.
- Personal conversation between the two heads of state (customary); heads of government might give a press conference after this.
- Private lunch for the two heads of state and their spouses (customary).
- The laying of a wreath at a national monument, the grave of the unknown soldier, or at the grave of the nation's founder (customary).
- A visit to the mayor of the capital city (customary); the visiting head of state will often sign the guestbook or be given the key to the city.
- Tête-à-tête with the prime minister (customary).
- Courtesy visit to members of the national legislature – in the United States, the Senate and the House of Representatives for example

(customary); if the visiting head of state is also the head of government, they might also want to deliver a speech in the legislature.
- State dinner; generally white or black tie for men, and long dresses for women (integral), decorations are worn according to protocol. In all cases, decorations are worn when the men are wearing white tie.
- Government lunch, given by the prime minister and members of government (customary).
- Visit to institutions, provinces, and businesses (depending on the interest of the visiting head of state and time available).
- Reception for the foreign community, being the nationals of the visiting head of state living in the host country (customary).
- Return dinner, reception, or cultural event (customary).
- Partner programme (customary).

When dealing with an official visit, rather than a state visit, its length and the number of events that take place is often lower. At an official visit, the Guard of Honour might be diminished, the visitors might not lay wreaths, and decorations are generally not exchanged. In the place of a gala dinner, a lunch might be held instead. Sometimes the return dinner and reception are replaced by an audience at the beginning, or end, of the visit. In many cases, a delegation meeting will be included in the programme. Generally, accommodation for official visits is similar to state visits, usually at a royal palace, a 'government guesthouse', or a hotel.

Arrival and Departure Ceremonies

Arrival and departure ceremonies are seen to be the highest possible forms of respect for a visiting head of state at their arrival at an airport, railway station, harbour, presidential or royal palace. The form and content of this ceremony is dependent on the kind of visit that the head of state is making. The highest form is the state visit, followed by an official visit. The visit can also take on the character of a working visit, a courtesy visit, or a private visit. Finally, it is possible that a foreign head of state might use a country as a stopping point to a next destination. In this case, the head of state of the transit country might send a representative to the airport to send their best wishes to the visiting head of state.

It is easy to imagine that the higher the level of visit, the more elaborate the ceremony. Every country therefore makes its own adjustments and tailors the level of ceremony and the protocol surrounding it to the different levels of visits.

In the case of the visiting head of state arriving in a presidential or royal airplane, the airplane will be escorted by two or more military aircrafts from the moment it enters the country's airspace to its landing. This is done as the first gesture of respect to the visiting head of state. At the aircraft steps, the jetway, or at the train doors, a Guard of Honour will be present, made up of two soldiers in ceremonial garb. In the Netherlands, this is done by the Royal Constabulary (*Koninklijke Marechaussee*) and in Italy by the *Carabinieri*.

The moment of arrival by the visiting head of state and their aircraft is coordinated beforehand and is signalled with the words 'doors open.' This is, unsurprisingly, the moment that the doors of the aircraft open. If the welcome ceremony takes place on the airfield, and the host head of state is present, it is internationally customary that the chief of protocol together with the ambassador of the visiting country go on board the aircraft first. After they have paid their respects and given any relevant information to the visiting head of state, they exit the aircraft. The visiting head of state then alights from the aircraft and sets foot on the host country's soil. At that moment, a 21-gun salute is given. This also takes place on the arrival and greeting by the receiving head of state at a railway station, harbour, or the presidential or royal palace. Later on in this chapter, gun salutes will be further explored.

Greetings

Because the 21-gun salute lasts quite a long time, the ceremony continues during it. The first person to greet the visitor is the receiving head of state, followed by their spouse, and then other high authorities, where after the distinguished party proceeds to the dais or whichever place they have been designated to receive their honours. At the greeting, flowers will often be given to the visiting head of state's wife, or to the head of state herself if she is female.

If the arrival ceremony and the official greeting by the head of state takes place at the presidential or royal palace later, the visiting head of state is greeted on arrival by a representative of the receiving head of state. This can be a member of the royal family or, as is customary in many countries, a member of the government, such as the secretary of state or the chief of protocol.

In many countries such as Italy, Lithuania and Turkey, the visiting head of state is greeted first by a member of the government, the visiting country's accredited ambassador to the host country, the host country's accredited ambassador to the visiting country, and some military authorities. They are all introduced by the chief of protocol. The official greeting by the head of state takes place later at the presidential palace.

In Germany, the chief of protocol greets the visiting head of state in the name of the president. Under these circumstances, there is only a short ceremony at the airport which is limited to an honour guard and a red carpet. In this case, the visitors are then taken to the VIP lounge where their motorcade is waiting. The inspection of the honour guard then takes place at the presidential palace, where the guests are greeted. The leaders of the visiting entourage often take their places in the ceremony well ahead of the visiting head of state's arrival, so as to be ready in advance.

In the Russian Federation, the official first greeting takes place at the airport and is conducted by the chairman of the government and the minister of Foreign Affairs. In contrast to other countries, arrival and departure ceremonies take place at the airport even if the president is not there himself. At the Kremlin, there is a second arrival ceremony where the president greets the visitor. The *Protocol of the Russian Federation* describes how arrival and departure ceremonies are conducted at Russian airports:

> *For the occasion of the arrival of an eminent guest, the state flags of the Russian Federation and the visitor's country are raised at the airport. On the airfield the guards of colour representing the three branches of the armed forces are lined up. After the landing of the plane the staff of the embassy of the visitor's country are invited to take their place in front of the airport building. Approaching the plane ladder are the Chairman of Government of the Russian Federation or the Deputy Chairman of the Government, the Ambassador of the visitor's country in Moscow and the Director of the State Protocol Department of the Foreign Ministry of Russia. The Director of the State Protocol Department of the Foreign Ministry of the Russian Federation and the Ambassador of the visitor's country in Moscow ascend aboard the plane and invite the head of the foreign state to leave the plane.*
> *At the foot of the ladder the visiting head of state is greeted by the Chairman of Government of Russia or his Deputy. Photographs are taken. If the eminent guest is accompanied by the spouse, she is greeted at the ladder by the spouse of the Chairman of Government of the Russian Federation who presents the guest with a bouquet of flowers. After the national anthems are played, the guest's spouse occupies a place among the officials accompanying the visiting head of state. The Director of the State Protocol Department of the Foreign Ministry of Russia invites the visiting head of state and the Chairman of Government of Russia to approach the guards of*

colour. While they walk, this visiting head of state remains to the left of the Chairman of Government of the Russian Federation. After the guest and the Chairman of Government occupy their position on the carpet (facing the airport building), the commander of the guards of colour reports to them. Then the visiting head of state and the Chairman of Government of Russia turn to the formation of the guards of colour. The national anthems of the visitor's country and the Russian Federation are played. The visiting head of state and the Chairman of Government of Russia pass in front of the guards of colour. Thereupon the visiting head of state and the Chairman of Government of the Russian Federation take leave of the commander of the guards of colour with a light nod. The visiting head of state and the Chairman of Government of Russia head for the airport building. The Chairman of Government of the Russian Federation greets the visiting officials, while the guest greets the Russian officials, senior diplomats and the staff of the Embassy of his country. The Director of the State Protocol Department of the Russian Foreign Ministry invites the eminent guest and the Chairman of the Russian Government to take their position on the carpet. The visiting head of state stands next to the Chairman of Government. The guards of colour march by in formation. If the guest is headed for the residence provided by the Russian side, the Chairman of Government of Russia or his Deputy accompanies him to the residence in the same car. The car is equipped with the flags of the guest's country and the Russian Federation. In the case of a state visit or official visit the car is accompanied by an escort of nine motorcycles.

The official welcome ceremony by the President of the Russian Federation, takes place in the Catherine Chamber of the Kremlin Residence.

At the appointed time the foreign head of state arrives at the visitor's entrance in the inner courtyard of the Kremlin residence of the President of the Russian Federation, then passes through the lobby and ascends the main stairway into the Catherine Chamber. In the lobby and on the stairs the guards of colour salute the visitor. By that time, the Russian participants and the officials accompanying the guest gather in the Catherine Chamber. Both groups line up to the left of the main entrance. The Russian delegation stands closer to the heads of state, further on is the visiting delegation. As he walks from the Conference Room, the President of the Russian Federation approaches the guest to the sound of presidential fanfares. Meeting in the middle of the Chamber, the President of the Russian Federation and the guest exchange handshakes, then proceed to the place indicated by the

Russian flag and the flag of the visitor's country. The guest occupies the place to the right of the President of Russia, facing the main entrance. Photographs are taken. The national anthems of the guest's country and the Russian Federation are played. The President of the Russian Federation and the visiting head of state proceed for the introduction of Russian and visiting officials. After the introduction ceremony the President of the Russian Federation and the visiting head of state leave the Chamber.

Inspection of the Honour Guard

In the event of the ceremony taking place in the presence of the receiving head of state, both heads of state take their places at a podium after the official greeting, where after both national anthems are played. First, the visiting country's anthem is played, and then the host country's. At the departure ceremony, some countries play their own (the host country's) national anthem first, and then that of the visiting country. After the playing of the national anthems, the commander of the Honour Guard reports to the visiting head of state and invites the visiting head of state to inspect the Honour Guard. The inspection of the Honour Guard is the most important part of the arrival ceremony. It is important that the visiting head of state who is carrying out the inspection realises that they are there as a sign of respect for their position. During the inspection, the visiting head of state will walk on the left side of the receiving head of state, and they will be led by the commander of the Honour Guard. During the inspection, a tribute will be brought to the flags, 'the colours'. These can be national flags, but they are also often banners or standards that have been given to the military units in question by a head of state in recognition of military acts of valour. In the past, flags were carried in military operations in order to mark the place of the commander as well as assembly points. The tribute to the colours can be made to the front of the flag with an incline of the head, or saluted by the visiting head of state if they are dressed in military uniform. In some countries, the visiting head of state does not stop to salute the colours if dressed in military uniform, but instead continues marching while facing the flag, and saluting it.

Why do military events take such an important role as a form of respect for a visiting head of state? Why do countries allow foreign heads of state to inspect their soldiers? The presence of the military can be seen as a show of power, but in fact, allowing a visiting head of state to inspect a host country's military is the highest possible show of respect and trust. During the departure of the visiting head of state, the same ceremony takes place as a send-off. After the inspection of the Guard of Honour, a parade can also take place. This is customary in many countries such as the United Kingdom and the United States, whereby the Guard of Honour marches alongside the two heads of state, and more honours are presented. In most countries, after this parade, or directly after the inspection, the receiving head of state and their spouse introduce a number of authorities to the visiting head of state and their spouse, and the visiting head of state and their spouse introduce their official entourage to the receiving head of state. This presentation can also take place later, at the presidential or royal palace.

After the exchange of honours, the attendees go to the VIP lounge or go directly to the cars in the motorcade, where they then go to the first scheduled event, or to the presidential or royal palace.

Motorcades

The motorcade is the official designation for a combination of vehicles where the head of state and the entourage travel through the host country. Motorcades for heads of government and heads of state can consist of dozens of vehicles, being made up of armoured cars, SUVs, and police motorcycles. The receiving head of state will invite the visiting head of state to ride in his or her car, with the right rear seat being taken up by the visiting head of state in countries where traffic is on the right, and the left seat if traffic is on the left. The standard of the guest will be placed on the side of the car where the guest is seated. For more on this, see the chapter on flag protocol.

Each country has its own protocol for the arrangement of a motorcade, depending on the level of security needed. The composition of the security cars depends on the current policy on security matters. The car in which both chiefs of protocol are seated is usually placed in front of the presidential or royal car. It is important that the members of the entourage ride together with the authorities of the receiving country. It is also possible to use small busses instead of cars to limit the length of the motorcade. In order to quickly board the cars and busses after the arrival ceremony, the arrangement of the motorcade will often be communicated beforehand, and the cars are designated by a letter or a number.

In the Netherlands, a royal bus is sometimes used for the heads of state and members of the visiting delegation for some parts of the programme.

Depending on local customs and the distance travelled, the motorcade will be accompanied by an honour escort which can be made up of cars, jeeps, horses or even camels. Honour escorts will be further explored later in this chapter.

Laying of wreaths

Another important part of state visits is the laying of wreaths. A wreath laying at a monument is a ceremony where respect is given to the remembrance of soldiers and citizens killed in a time of war. Flowers and wreaths play an important role around the world as a gesture of respect and remembrance of the dead.

On the website of Arlington National Cemetery in Arlington, Virginia, the following is written about wreaths and flowers:

> *The gift of flowers at a memorial site is a ritual that occurs around the world, understood in every culture. The floral tributes at funerals bespeak both the beauty and the brevity of life and evoke memories of other days. These types of memorials are made each day at Arlington National Cemetery, at the dozens of funeral services occurring there and in solitary communion with a departed loved one. More formal ceremonies involve the laying of a wreath and the attendance of others at this ritual. These, too, are held frequently at Arlington.*

A national monument or tomb can be found in almost every country in the world. National monuments are intended to remember the dead of specific wars and to honour the suffering of the nation.

In the Netherlands, the National Monument at Dam Square in Amsterdam was unveiled by Queen Juliana on 4 May 1956 to remember every Dutch person who died as a result of the Second World War. Since then, the monument has played a central part in the Dutch National Remembrance Day, which has taken place since 1961 to remember the Dutch victims of war and peace-keeping operations since the Second World War. The yearly remembrance ceremony takes place in the presence of the king and queen.

The laying of a wreath is part of the ceremony on the first day of a state visit in many countries. The visiting head of state will be briefed extensively beforehand on the ceremony by the organiser of the ceremony – often a military authority. One or more flags will be flown from a monument, an Honour Guard of soldiers will stand ready, and a military band will be present for musical accompaniment. A trumpeter is prepared to play, as is customary in many countries, the *Last Post* – a bugle call used in many armed forces around the world. The call, which is usually played at the end of the day during the inspection of the guard, is currently used internationally at military remembrances and funerals. The signal will be ended with the bugle call *Reveille*. In the Netherlands, the call *Taptoe* is played followed by

Voorwaarts. The mood of the *Last Post* and *Taptoe* are the same. The *Last Post* means a last greeting. In the Netherlands, the call *Taptoe* has taken on a ceremonial character as a moment of thought and remembrance. In France, *Aux Morts* is played instead.

During the ceremony, the royal or presidential couple will be brought to the monument or tomb by one or more authorities. This can vary from the prime minister to the minister of defence, or a high-ranking military official. The wreath, which is arranged beforehand by the ambassador of the visiting head of state to their specifications and wishes, either lies ready near the monument or the tomb and is presented to the visiting head of state on arrival, or is brought with the delegation in the procession. When arriving at the monument or tomb, the royal or presidential couple will take their positions at the base of the monument or the tomb where the wreath is being laid. The official or officials leading the presidential or royal couple to the tomb or monument stay behind. As soon as the royal or presidential couple arrives at the base of the monument or tomb, two soldiers place the wreath against the monument, or on a wreath holder on the tomb.

After this, the couple goes to the wreath and arranges ribbons on it. Then they take a step back, stand to attention and observe a moment of silence. As mentioned earlier, the moment of silence is signalled with the *Last Post*, and ends with the *Reveille*, or whichever calls are appropriate depending on the country.

After this, the couple turns back to face the officials leading them to the monument or tomb, and the attendees return to their cars or the building from which they arrived.

In the Netherlands, the visiting head of state and their spouse will lay a wreath on the National Monument in Amsterdam, in the presence of the prime minister and the mayor of Amsterdam. In some countries, the ceremony takes place at the Tomb of the Unknown Soldier or the tomb of the nation's founder. This is the case in the United Arab Emirates, where a remembrance ceremony is held at the Grand Mosque in Abu Dhabi, where the founder of the nation is buried. In Ankara, Turkey, a wreath is laid on the tomb in Anıtkabir, the official name for the Mausoleum of Mustafa Kemal Atatürk, the leader of the Turkish War of Independence and the founder of the Republic of Turkey. In the United States, a wreath is laid at Arlington National Cemetery. The following is written about this on the Arlington National Cemetery's website:

> *The most solemn and august of these occur on* **state occasions** *where the president or his designee lays a wreath to mark the national observance of Memorial Day, Veterans Day or some other special occasion. As a general*

rule, these take place at the Tomb of the Unknown Soldier, attended by ceremonial units from the uniformed services.
Also marked by a high degree of ritual and joint service participation are wreath layings that occur during **state visits**. *A visiting head of state will pay formal respects to the sacrifice of America's veterans in foreign wars by placing a wreath before the Tomb. Similarly, other foreign ministers may also include a wreath laying here as part of their official itineraries.*

Presentation of credentials

What are credentials, and what is the meaning behind them? The presentation of credentials is the first official act that a representative of a country performs after arrival in the country where they will fulfil their function as ambassador. In international law, credentials authorise the head of a diplomatic delegation to represent their state. The head of state of the country sending ambassadors gives the ambassador or envoy credentials which are addressed to the head of state of the receiving country. The permanent chargé d'affaires, appointed to be permanent head of mission in the absence of the ambassador, receives credentials from their foreign minister and forwards them to the receiving country's foreign minister. Article 13 of the Treaty of Vienna of 1961 stipulates that once the required acts are fulfilled, the head of the delegation is formally accredited.

As mentioned earlier, the hierarchy of ambassadors in a receiving country is of essential importance in the application of the rules of international protocol. Where earlier, the power of a country was the deciding factor in precedence, the Congress of Vienna, 1814-15, in Appendix 17 of the act, stipulated strong rules for the order of precedence in the hierarchy of diplomatic representatives. These rules prescribe three classes of diplomatic representatives: ambassadors, envoys, and chargés d'affaires. Within each class, the date of arrival in the city concerned determines primacy in the hierarchy. On the basis of this hierarchy, ambassadors are given the opportunity to present their credentials to heads of state – they include the letter of recall for the previous ambassador wherein the new ambassador is recommended as the new diplomatic representative. The presentation of these letters to the head of state is a formal right of the newly appointed ambassador.

In many countries, the presentation of credentials to the head of state is accompanied by a ceremony that includes the inspection of the Guard of Honour. This is the case in a.o. Denmark, Lebanon, Morocco, the

Netherlands, and Turkey. In other countries such as Norway, the Russian Federation, Spain, Sweden, and the United Kingdom, no inspection takes place. The visiting country's national anthem is played in Egypt, Lebanon, the Netherlands, and Spain, but not in Denmark, Norway, the Russian Federation, Sweden, or the United Kingdom. In some countries, an audience can be a part of the ceremony, such as in Denmark, the Netherlands, Norway, the Russian Federation, Sweden, and the United Kingdom, but not in other countries, such as Egypt, Lebanon, Morocco, and Spain. It is clear, therefore, that every head of state decides how they wish to conduct this ceremony and that there is no uniform, internationally agreed arrangement for it.

In the Netherlands, the presentation of credentials takes place at Noordeinde Palace in The Hague, the office of the king of the Netherlands. On certain, fixed mornings, the king receives at most three ambassadors, all with the same ceremony. The ambassador, along with their spouse and head of staff (a maximum of four) will be led from his or her residence or chancellery by the chamberlain or the aide-de-camp to His Majesty the King. The ambassador, their spouse and the chamberlain or aide-de-camp leading them will be taken to the palace in a Berline carriage. The ambassador is seated on the right side in the direction of travel. His or her spouse is seated on the left. The chamberlain or aide-de-camp sits opposite. The name of the carriage comes from the French, and originates in Berlin where in 1662, the first Berline was designed. It is a closed, four-seater carriage drawn by two to four horses. The carriages are painted black and ox-blood red. They are upholstered in red cloth. The embassy staff is transported in a second carriage. The procession is led by a small mounted escort.

When arriving at the palace, the ambassador, together with the spouse and led by the chamberlain or aide-de-camp, takes his or her place in the courtyard before a Guard of Honour. First, the ambassadors receive four drum rolls as the highest honour, followed by the playing of the national anthem of their country. After this, the commander of the Guard of Honour presents himself to the ambassador and invites him or her to inspect the Guard of Honour. After returning to his designated place, the commander takes leave of the ambassador. At a signal from the master of ceremonies of His Majesty the King, the ambassador and his entourage enter the palace. Inside, the ambassador is greeted by the grand master of the Royal Household, and if the ambassador's spouse is present, also by the mistress of the robes of His Majesty the King.

The grand master leads the ambassador to the balcony chamber where the presentation takes place. The embassy staff follow, led by the master of ceremonies. If the wife of the ambassador is present, she will stay behind with the mistress of the robes and be invited to join the party later. If the ambassador is female and is accompanied by her husband, the chamberlain will fulfil this role. At the presentation of credentials to the king, the foreign minister or their representative will be present next to the grand master, the master of ceremonies and an aide-de-camp. The presentation of credentials is limited to a short exchange in which the return and recall letters are included.

Presentation of Credentials at Noordeinde Palace

After this, the king greets the ambassador with a handshake and invites him to present his or her staff. After a short conversation, the ambassadorial staff leaves the room, led by the master of ceremonies. The king then invites the ambassador to take his or her place.

An audience then takes place in the presence of the foreign minister and the grand master. Midway through the conversation, the spouse of the ambassador joins them by invitation. After the audience, the ambassador proceeds to leave the palace with their spouse. In front of the courtyard, they receive four more drum rolls as an honour. The distinguished party, together with the chamberlain or aide-de-camp, then go to the carriages and return to the residence or the chancellery. The two following ambassadors then receive the same ceremony.

It is customary in the Netherlands for each ambassador to be received separately. In many other countries, multiple ambassadors are received simultaneously. In still other countries, large groups of ambassadors are given their credentials on a single morning, with the difference that every ambassador meets personally with the head of state, while no audience is held after the presentation of credentials. In other capital cities, such as Brussels and Moscow, where many ambassadors are accredited, practical matters are taken into consideration. The benefit of this is that the arriving foreign ambassadors do not need to wait too long to be accredited. After all, ambassadors are generally not allowed to practice their public functions until they have been accredited, unless extraordinary circumstances apply.

Other countries have their own procedures for the presentation of credentials. In the *Protocol of the Russian Federation*, the following is written on how credentials are bestowed in the Russian Federation.

> *On the day of the presentation of credentials, the Russian side provides the Ambassador of a foreign country with a presentational automobile, whereby he arrives in the Kremlin accompanied by an official of the State Protocol Department of Russia's Foreign Ministry. At the appointed time (twenty minutes before the ceremony at the latest) the Ambassadors of the foreign countries enter by car to the inner court of the Kremlin-residence of the President of the Russian Federation. They enter from the visitors' entrance and ascend through the main stairway to the second floor. The guards of honour are placed along their way. All Ambassadors are assembled in the Exhibition hall. Several minutes before the ceremony the Ambassadors of the foreign countries are lined up at the Catherine Chamber, where the president will enter the room accompanied by a deputy head of the Administration of the President and the Minister of Foreign Affairs or the First Deputy Minister. The Minister of Foreign Affairs stands to the right of the President and the Deputy Head of the Presidential Administration on foreign policy matters stands to his left. The Director of the State Protocol Department at the Foreign Ministry of Russia announces the Ambassador who is to present his credentials. The Ambassador walks along the strip of carpet towards the President of the Russian Federation, presents his credentials and, upon a handshake, occupies a position to the right of the President and a photograph is taken before the Ambassador returns to his place in the line. Upon the presentation of credentials by all Ambassadors of foreign countries present at the ceremony, the President addresses them with a brief speech (Champagne is served). Then the President has an informal conversation with the Ambassadors after which the ceremony of the presentation of credentials is over. Note: After the reconstruction of the Grand Kremlin Palace, the ceremony of the presentation of credentials*

will again be held in one of the new halls of the Palace. It will acquire new characteristics and will surely remain one of most eminent events of the presidential protocol.

In the American book *Protocol* by Mary Jane McCaffree, Pauline Innis, and Richard Sand, the presentation of credentials by the foreign ambassador to the president of the United States is described thus:

A Protocol officer calls at the residence or chancery of the Ambassador who is to present his credentials to the President. A White House car, with the United States and foreign national flags displayed, is used. A motorcycle policeman escorts the car to the White House. The car enters the southwest gate and drives slowly around the south driveway (counter clockwise), stopping at the Diplomatic Entrance. The driveway is lined with an Armed Forces Honor Cordon. Each individual presents arms as the car reaches its position. The United States and foreign national flags are displayed at the Diplomatic Entrance. The Ambassador is greeted by the Chief of Protocol and the Assistant Secretary of State concerned. The Chief of Protocol escorts the Ambassador through the Diplomatic Reception Room, the lower hall, the outside corridor, and into the Cabinet Room. The Ambassador is asked to sign the guest book. Press photographers and reporters are assembled in another room. The President enters and stands with his back to the south wall. He is flanked by the United States and presidential flags. The Chief of Protocol stands to the President's left. The accompanying Protocol Officer escorts the Ambassador to the door to the Oval Office. The Chief of Protocol announces the Ambassador, who enters, followed by the Assistant Secretary of State. The President shakes hands with the Ambassador. They exchange informal greetings while photographs are taken. The Ambassador hands the Letter of Recall, his credentials, and the written remarks to the President. The President accepts these and passes them to the Chief of Protocol, who in turn hands the President, the President's written reply. The President gives his reply to the Ambassador. The Chief of Protocol escorts the Ambassador back to the Diplomatic Entrance, retracing their route. The Ambassador enters his car and accompanied by the Protocol Officer, departs from the White House by way of the southwest gate.

State funerals

A state funeral is a solemnity in a country whereby a significant person is honoured after his or her death. This solemnity is performed with much ceremony, and generally has a very public character. Religious beliefs and military traditions play an important role. A state funeral can occur after the death of a head of state, a member of a royal family, or an important statesman. Many countries hold state funerals along much the same lines. Belgium, the Czech Republic, Finland, France, Ireland, Italy, Malta, Poland, the Russian Federation, and the United Kingdom hold similar state funerals. In Belgium, for example, funerals of members of the royal family are of a public nature. Members of the royal family are always buried in the crypt underneath the Church of Our Lady in Laeken. Funerals such as these can never be conducted in private in Belgium. Ministers of state are buried with the same state ceremony, unless the family of the deceased wishes otherwise. The death of a member of the royal family in the Netherlands is not treated as a state funeral, but is rather an entombment in the Royal Crypt. This is seen as a private matter undertaken by the royal family, of which the government pays a part of the cost and takes on some of the organisation where state organs are necessary. Several functionaries fulfil a role in the organisation of a royal burial, including the prime minister, the minister of defence, the governor of the residence, and members of the royal household. The grand master of the Royal Household is charged with coordination of the funeral and is supported by the chief of the military house, the master of ceremonies, and the crown equerry. The master of ceremonies fulfils an essential role in the planning and execution of the funeral service, and the entombment in the royal crypt.

The ministry of Foreign Affairs and the representatives of the Kingdom of the Netherlands abroad are responsible for informing about the death and inviting heads of state to attend the funeral. Accredited diplomatic representatives of the Netherlands, the president of the International Court of Justice, and the heads of international organisations are also informed. The funeral takes place with great ceremony. A few days before the funeral, the royal family invites the Dutch people to pay their respects to the deceased at Noordeinde Palace in The Hague where a *chapelle ardente* is installed. The coffin containing the body of the deceased is brought from the residence to Noordeinde Palace in a small motorcade, led by an escort of sixteen motorcycles ridden by the Royal Constabulary, *Koninklijke Marechaussee*, to the central section of Noordeinde Palace, where a vigil is held by the coffin. Furthermore, an Honour Guard is stationed at the *Nieuwe*

Kerk in Delft, where the entombment takes place. The military organises a large military ceremony in which all the components of the military, including the Royal Army, the Royal Navy, the Royal Air Force, the Royal Constabulary and veterans, contribute. On the day of the funeral, along the road from The Hague to Delft, a line of soldiers stands in honour of the deceased, accompanied by a procession of military bands and detachments on foot and horseback. From the moment of the procession's arrival in Delft to the moment of burial, a gun salute is given every minute. The funeral service and the entombment in the Royal Crypt are attended by royals, foreign missions, heads of large international organisations, Dutch authorities, and personal invitees. The organisation of the foreign missions is the responsibility of the ministry of Foreign Affairs.

The kind of state funeral customary in the United States is described thus on Wikipedia, at the time this book was written:

State funerals in the United States are public funerals held in the nation's capital, Washington, D.C. that are offered to a sitting or former President of the United States, a President-elect, as well as other people designated by the president. Administered by the Military District of Washington (MDW), state funerals are greatly influenced by protocol, steeped in tradition, and rich in history. However, the overall planning as well as the decision to hold a state funeral, is largely determined by the president before his death and the First Family.

And in the United Kingdom as follows:

In the United Kingdom, the term State Funeral is used primarily for the funeral of a monarch. The last such funeral was in 1952 for King George VI. In addition, very exceptionally, a State Funeral may be held to honour a highly distinguished subject, by leave of the monarch and with Parliament's approval (of expenditure of public funds). This last happened in 1965 for Sir Winston Churchill. Other funerals (including those of senior members of the Royal Family and high-ranking public figures) may share many of the characteristics of a State Funeral without being called as such; for these, the term 'Ceremonial funeral' is used. In the 21st century, the funerals of Queen Elizabeth The Queen Mother (2002) and Baroness Thatcher (2013) have fallen into this category. Along with the funeral service itself (which will be a large-scale national occasion), these events tend to be characterised by the use of a gun carriage to transport the coffin between locations, accompanied by a procession of military bands and detachments along with mourners and other officials.

Inauguration / Swearing-In and Coronation

It would be nice to change tone from a discussion of death and move on to the installation of new heads of state. The ceremony surrounding this differs from country to country. In some countries, monarchs as well as presidents are described as being 'inaugurated', while in other countries monarchs are only described as being 'crowned.' As may have become clear, each country has its own way of conducting ceremonies. It is important though to distinguish the essential differences between inaugurations / swearing-ins and coronations.

Coronation

A coronation is the solemn initiation of an emperor, an empress, a king or a queen, often paired with a religious ritual. The service or mass is broken up by secular activities such as oaths, being seated on the throne, and a salutation. The salutation is the part of the solemnity when the most important authorities and members of parliament indicate that they recognise the new monarch by paying homage. Generally, coronations take place in countries where church and state are not separated. An exception to this is Denmark, which has a Lutheran state church, but, since 1850, its kings and queens have been inaugurated rather than crowned. The actual coronation, when the crown is placed on the monarch's head, is sometimes performed by the monarch themselves, but it is most often performed by a clerical dignitary, often an archbishop. This indicates that the monarch rules by the grace of God. The coronation is often preceded by an unction in the case of Roman Catholic monarchs, but also at the coronation of Anglican kings and queens in the United Kingdom. The monarch commits him or herself to fulfilling their constitutional and sometimes religious duty. After the crowning, the monarch is adorned with the royal regalia.

In the United Kingdom, after the death of the incumbent monarch, the crowning of the new king or queen often takes place many months later. It is seen as inappropriate to conduct a festive and celebratory coronation during a period of national mourning. As such, Queen Elizabeth II was crowned on 2 June 1953, long after she had technically ascended to the throne on 6 February 1952. The coronation is performed by the Archbishop of Canterbury, the highest authority of the Church of England. The monarch is first presented to the people and recognised by them. Then the monarch takes the oath on the church and the constitution. After this, they are anointed, crowned, and adorned with the regalia.

Inauguration / Swearing-In

The word inauguration has two meanings. An inauguration can be a ceremony in which a monarch publicly assumes his or her role, swears an oath, and gives a speech. This is often a ceremony that replaces or supplements a coronation. During the ceremony, the royal regalia, such as the crown, orb, sword, and sceptre (sometimes just the crown) are displayed. After this inauguration, the monarch is officially honoured for the first time in public by their subjects when they appear on the balcony of the royal palace. This occurs after the monarch accepts the position and swears an oath on the constitution.

Generally this occurs in monarchies where church and state are separate. For example, the Dutch Sovereign Monarch William I and the King of Holland Lodewijk Napoleon were both inaugurated, as all the Dutch monarchs have been after them. As such, on 30 April 2013, King Willem-Alexander was inaugurated. In the Netherlands, inauguration takes place at the *Nieuwe Kerk* in Amsterdam, at a united assembly of the Upper and Lower Houses of the States-General, and delegations of the Caribbean parts of the kingdom, where the members pledge their allegiance to the monarch after they have sworn an oath on the Dutch constitution, in accordance with Chapter 2, Article 49 of the Dutch constitution. An inauguration is usually preceded by the abdication of the incumbent monarch. In the Netherlands, the official abdication takes place on the day of the inauguration, in the *Mozeszaal* of the Royal Palace in Amsterdam. From that moment on, the new monarch has governmental power, which is confirmed by the inauguration. After the official inauguration the royal couple appears on the balcony of the Royal Palace.

An inauguration can also be a formal ceremony marking an event, such as the beginning of a presidential term. It usually takes place in a formal investiture during which an individual accepts a position. These can be heads of state, heads of government, but also people in other positions such as professors. During an inauguration, the individual receiving a position makes an inaugural address. This is how the president of the United States and the president of the French Republic and many other heads of state are inaugurated.

In the Kingdom of Belgium, the ceremony surrounding the accession to the throne is limited to the signing of the deed of abdication by the outgoing monarch in the presence of seventeen witnesses, followed by the new monarch taking the oath on the constitution in parliament. After being sworn in, the new monarch makes their first royal speech. The day is ended with the appearance of the royal couple on the balcony, a salute to the Unknown Soldier, an inspection of the troops, and a grand parade.

Gun salutes

In most countries, 21-gun salutes are given as signs of welcome and respect at arrival ceremonies, at the moment that the guest sets foot on the country's soil. This is a symbolic gesture for disarming the cannons. Just as in the past it was customary to greet a visitor with an open hand in order to show that no weapon was present, gun salutes were given in a safe direction by old warships sailing into foreign ports.

Gun salutes are generally fired with pauses of ten seconds, and today are meant as a show of honour and respect for an important authority. Most countries keep the number of shots to twenty-one as a show of honour for visiting heads of state.

The website of Arlington National Cemetery writes the following on the origin of the 21-Gun International Salute:

All personal salutes may be traced to the prevailing use in earlier days: to ensure that the saluter placed himself in an unarmed position, and virtually in the power of the saluted. This may be noted in the dropping of the point of the sword, presenting arms, firing cannon and small arms, lowering sails, manning the yards, removing the headdress or laying on oars. Salute by gunfire is an ancient ceremony. The British for years compelled weaker nations to render the first salute; but in time, international practice compelled 'gun for gun' on the principle of equality of nations. In the earliest days, seven guns was the recognized British national salute. Here again we see that the number seven had a mystical significance. In the Eastern civilization, seven was a sacred number: astronomy listed the seven planets, the moon changed every seven days, the earth was created in seven days, every seventh year was a sabbatical year, and the seven times seventh year was a jubilee year. Those early regulations stated that although a ship would fire only seven guns, the forts ashore could fire three shots (again the mystical three) to each one shot afloat. In that day, powder of sodium nitrate was easier to keep on shore than at sea. In time, when the quality of gunpowder improved by the use of potassium nitrate, the sea salute was made equal to the shore salute; 21 guns as the highest national honor. Although for a period of time, monarchies received more guns than republics, eventually republics gained equality. There was much confusion because of the varying customs of maritime states, but finally the British government proposed to the United States a regulation that provided for 'salutes to be returned gun for gun.' The British at that time officially considered the international salute (to sovereign states) to be 21 guns, and the United States adopted the 21 guns and 'gun for gun' return, Aug.18, 1875. Previous to this time our national salute had been variable; one gun for each state of the Union. This practice was partly a result of usage, for John Paul Jones saluted France with 13 guns at Quiberon Bay in 1778 when the Stars and Stripes received its first salute. The practice was not officially authorized until 1810. When India was part of the British empire, the king-emperor would receive an Imperial salute of 101 guns. Unless rendered to a president or the flag of a republic, 21 guns is called a Royal Salute in the British Isles, and even then it is called (colloquially) 'royal' in the British Commonwealth. In short, it would be said of the president of the United States, if saluted in Canada, that he received a 'royal salute'. The United States also has an extra-special ceremony known as the 'Salute to the Nation', which consists of one gun for each of the 50 states. The mimic war is staged only at noon on the Fourth of July at American military ports, although it has been given on a few other occasions, such as the death of a president. The Navy full-dresses ships and fires 21 guns at noon on the Fourth of July and Feb. 22. On Memorial Day, all ships and Naval stations fire a salute of 21-minute guns and display the ensign at half-mast from 8:00 a.m. until completion of the salute. (source: Lovette, 1960)

It is clear that gun salutes not only take place as a part of the ceremony surrounding a visiting head of state but also at other times as a form of respect. Many countries have their own protocol for this. This is how gun salutes are given in the following countries:

China
The 21-gun salute is used in the Republic of China in honour of the president during National Day celebrations. After three trumpets blow, the audience is asked to stand up as the president arrives. When he has taken his position at the dais, the gun salute starts while the gun salute music is played. In some celebrations, it is done while the national anthem is played.

Denmark
Gun salutes are used for a variety of occasions, mostly in honour of the Danish royal family. There are permanent salutary guns in place at

Kronborg Castle in Elsinore, the Sixtus battery at Holmen naval base in Copenhagen, as well as at the naval base at Kangilinnguit in Greenland. A 27-gun salute is used in honour of majesties, whereas the 21-gun salute is used in honour of other members of the Danish royal family.

Gun salutes occur on:
- 16 April – Birthday of HM the Queen
- 11 June – Birthday of HRH the Prince Consort
- The occasion of royal births
- The occasion of royal funerals

Gun salutes also occur during naval visits and when a foreign head of state arrives on a state visit.

France
The 21-gun salute, accorded to the president of the French Republic, forms part of the military honours (*honneurs militaires*). The salute is given during the inauguration ceremony (by two 75mm guns) and during naval visits. These honours are extended to foreign heads of state during state visits. All French Navy vessels anchored in a French harbour on Bastille Day must issue a 21-gun salute at noon, subject to local regulations.

The Netherlands
In the Netherlands, gun salutes are given for the following people or events:
- For HM the King: 35 shots
- For the Prince or Princess of Orange (heir to the throne): 33 shots
- For general princes and princesses of the Netherlands: 21 shots
- For a governor of an overseas territory: 21 shots
- For a foreign head of state: 21 shots
- For a foreign reigning monarch: 21 shots
- At the birth of a heir to the throne: 101 shots
- At the transportation of the physical remains of a member of the royal family from Noordeinde Palace to the *Nieuwe Kerk* in Delft to be laid to rest in the Royal Crypt (with pauses of one minute)
- On the day of the Joint Session of the States General, *Prinsjesdag*, from the moment the King leaves Noordeinde Palace for the Hall of Knights until the moment the King returns at Noordeinde Palace (with pauses of one minute)

Sweden
21-gun salutes mark special royal occasions throughout Sweden, referred to as a *Kunglig Salut* (Royal Salute). The number of rounds fired in a salute depends on the place and occasion. The basic salute is twenty-one rounds. However, when a birth takes place within the Royal House of Sweden, and the child is the firstborn to either the reigning monarch or to the heir to the throne, an extra twenty-one rounds (for a total of forty-two) are added to the normal salute. At all other births twenty-one rounds are fired.

United Kingdom
The following protocol is used in the United Kingdom, as published on the official website of The British Monarchy:
- Today, gun salutes mark special occasions on certain days of the year, many of them with royal associations. Royal salutes are fired from locations in London and authorised stations in the United Kingdom. The number of rounds fired in a royal salute depends on the place and occasion.
- The basic royal salute is 21 rounds. In Hyde Park an extra 20 rounds are added because it is a Royal Park.
- At the Tower of London 62 rounds are fired on royal anniversaries (the basic 21, plus a further 20 because the Tower is a royal palace and fortress, plus another 21 'for the City of London') and 41 on other occasions.
- The Tower of London probably holds the record for the most rounds fired in a single salute: 124 are fired on 10 June when The Queen's official birthday (62 rounds) coincides with The Duke of Edinburgh's birthday (also 62 rounds).
- Military saluting stations are London, Edinburgh Castle in Scotland, Cardiff and Hillsborough Castle in County Down, Northern Ireland.
- In London, salutes are fired in Hyde Park and at the Tower of London. On state visits, at the State Opening of Parliament and for The Queen's Birthday Parade, Green Park is used instead of Hyde Park.
- The salute is fired by The King's Troop, Royal Horse Artillery. The first round is fired at noon (11.00 am on The Queen's official birthday).
- At the Tower of London, the salute is fired by the Honourable Artillery Company at 1.00 pm.
- Gun salutes occur on the following royal anniversaries:
    6 February (Accession Day)
    21 April (The Queen's birthday)
    2 June (Coronation Day)

10 June (The Duke of Edinburgh's birthday)
The Queen's official birthday (a Saturday in June)
14 November (The Prince of Wales's birthday)
The State Opening of Parliament (usually November or December).
Gun salutes also occur when parliament is prorogued by the sovereign, on royal births and when a visiting head of state meets the sovereign in London, Windsor or Edinburgh.

United States
In the United States, as naval customs evolved, twenty-one guns came to be fired for the presidents of the United States, former presidents and presidents-elect, heads of state, heads of government, and reigning monarchs with the number decreasing with the rank of the recipient of the honour. While the 21-gun salute is the most commonly recognised, the number of rounds fired in any given salute will vary depending on the conditions. Circumstances affecting these variations include the particular occasion and, in the case of military and state funerals, the branch of service and rank (or office) of the person on whom honours are being bestowed.

Guard of Honour / Ceremonial Guard

An honour or ceremonial guard is a ceremonial military unit that is assembled during state solemnities, or is inspected by the visiting head of state during a state visit.

The Guard of Honour is generally formed from several detachments of the military. In some countries, the Guard of Honour is solely composed from a presidential or royal palace guard. In principle, the inspection of the Guard of Honour takes place at state visits, when a receiving head of state greets the guest and leads them to this inspection. In the Netherlands, this normally takes place at an airfield, before the Royal Palace in Amsterdam, or at Noordeinde Palace in The Hague. In Italy, it takes place in the Quirinale Palace Courtyard in Rome, and in Germany at Schloss Bellevue in Berlin.

Below are some examples of different compositions of Guard of Honour for ceremonial functions around the world.

Argentina
In Argentina, the Guard of Honour is made up of the Regiment of Mounted Grenadiers, still serving as part of the Argentine army. At present, the

regiment acts as the Presidential Guard of Honour and fulfils ceremonial protocol functions.

Brazil
The Brazilian armed forces and police have several troops for ceremonial use. The most important of them is the Brazilian president's Guard of Honour. It is composed of the 1st Guards Cavalry Regiment – 'Independence Dragoons', the Presidential Guard Battalion and the Cayenne Battery (formally, the Historical Cayenne Battery.)

China
Guards of Honour, known as the Combined Honour Guard of the People's Liberation Army, are provided by the Capital Garrison in Beijing, under the Beijing Military Region and report directly to the general staff.

France
The Republican Guard of the French Gendarmerie provides both foot and horse-mounted guards of honour.

Germany
The primary mission of the Wachbataillon is to perform military honours for the German federal president, federal minister of defence and the inspector general of the Bundeswehr during state visits or on similar occasions. In addition, the Wachbataillon takes part in military events and ceremonies of major importance.

Italy
The Guard of Honour for state visits in Italy is made up of individuals from the army, the navy, the air force and the *corazzieri* (presidential guard).

Mexico
The Guard of Honour in Mexico is made up of individuals selected from the navy, army, or air force. Some of their duties include guarding the Mexican flag in the Zocalo, the main square in central Mexico City and the raising and lowering of it.

The Netherlands
At state visits in the Netherlands, the Guard of Honour is made up of military detachments from the navy, the army, the air force, and the Royal

Constabulary, as well as a military band and the colours. The Guard of Honour for official visits is made up of one detachment.

Russian Federation
Russia's primary Guard of Honour is the Kremlin Regiment of the Federal Protective Service of the Russian Federation, established in 1936.

Sweden
All units of the Swedish Armed Forces carry out Guard of Honour service, although the Life Guards regiment makes up the main part of Guard of Honour services. The Grenadier Company of the Life Guards is used as a Guard of Honour at welcoming ceremonies during state visits. A detachment of grenadiers is also used as a Guard of Honour at the opening of the Riksdag, when an incoming foreign ambassador meets the king at an audience to present letters of credence and when the king attends an annual meeting of one of the Royal Academies. *Drabantvakt* (Royal Bodyguard), commonly known as Karl XI's *drabanter* (Charles XI's Bodyguard) and Karl XII's *drabanter* (Charles XII's Bodyguard) is a ceremonial guard used on state occasions such as state visits, investiture of a monarch, royal weddings and funerals, etc. The guard was formed in 1860 based on historical royal bodyguards. The guard consists of twenty-four soldiers and one officer selected from the Swedish Life Guards.

United States
Each military branch has its own Honour Guard: the army, the marines, the navy, the air force, and the coast guard. Most state national guard units have a ceremonial guard as well. The official Honour Guard of every branch is based in Washington, DC, though nearly every military installation has its own Honour Guard for local ceremonies and events. The Honour Guard units in Washington, DC represent the military as a whole and the United States as a nation, and perform numerous ceremonies on behalf of the president of the United States. The U.S. 3rd Infantry Regiment (The Old Guard) is the pre-eminent Honour Guard and also the presidential guard.

Escorts of Honour

An Honour Escort is usually composed of a motorised escort, including a group of police or army motorcyclists that lead the car carrying a head of state or other high authority, and serves as a sign of honour to the visitor and his or her status. In the Netherlands, the Royal Constabulary escorts heads of state and members of the royal family.

After a visiting head of state officially arrives for a state visit, seventeen motorcyclists (sixteen and one team leader) accompany the head of state. The number of motorcyclists is nine (eight and one team leader) during an official visit, and for all other visits five (four and one team leader).

Besides the Honour Escort on arrival, there will also be an escort of eight motorcyclists for state visits and four motorcyclists during other transportation as according to protocol and motorcyclists from the police for the technical traffic support team.

In France, the Honour Escort is carried out by the *Gendarmerie*, and in Italy, it is the responsibility of the *Carabinieri*. Every country has its own protocol, and in the Russian Federation the visiting head of state, whether during a state visit or an official visit, is accompanied by nine motorcyclists. In Germany, the visiting head of state is escorted by seven motorcyclists. In some countries, the motorcyclists ride behind one another in front of the guest's vehicle, or in a V-formation. In others, they ride in front, next to and behind the guest's car. Generally, the size of the escort will be scaled down during the visit. Besides the Honour Escorts, a technical traffic support team of motorised policemen escort the motorcade during the visit.

In some countries, Honour Escorts are composed completely differently, sometimes comprising jeeps, horses, and even camels. In Sweden, and formerly in the Netherlands, it is customary to transport the visiting head of state to the royal palace in an open carriage, accompanied by a mounted escort. This mounted escort can be made up of a cavalry regiment. The use of mounted escorts is also found in some countries in South America and other countries, to escort the head of state to a ceremony, like a wreath-laying in Belgium and the joint assembly of both houses of the States-General (the upper and lower houses) in the Netherlands where, every third Tuesday of September (named *Prinsjesdag* in Dutch), the king gives a speech – *de Troonrede* in the *Ridderzaal*.

Suite of Honour

A Suite of Honour is normally assigned by the host head of state to the visiting head of state, and will accompany the visiting head of state (and spouse) at all times, except for private engagements. One or more relevant

persons can be attached to the visiting head of state (and spouse) for their support, assistance and convenience, such as:
- a family member of the host head of state (mainly in case of monarchies);
- a cabinet minister;
- an aide-de-camp (ADC);
- a lady-in-waiting (for female guests);
- other member(-s) of the royal household.

Silent processions

A silent procession functions as a remembrance of a person or a tragic event. In many countries, silent processions are held to remember the victims of war. Since the 1990s, silent processions have been held in the Netherlands after incidents of senseless violence. A silent procession, often a spontaneous citizens' initiative with support from local authorities, is conducted silently, with or without flowers, and if the procession takes place at night, with lit candles or tea lights. Generally, mayors and politicians also attend. In many countries, silent processions also take place as an expression of protest. In this case, silent processions are organised as a protest against the actions of the government, a political decision, political killings, unjust arrests or convictions, and restrictions of freedom of speech and expression. The protest march has a long history. At the beginning of the 20th century, marches were held often in the United States. On 29 July 28 1917, a silent procession took place in Harlem, New York, by 8,000 – 10,000 African-Americans. The purpose of this parade was to protest against lynching and anti-black violence.

After the terrorist attack at the headquarters of the satirical magazine Charlie Hebdo in Paris in January 2015, where 17 journalists, cartoonists, shoppers and police were killed over three shocking days, more than a million Parisians came to pay their respect to the dead in a silent march, united behind a peloton of 50 heads of state and government in a vast human tide that reaffirmed the universal values of the French Republic: *liberté, égalité, fraternité.*

Mr Andrea Miliccia, former Protocol Manager for the London 2012 Opening Ceremony

Andrea Miliccia, born in Cuneo, Italy, is the chief of protocol & VIP guest management at the King Abdulaziz Center for World Culture, a fully integrated institution for knowledge, creativity, and cross-cultural engagement inspired by Saudi Aramco, the state-owned oil company of the Kingdom of Saudi Arabia.

His Olympic experience started in Torino with the 2006 Olympic Winter Games where he fell in love with the Olympic movement and the world of protocol. Included in the IOC delegation for both Beijing 2008 and Vancouver 2010, he was behind the successful delivery of the protocol operations for the London 2012 opening ceremony. Andrea also worked in Rome at the presidency of the Council of Ministers of Italy for the 2009 G8 summit and, more recently, in Brazil for the 2014 FIFA World Cup.

His extensive experience in designing and coordinating VIP visitations, ceremonies, and special events at major international happenings led him to establish his own management and consulting firm, Protocol AM, in 2013.

After a master degree in political sciences and postgraduate studies in international relations, he completed his education with an internship at the Permanent Mission of Italy to the United Nations in New York. Lecturer at the LUISS Business School of Rome for the course in event management, Andrea has been currently attending a Master of Arts in Protocol and Soft Diplomacy Skills organised by the International School of Protocol and Diplomacy in Brussels.

Protocol at the Olympic Games by Mr Andrea Miliccia

Ten years ago, when I first started to work as venue protocol manager for the Olympic Winter Games of Torino 2006, I had no familiarity with the sport event industry and very little knowledge of the protocol world. In no time, surely because of my personal inclinations but mainly thanks to the teaching and guidance of an extremely inspired and inspiring leader such as Paul J. Foster,[10] I discovered a passion and found my way. Paul, who over time has become my mentor and one of my dearest friends, had the merit of instilling in me his true love for the 'Games', and for making me understand and appreciate why protocol is crucial in correctly communicating the Olympic values and spirit.

Since the first edition in Athens in 1896, the modern Olympic Games have become the world's most popular and best-beloved international multi-sport event. With more than 200 National Olympic Committees[11] from across five continents participating – the United Nations counts 193 member states – they are not just the stage for the world's top elite athletes to compete. In addition to being the greatest festival of sport, they are a recurring celebration of humanity, encompassing a wide array of deep-rooted rituals and traditions that set them apart from all other global sporting events. The respect of a definite set of rules, that is the Olympic protocol, preserves the power of these rituals and gives a sense of continuity to these traditions.

The gradual assimilation of their ceremonial elements over the years shaped the Olympic protocol as we know it today. Not all editions of the Olympic Games equally contributed to its development, though; the most significant period for the introduction of these ceremonial features dates back to the first half of the 20th century. Antwerp 1920, for example, saw for the very first time the Olympic flag with the five rings being raised during its opening ceremony; Paris 1924 is remembered for establishing the ritual of raising the next host country flag, as a symbolic handover, during its closing ceremony. Amsterdam 1928 is often evoked for the first fire lit in a stadium's cauldron but, also, for the 'Greece first, host nation last' protocol innovation for the athletes' parade. While Los Angeles 1932 went down in history for introducing the raising of the medal winners' flags during the victory ceremony, the idea of a torch relay saw the light on the occasion of the Berlin 1936 Games, where a lit torch was carried from Olympia, Greece, to the newly built *Olympiastadion.* After this fruitful

---

10   Head of Protocol for the XX Olympic Winter Games of Torino 2006; later appointed Head of Protocol, Hospitality and Events at the International Olympic Committee (2006-2011).
11   There are currently 206 recognised National Olympic Committees (NOCs), representing both sovereign states and other geographical areas. Each NOC has the mission to develop, promote and protect the Olympic Movement in their respective countries, in accordance with the Olympic Charter. NOCs are responsible for organising their athletes, coaches and officials participation in the Olympic Games.

period of two decades, nothing substantially changed until the Olympic Games of Melbourne 1956, where the athletes marched together during the closing ceremony as a symbol of global unity – previously they used to enter the stadium in alphabetical order by country – and the Games of Rome 1960, where the official Olympic anthem was first played.

From this brief historical overview, it becomes clear that many elements of the Olympic protocol are epitomised in the opening ceremony, which is probably the most powerful vehicle for the IOC[12] to promote the image and preserve the magic of the Olympic Games. The entry by the head of state, the playing of the host country national anthem, the athletes' parade, the symbolic release of doves, the opening declaration by the head of state, the raising of the Olympic flag accompanied by the playing of the Olympic anthem, the oaths, and the lighting of the cauldron are all poignant moments of the highest solemnity drenched with protocol. They are the opening ceremony. The artistic performance, however astonishing and essential in characterising and making it unique, is simply a wonderful addition to it.

As protocol manager for the London 2012 opening ceremony, I was responsible for supervising and coordinating the arrival and departure operations, the seating, and the hospitality services dedicated to the 10,000 Olympic Family[13] members at the Olympic stadium. My focus, however, was on the 1,100 key dignitaries and members, including but not limited to: the IOC Presidential Box[14] guests (i.e. Her Majesty The Queen and other members of the British royal family, the highest offices of the British government, the IOC president and executive board members); the heads of state and government; the IOC members; the presidents and secretaries general of the International Sports Federations.[15] The formal planning process started one year in advance, and the latest details were finalised only few days before the event. It was the most incredible, complex, and challenging project I have ever worked on. As a team, we

12   The International Olympic Committee (IOC) is the supreme authority of the Olympic Movement.
13   The Olympic Family consists of all Institutions and their official representatives that sustain and support the Olympic Movement and, therefore, Olympism and the Olympic Games.
14   The IOC Presidential Box is the most important seating area of the Olympic Stadium for the Opening and Closing Ceremonies. Equally shared between the IOC and the Organising Committee, accommodates, in order of precedence, the two organisations' most eminent representatives and distinguished guests.
15   As stated in the Olympic Charter, an International Sport Federation (ISF) is an 'international non-governmental organisation administering one or several sports at world level'.

had to design, develop, and agree client journeys, hospitality services, seating arrangements, transportation, and security plans with all major stakeholders such as Buckingham Palace, Foreign and Commonwealth Office, Metropolitan Police, and the International Olympic Committee. The seating plan was, as always, particularly delicate, but we managed it well because of the goodwill of all parties involved; everyone had to relinquish something for the overall success of the event. Our plan and the people who executed it were unquestionably the two major reasons for this tremendous accomplishment. The planning was accurate, took into consideration all variables and, most importantly, was the result of a genuine consensus. However the people on the ground turned a very good plan into a great one, and made it work extremely well. The contributions of all the other protocol officers and members of the international relations team, everyone with a specific task inside or outside the stadium, together with more than 100 volunteers, were simply extraordinary. The commitment, energy, and enthusiasm of all those friends and colleagues are definitely the best memory I keep of that incredible night. As an interesting fact, you may be surprised to know that the seventy heads of state and governments attending the opening ceremony were bussed to the Olympic stadium from Buckingham Palace, where they took part in the reception given beforehand by the Queen. What would normally be considered a heresy – think about state protocol – is here considered not only a best practice, but really the only way to make an event with such a concentration of high-calibre dignitaries happen.[16]

Apart from the opening ceremony, there is a lot of protocol involvement with a broad range of other meetings, special events, and ceremonies happening just before or during the Olympic Games.[17] On this occasion, however, I would like to talk about the protocol activities and services dedicated to the Olympic Family at venue only. Before doing so, I will briefly try to explain why we refer to our client group as Olympic Family, avoiding the use of the word VIP. The difference may seem subtle, but it is quite substantial. A VIP guest is usually a celebrity invited to give lustre to an event simply because of their name, whereas an Olympic Family member, whether or not a public figure, is someone participating in the

---

16   It may be worth clarifying that the Heads of State and Government attend the Opening Ceremony in their capacity as official guests of their respective National Olympic Committees to honour their athletes, rather than in their official civil authority.

17   Opening Ceremony of the IOC Session, IOC Session, IOC Executive Board Meeting, Presentation of the IOC Members to the Head of State, Team Welcome Ceremonies, Victory Ceremonies and Closing Ceremony of the Games.

Olympic Games because of their function. Also, the term 'family' suggests the idea of a group of persons with something in common, revealing a very close relationship with the cause of the event.

So, what are these venue protocol activities then? At competition venues, they mainly encompass the correct application of the Olympic protocol such as ensuring the accurate display of flags; the management of all areas dedicated to the Olympic Family, namely drop-off points, lounges and tribunes; the provision of various services including meet and greet, hospitality, seating management, and flag support for victory ceremonies. Totally different operations mark the non-competition venues. At the Olympic village, for example, they mainly include the organisation of both protocol tours (for dignitaries) and Team Welcome Ceremonies (for athletes and officials). At the airport, they simply consist of appropriate meet and greet services and smooth arrival and departure operations. Compared to other protocol-heavy working environments (i.e. the diplomatic world), I would probably say that more emphasis is here given to the operational aspects of the protocol officer role compared with its political nuances – that are still very much present. 'What we do is like a fine thread that runs through all the very different fabrics of nations that make up this unique event, smoothes the edges and ties it into a most colourful patchwork of humanity. It is a challenging and yet highly rewarding job to balance the diverse elements, expectations, cultures, and to communicate the Olympic values of excellence, friendship, and respect through protocol.' This is how a brilliant former colleague lyrically summarised our job in one of our recent conversations. I could not have said it any better. In general, one of the biggest challenges of the protocol team in the lead-up to the event is educating the future domestic and international guests about the Olympic protocol peculiarity and potential discordance with the host country protocol. During the Olympic Games in fact, national and state protocol is not dismissed but, in case of conflict, Olympic protocol takes priority. In the order of precedence, for example, a minister for sport will always come before any other government minister, even those who traditionally have a heavier political weight.

Having had the chance to work on various editions of the Olympic Games I can easily say that they are the world as we dream it. Enhancing the Olympic values and somehow contributing to building a better world through sport, protocol is crucial in bringing the world together on equal standards in peace and solidarity. Also, protocol is the only credible answer to the increasing demand of correctly managing international events in which authorities and dignitaries are present. The application of some specific rules and internationally recognised procedures in fact protects officials and their role, reducing the risk of mistakes and misunderstandings. After all, protocol is a matter of respect, and to me, an understated form of art too.

Ushers preparing for an event

8. The protocol officer

Introduction

In the previous chapters, different kinds of elements of protocol have been presented. In this chapter we will describe the role of the protocol officer in making sure that the elements of protocol are embedded well in a successful event, meeting, or encounter. A protocol officer should be aware of the guidelines described in the previous chapters, but on top of that he or she should understand the bigger picture; the goal of the meeting and even the vision and mission of the organisation. Organisations and their leaders cannot survive without a good network and without knowing the right people. This need for a good network has created the need for good network management. And another word for network management is protocol. Protocol is the basis of efficient relationship management, in the private sector as well as in the public sector. In essence, protocol management has always been about optimising relationships by maximising personal attention and systemising – by means of rules and procedures – logistics. The success of an event lies in building authentic relationships that are based on the intrinsic belief of operating in the common interest. As Eric Niehe, former ambassador of the Netherlands in India, puts it: 'Protocol translates organisational strategy into effective relationship management.' In this respect, strategic thinking needs to be combined with tactical performance in which the protocol officer should find the right balance between being an event manager and a policy officer.

Event management at the highest level is all about nitty-gritty details. A protocol officer should always keep in mind that any insignificant detail can affect the entire event. As the well-known British historian Harold Nicholson (1886-1968) once noted during a large international conference: 'The matters of organisation and procedure become no less important than the political issues. If poorly handled they can become a major disintegrating factor.'

A protocol officer cannot manage an event alone; cooperation is needed with others. And one cannot expect people to do a good job for you unless it is clear what they are supposed to be doing. It is vital to have everyone working together as a team to get the event up, running, and – in the end – successful. Too often people involved in an event operate in a vacuum. The success of an event will be greatly enhanced if people know how their task contributes to the overall execution. All members of the team should be treated as goodwill ambassadors or PR officers for your organisation. Colleagues from all layers and divisions should be motivated to contribute to the desired strategy, because if they do not come off as professional and hospitable, it reflects badly on your organisation. Too often account managers in the business sector just meet up with their colleagues instead of mingling with the guests, which they are supposed to be doing to increase the effectiveness of the event. Let them know they are a valuable part of your organisation's success, and hold one or more meetings with them in advance of the event to brief them on the goals for the event and their clearly defined responsibilities that fit within those goals.

The use of protocol could be a tool to increase the effectiveness of network meetings. The responsibility for relationship management should be embedded well in the organisational structure and culture. When conducting business in various types of organisations and industries, it is useful to understand the way business is conducted, the culture of the environment and the structure of the organisation, and the importance of protocol in this context towards external stakeholders and clients.

For example, banks divide their personal attention among several groups of clients: retail, preferred banking, private banking, and private wealth management. The more interesting a client is to the bank, the more personal attention is given to him/her, so the more guest engagement is realised. Different categories require different engagements. In protocol these groups are called 'echelons'. The first echelon comprises the most important clients or guests, like the guest of honour, and they receive the best service. The second echelon includes other important guests and should receive good service, but necessarily less personal attention from the host than the guests in the first echelon. In the third echelon all the remaining guests could be placed and they should receive a proper standard of service.

The focus of a protocol officer

As mentioned before, a protocol officer should find the right balance between being an event manager and a policy officer. Not just a good and interesting programme is necessary to make an event successful; protocol and personal attention are certainly similarly essential. On the one hand, the content of a seminar or audience for example, should be well defined, but also the venue and food & beverage aspects should perfectly fit the circumstances. A protocol officer should, however, focus on much more than that. He/she is responsible for the overall success of the event and therefore should consider all the movements of guests and hosts from A till Z as well. No matter what kind of event, all of them consist of at least an arrival and farewell, and one or more movements between different areas (e.g. rooms, halls).

Let us give an example of the focus of a protocol officer during an event that comprises of a seminar, followed by a reception and afterwards a dinner.

Arrival	**Seminar**	Movement	**Reception**	Movement	**Dinner**	Farewell
Welcome			Introductions	Seating		Departure
Seating						

Engagements on arrival

- Highest-ranking persons (first echelon) are supposed to arrive last; all other guests will arrive beforehand.
- Doors of cars will be opened by employees in front of the building and the guests will be welcomed by a protocol officer. Use correct forms of address. Guests will be escorted to the main entrance. From there they will be guided to the cloakroom and the registration desk. Assist where needed along the way.
- Give guests directions or brief guests while escorting. A protocol officer should accompany the guest always on the guest's left hand side, since the right side is the most important.
- Show hospitality and respect.
- Be properly dressed and stand and walk upright.
- Do not stand with your hands in your pocket and do not chew.
- Make eye contact and look at the guest friendly.
- Keep conversation short and complete.
- Speak clearly and articulate well.
- Take initiative.

Welcome

- After registration, the protocol officer escorts the guest to the host or hostess. Upon arrival at the host/hostess, the protocol officer announces the name of the guest.
- If guests are not escorted, it is also possible to give them directions how to reach the host. In that case, names are normally not announced.
- It is the responsibility of the protocol officer to prevent long queues or that guests will be forgotten to be introduced to the host.
- Personal greeting by the host.

- Who takes the initiative to extend his or her hand first? Normally the most senior in position, the eldest, or the woman would do.
- At some events, the host or hostess only welcomes a limited number of guests personally. These are normally the ones in the 1st echelon, such as dignitaries or the main sponsors. In that case the host/hostess is positioned in a separate room to which the VIPs will be escorted by a protocol officer. At the registration desk, a selection should be made who will be escorted and who should proceed to the main reception area or directly to the seminar room.
- If the host/hostess is not supposed to welcome all guests, one could decide to appoint one or more co-hosts in order to make it possible that all guests will be welcomed by a representative of the organisation. For example other members of the board of directors or account managers can fulfill this role.

Seating arrangements for seminar

- Seating instructions are normally handed out at the registration desk (e.g. seating card with number of chair, row and/or bloc).
- When the guests enter the seminar room they will be supported by a protocol officer who can give directions. The first and probably second echelons might have reserved seats in the first rows, while the other participants could have free seating.
- At the reserved chairs and rows, cards are placed with the names of the guests or 'reserved for (e.g. Diplomatic Corps)' if certain guests are seated as groups, or just 'reserved.' The protocol officer should possess a seating list and chart in order to give the right directions.
- Just before the programme starts, the protocol officer should check if there are any empty spaces at the front row(s) and if so, try to fill them with staff members.

Movement

- Host and high-ranking guests will be escorted out of the meeting room. From there they will be guided to a holding area for a little while or straight to the reception area. Other guests will be directed to the reception area, without escort. Assist where needed along the way.

Introductions during reception

- In case special introduction rounds are foreseen for high-ranking guests during the reception, the host remains with this guest of honour at all times and co-hosts could take care of the other guests.
- These special introductions should be arranged in advance and should look as informal as possible in order to create an atmosphere in which everyone feels comfortable. Quite often the guests who are participating in the introduction rounds will be informed accordingly in advance. Upon arrival at the seminar, they will be briefed by the protocol officer about the procedure. After the seminar the protocol officer will await the guests at the designated space in the reception area. The protocol officer is responsible for having all the guests positioned at the correct spot at the right time. The host then escorts the guest of honour to the designated space and introduces the guests to the guest of honour.
- Look around and show initiative: take care of any guest who is just standing on his or her own. Make conversation and try to put people in contact with each other.

Movement

- Host and high-ranking guests will be escorted out of the reception area. From there they will be guided to the dining hall. Other guests will be directed to the dining hall, without escort. Assist where needed along the way.

Seating arrangements for dinner

- Seating instructions are normally handed out at the registration desk (e.g. seating card with table number or table name).
- When the guests enter the dining hall they will be supported by a protocol officer who can give directions. The first and probably second echelons might have reserved seats on the main table(s), while the other participants could have free seating.
- Keep precedence in consideration (most often as a guideline for diplomatic and government affairs), but try to mix guests as well based on mutual interest in order to increase effectiveness (most often the case in the corporate world).

- At the main tables, cards are placed with the names of the guests. The protocol officer should possess a seating list and chart in order to give the right directions.
- Just before the dinner starts, the protocol officer should check if there are any empty spaces at the main table and if so, try to fill them with staff members, or make sure that cutlery and glasses will be removed.

Engagements during farewell and on departure

- Farewell and departure are as important as the arrival and welcome due to the fact that the first and last five minutes leave a long-lasting impression.
- The protocol officer should make sure that the host/hostess is positioned in such a way that guests can easily say goodbye to him/her on the way out.
- Give directions to the exit and assist where needed at the cloakroom.
- If possible, escort guests to the exit and enquire if the event met their expectations. This is valuable information for the evaluation and follow-up.
- Is a give-away appropriate upon departure? Make sure it adds to the goal of the event, otherwise refrain from providing one.
- Doors of the main exit will be opened by employees and the guests will be escorted to their car by a protocol officer.
- Doors of the car will be opened by employees in front of the building and the protocol officers will say goodbye.
- Highest-ranking guests are supposed to leave first; other guests follow afterwards.

Four stages for a successful high-level event

This section offers a comprehensive overview of the different elements to be considered when planning a high-level event. Realising the organisation's strategy by means of the event and with support of protocol should be the focus of answering the question: how to obtain the best possible return from your network?

The four stages of successfully realising a high-level event are:
- Initiation
- Planning & Preparation
- Execution
- Evaluation & Follow-up

Initiation

- Why do you want to organise the event? What do you want to achieve?
- What will happen if you do not organise the event?
- What is the purpose of the event? How is that tied in to your organisation's vision, mission, and strategy?
- Make sure that the content and the hospitality aspects are in line with each other.
- From the beginning, policy officers should work closely together with protocol officers to create the most enhanced and successful programme.
- Who is initiating the event? You or someone else? And is the one who is initiating also the one who is organising the event?
- Which internal and external stakeholders will be involved?
- Who will invite? And how?
- Who is on the guest list? Which guests support the organisation's goal(s)?
- How is the invitation route organised?
- Is the event attractive as a network event? Will the right people be attracted? Why will they care about this event? Understand your event's audience. What are their wants and needs?
- Does the event add value to guests as well as host?
- Who are acting as hosts? And as co-hosts? How are they trained and briefed?
- What location is most suitable for the event? The outcome of the event can be greatly influenced by the choice of location. It is all about the right atmosphere.
- Which configuration do you make? Which set-up of rooms do you choose?
- Keep aspects such as accessibility, parking spaces, valet service, and security in mind.
- Which dates and timings are most suitable? Take national or religious days in account.
- Keep a close eye on timing such as time zones, days of the week, etc.
- Save the date well in advance!
- What is the best duration for the event?
- What programme is foreseen? Make sure that the event's format is appropriate. Why will an event for example work better as luncheon than as a dinner or cocktail party (which typically fosters more conversation)?
- Do you need to take a formal or an informal approach?
- Maintain or create a unique identity: do not just 'copy-paste' nice ideas from others; you can learn from them, but take your own cultural, historic, religious, or corporate background, etc. into account, because

what might be appropriate in one country or organisation might be frowned upon in another.
- Be creative, but do not go to too many extremes. Start a process of brainstorming, creating, developing, and implementing an event concept. Less is most often more!
- Does the time schedule allow for people to meet? Does the organisation facilitate encounters?
- What is the budget? Who is paying?
- Do not sacrifice quality for cost: organise it right, or do not organise it at all.
- What process is needed to organise the event?
- What are you doing yourself and what do you outsource? Keep in mind that some responsibilities can only be fulfilled by yourself, but make use of expertise of others.
- Compose a clear organisation structure; the protocol officer should create precise job descriptions for each employee involved.
- Use clear agreements to show each other's responsibilities.

Planning & Preparation

- Time management; prepare a schedule, try to maintain it, and be realistic:
  - Long-term preparation: tactics, components;
  - Short-term preparation: implementation, confirmation;
  - Countdown: detailed scenarios;
  - Last moment arrangements: final rehearsal, walk in the shoes of your host and guests.
- Timelines change according to the kind of event; a timeframe for the preparations of a global conference is of course much longer than for an audience with a small number of local officials.
- Make realistic deadlines for the completion of tasks and have a logical order in them: e.g. you cannot set a menu until you hire a caterer.
- Composition of committees or working groups: make use of an organisation chart: a protocol officer with overall responsibility and underneath the different committees (such as logistics, security, media, food and beverage, agenda, VIPs, etc.).
- Role of the protocol officer is to define responsibilities for both internal and external parties. Make use of checklists and compose a detailed scenario.
- Conduct site visits with all relevant parties involved.
- Make relevant drawings / overviews / pictures / maps related to the event.

- If the event is taking place abroad, make sure you think of the following logistical and medical aspects:
  - Travel arrangements.
  - Passports (diplomatic?) and visas.
  - Currencies / financial aspects / ATMs.
  - Use of mobile phones / roaming service.
  - Telephone list.
  - Electricity / voltage / adapters.
  - Network / radio frequencies.
  - Luggage arrangements.
  - Time differences / climate.
  - Vaccinations.
  - General / specific country information.
- Give staff briefings and do a rehearsal with the key players before the event.
- Conduct regular meetings and produce status reports to see whether you are still on track.
- Send out invitations in which all expectations are made clear.
- Prepare seating cards and/or nametags (they have to be functional, so only use them when really necessary) upon arrival at the registration desk.
- If necessary, send confirmation letters (including practical information).
- Make sure that good cooperation between protocol and security officers is taking place. Several areas of responsibility in the preparation stage and during the execution could be the securing of the premises, credential examination for all employees and suppliers, and the personal protection of VIPs. Security measures always depend on the foreseen level of threat for the event or individuals attending the event. During the Nuclear Security Summit in 2014 in The Hague for example, armoured vehicles were used for certain heads of state, while others were just crossing the city on foot surrounded by just a small number of security officers.
- Promote the event, if appropriate, by means of publicity, press releases, published announcements, website, social media, etc.
- Make sure that good cooperation between protocol and the media is taking place. Find the right balance between exposure and defending a certain level of privacy of high-ranking officials. Decide on the press arrangements during the event: Where are they allowed? Should there be a press office? Are press briefings or interviews foreseen? Is a private photographer required?

Execution

- Keep a close eye on the flow of events from arrival to departure; it is all about hospitality from A to Z: check, check, double-check!
- Communication: have a contact sheet of everyone involved.
- What happens behind the scenes? If things go wrong back-of-house, this might influence the atmosphere or proceedings front-of-house as well.
- Make sure that meaningful encounters are staged at the event.

Evaluation & Follow-up

- After the event has finished, it is important to find out the outcome of the event. Compose a post-event report based on a debriefing with all relevant internal and external parties.
- Questionnaires for participants could be appropriate for events like conferences, seminars, etc.
- Send out thank you letters and / or gifts to relevant parties.
- Were expectations met?
- What was the event's greatest accomplishment?
- What was the event's weakest moment?
- What were obstacles faced?
  How are the results measured? What is the follow-up?
- Ask the host and co-hosts what has been discussed.
- Define suggestions for future improvements (including preventive measures).
- If applicable, was media coverage sufficient?
- Did you stay within your budget?
- Should the event be held again? Reflect on vision, mission, and strategy of the organisation.

Unforeseen circumstances

Inspect what you expect and expect the unexpected.

Even if you made sure that everything was organised in the smallest detail, it might happen that unforeseen circumstances arise. For example what to do in case of disastrous weather, national mourning, or an act of international terrorism occurring just before the event? Or on a different scale; the guest of honour or the caterer does not show up. Or what happens if too many people show up? This book is not intended to answer all these questions, but it is worthwhile to keep these kinds of issues in mind while preparing an event. If necessary, prepare some doom scenarios and make a contingency plan.

Nickson and Siddons (2006) determined these kinds of unforeseen circumstances to be 'external events' that happen outside your sphere of influence. They asked the question why do mistakes, disasters or ad hoc changes happen in event management and came up with the following six causes:
- Inadequate information;
- Unclear / wrong goals and requirements (false assumptions);
- Failures of communication and management (including misunderstandings, cultural mismatches, lost messages, poor planning, and poor setting of objectives);
- Inadequate resources (funding, people, and equipment);
- Unproven technology (trying something for the first time);
- External events (e.g. politics, natural disasters, international crises).

In conclusion, **to organise a successful high-level event, the focus of a protocol officer should be on:**

vision and Strategy
contenT
pRecedence
guest lists And invitations
assisting hosTs
logistical and technical prEparations
briefinG colleagues
reciprocIty
Cultural differences

persoNal attention to guests
an immaculate Execution
the right aTmosphere
keeping calm and folloW protocol
cooperating to reach expOsure
coopeRating to ensure security
diplomatic sKills
unforeseen cIrcumstances
thorough evaluatioN
measurinG results and follow-up
!

Speech by Ivo van Vliet, Jeroen Koks, and Ruben Nederpel

Below speech was held during a protocol seminar related to *Prinsjesfestival*, September 2014, Former Hall of House of Representatives, The Hague.

Ivo:
Your excellencies, ladies and gentlemen,
My name is Ivo and I am 20 years old.

Jeroen:
I am Jeroen and I am twenty-two years old.

Ruben:
My name is Ruben and I am twenty-one years old.

Ivo:
We are all still studying or have just finished our study.
And we all work as ushers for the Protocolbureau in The Hague.
My career in protocol started by opening doors, telling people to turn left a hundred times, handing out badges, and just smiling a lot.
Apparently I did well and I boosted my career in protocol. I still smile a lot but I now also seat the guests and escort dignitaries.

Jeroen:
To work in protocol is just the best thing for a student. It is cool to be at exclusive events and meet famous people. But I also benefit from the skills I developed... I have become so much better at telling difficult things in a very charming way.

Ruben:
Most of all, working in protocol shaped our vision. And that is what our short presentation is all about.
This seminar is about the future? We are the new future in protocol.
And we are very pleased to have this opportunity.

Ivo:
First of all, I never realised protocol has such a negative meaning for a lot of people. I do not experience protocol as being formal.
In fact, protocol prevents events from being formal. Protocol guarantees it all runs smoothly and brings clarity and peace.

Jeroen:
Secondly, most people think somewhere there is a very big protocol book with a solution for every situation. People think protocol is fixed and never changes.
It is my experience that protocol is a vision, a way of working, a basis. But protocol is different in every situation.

Ruben:
Thirdly, strangely enough protocol is often seen as something for royals and ministers only.
But I have used protocol at business events, fashion shows, and even dance events.
For example:
From a protocol perspective, a royal wedding and a dance event are organised by the same method.

Ivo:
Both have divided their guest list into three groups:
Echelon 1: the most important guests
Echelon 2: the other VIPs
Echelon 3: the rest of the guests

Jeroen:
At a royal wedding the first echelon are the bride and groom and the direct family.
At a dance event echelon 1 could be the CEOs of the largest sponsors and the alderman of culture.

Ruben:
Echelon 2 are the other VIPs
At a royal wedding, these are the representatives of other royal families and dignitaries.
At a dance event, echelon 2 are the rest of the sponsors, all the artists, the press, etc.

Ivo:
Every echelon has its own form of service.
At a royal wedding, this is determined by seating arrangements, greeting procedures, personal attention, time of arrival.
At a dance event this is exactly the same.

Jeroen:
Echelon 1 is welcomed upon arrival by the chairman of the dance festival.
Echelons 1 and 2 are seated in front of echelon 3.
Most dance events have a VIP area in front of the stage.
Every echelon has its own entrance, its own parking area, its own area of reception.

Ruben:
This method of protocol makes it possible to functionally focus your attention on the guests that are most important to us.
It is a tailor-made system of personal attention. And thus there is a great future for protocol.
But the modern era has created the need for a modernised image of protocol. An image that focuses on functionality instead of formality.

Ladies and gentlemen:
The protocol is <u>not</u> dead.
Long live the protocol!

Mr Jean Paul Wijers, Managing Director and founder of the *Protocolbureau*, and the Institute of Strategic Relationship Management

In 1996 Jean Paul Wijers graduated from the Hotelschool The Hague, one year after founding the *Protocolbureau*. Between 2001 and 2009 he worked for Gilbert Monod de Froideville, at that time the Master of Ceremonies of HM Queen Beatrix of the Netherlands, at royal weddings, state funerals, and royal baptisms.

Jean Paul Wijers has been called upon to assist at numerous official events and ceremonies. His vision on modern protocol management is the basis of the postgraduate programme on strategic relationship management.

Protocol is a basic principle of professional success by Mr Jean Paul Wijers

In our fast-moving, twenty-first century society, personal attention is the biggest gift you can give someone. Personal attention in the form of time: time to welcome people, time for a personal meeting. The internet revolution and the exponential growth of the use of social media come with an increasingly hectic modern life in Western countries, and the growing need for space and time for real, personal attention. Businesses and governments are conscious of this need and try to provide for it. Think about local authorities who want to be 'closer to the citizen', banks that have the 'ability to give you the personal attention you deserve', and the many, many network events that are organised at all levels today. These are well-intentioned attempts to provide personal attention, but they are not always as successful as they could be.

Simultaneously, time is a precious commodity. Who doesn't experience the daily tyranny of urgency? Everything has to be instant, dozens of questions and decisions beg for our attention – we have so much to do and so little time. There is also little time dedicated to giving personal attention to people, for maintaining our professional networks, regularly meeting with existing contacts and making new ones. Who would not rather have more time for that? We all know how important relationships are for success, both in our professional and in our personal lives. This is, for example, addressed in The Grant Study, a major study carried out over seventy-five years by Harvard students. This study showed that students who were able to maintain relationships were better at building successful careers. Another example is that of Jan Egeland, the Norwegian diplomat to the United Nations who received the Franklin D. Roosevelt Four Freedoms Award in 2008. In his acceptance speech he indicated that the success of the UN in developing countries largely depends on the success of building an effective network.

This article describes protocol management as the solution for today's strong need for personal attention and for the crippling sense of time deficiency that affects us daily. Protocol is often regarded as unnecessary formalities, but in my view protocol is rather a means to create and structure meaningful encounters. Modern protocol management is derived from classic protocol and is the keystone of a clearly formulated relationship management strategy. It is the most efficient and effective way for organisations to maintain their relationships.

Know your classics (and know how to use them)

Classic protocol was developed by and for the European monarchies in response to a question we still struggle with today: the king and his entourage had little time but had to see and speak to many. Searching for a more efficient method to manage time and to get more out of the events at the royal court, they developed protocol: rules and guidelines to structure events, with the goal of increasing the effect and the number of meaningful encounters. This protocol was also intended to show respect, at different moments and in coordinated ways.

Classic protocol still exists. For some, protocol has a negative image. The classic protocol officers put the rules of protocol above all and are only focused on matters like the correct order of the flags, the correct use of titles, and the correct placing of the cutlery. For a protocol fetishist, protocol is the ultimate goal and not 'why does the event take place, what is the goal, and what does this mean for protocol?' These are the questions asked in modern protocol management.

Modern protocol

Modern protocol is often perceived as a new form of protocol but in fact modern protocol is an incorrect term – the protocol itself hasn't changed. It is the approach that has changed or, rather, should change. Where the protocol fetishist says 'protocol is always the same', the modern protocol officer embraces the fact that protocol can be different every time. Protocol is, for him or her, not a goal but a tool with which a certain goal is reached. The translation of the goal into a different protocol every time is an important component of protocol management, which is itself a component of strategic relationship management.

Strategic relationship management

If protocol is not the goal but a tool, what then is the goal? This question brings us to strategic relationship management: acquiring, keeping, and strengthening professional relationships, on the basis of a previously formulated networking strategy. This networking strategy is an extensive translation of the communication strategy of a business or an organisation that is itself a translation of the overall vision and strategy. The vision and strategy of an organisation are translated into a communication and a relationship management strategy of which protocol management is a component.

Surprisingly, most businesses and organisations lack a networking strategy, even if relationship management is important and many network events are organised. That this leads to less effect and little room for networking is not surprising. To simply put 500 people in one room is not enough to create a networking opportunity. The Dutch organisation *Protocolbureau* has sent out hundreds of questionnaires to attendees of network events, and always received reactions like 'it was perfectly organised, but where was my account manager?' or 'who were all the other people who were invited?' An event only becomes an effective network meeting if it is arranged as such, structured, executed, evaluated, and followed up.

Protocol management

Protocol was and still is the perfect way to bring people in contact with one another. How to do this depends on the business or organisation along with the occasion and the goal of the event. Protocol management is all about analysing, translating, and applying. From an overall strategy to a networking strategy and, finally, to a protocol framework that works for each occasion or event. In other words, protocol management begins strategically and ends operationally.

The modern protocol officer – and also the event manager who regularly organises network and relationship management events – knows and understands the greater context in which the events are organised. He or she also knows why having a network is so important for a member of the board/CEO/minister/councillor and understands that without knowing the right people that person cannot be successful.

The modern protocol officer/event manager develops a protocol tailored for each event. This could be to structure meetings, for example between the mayor and his or her most important guests or between account managers and their key clients. Obviously, the correct people should be invited for this. That happens on the basis of stakeholder management: which relationships should we invite for what, which potential relationships and which 'beautiful people' (those who will never be a client but will serve to support the networking function of this event)? The protocol officer/event manager supervises all the parts of the operation, including taking care of the training and support of the hosts and hostesses, being available on the spot to monitor the progress of the event and with a plan to measure the results of the event.

What can go wrong?

Professionalising relationship management is somewhat tricky because of the many different ways it can go wrong, both on a strategic and organisational level as well as in the follow-up. Businesses and organisations can make crucial errors.

It has already been said that businesses and organisations often lack their own networking strategy, and if they do, the networking strategy is not always successfully translated into effective network events, and/or to the operational level. Relationship management should be consistently applied over a longer term, and the protocol officer/event manager responsible should be able to set up and control the internal project organisation that is necessary to implement a policy. This can be difficult if relationship management does not have a clear place within the organisation. Is relationship management the responsibility of communications, external relations or facilities, or do these departments all contribute a bit? On what level are the decisions made and what is the mandate of the protocol officer/event manager responsible?

On the operational level, too, there can be deficiencies if a network event is not operated like one. Experience shows that this happens a lot: network meetings in locations that are much too small, for which the wrong people have been invited, have packed programmes, music that is much too loud, long-winded speakers and lengthy dinners. These are all obstacles to real personal meetings.

Last, but not least, every network event is nothing more than a snapshot. The effectiveness of it hinges very much on a good follow-up. Many organisations fail to ask their employees afterwards: 'Who did you meet? Who did you speak to and what was the result?'

Conclusion

Those who dismiss protocol as nonsense are making a crucial error. Hundreds of important personal meetings are taking place every day, on all levels, and protocol is the tool to structure this. The structure makes it possible to build a meaningful network, which is the basis of successful leadership. For these reasons, today's protocol specialists – the modern protocol officers and event managers – are essential for businesses and organisations and are crucial to the success of their managers and leaders.

Inspection of the Guard of Honour by the former President of the Republic of Lebanon, HE Mr Michel Sleiman, at his state visit to the President of Brazil

Mr Lahoud Lahoud, Director-General, Chief of Protocol & Public Relations Department of the Presidency of the Council of Ministers of the Republic of Lebanon

Mr Lahoud Lahoud is holder of an M.A. in International Relations and a B.A. in Education from the Saint Joseph University in Beirut (USJ). He took up on-site internships at the offices of the United Nations Economic and Social Commission for Western Asia (ESCWA) in Beirut and the Lebanese ministry of Foreign Affairs. He stepped into the world of protocol in September 2008, when he was appointed deputy chief of protocol, then promoted to chief of protocol in August 2011. During his tenure as chief of protocol, he prepared and organised all the president's local, regional and international activities, visits, meetings, audiences, receptions, etc., as well as the president's participation in the UN General Assembly sessions and Security Council meetings. He actively took part –as an attendee and as a trainer– in numerous conferences, seminars and training programmes related, among other topics, to diplomacy, protocol, international relations, and civil service, in a.o. Belgium, China, France, Lebanon, the UAE, and the USA. He was awarded many high distinctions in recognition of his actions, notably from France (Officer of the French Order of Merit), Greece (Grand Commander of the Greek Order of the Phoenix), the Order of Malta (Pro Merito Melitensi) and Spain (Grand Officer of the Spanish Civil Merit).

Presidential Protocol by Mr Lahoud Lahoud

The first rules of Lebanon's protocol system were laid down in 1944, right after independence, in the aftermath of the French Mandate era, which lasted around a quarter of a century, and they were inspired by the French protocol system. Ever since, the Lebanese protocol system has undergone many amendments that made it more in line and harmony with the specificity of political life in Lebanon.

Lebanon shares many of the world-applicable rules in presidential protocol fundamentals with applicable world rules, such as the seating precedence, the location of national flags during meetings between high officials, the rules for the exchange of presents, etc. Nevertheless, to us, the major role of protocol remains that of an adjuvant to create an exemplary working environment for the president of the republic, whether through his daily activities, internal meetings or through international visits and participation in conferences and multi-faceted meetings.

It is worth noting that one of the basic specificities of the presidential protocol in Lebanon – and more so of the surrounding Arab states – is the typical generous welcome and human rapprochement for which our Arab societies are generally known. This feature particularly stands out during the audiences and meetings with international officials such as presidents and kings, who are quickly overwhelmed with this sense of warm welcome and high appreciation. This atmosphere to which the presidential protocol contributes makes the international political relations more humane and open.

Science and experience have shown that the accurate practice of presidential protocol fundamentals requires an accurate awareness of the habits, traditions, social conceptions, intellectual and political backgrounds of many of the states, personalities, and officials. Therefore, we have always worked carefully on the preparations for the president's meetings and numerous internal and external activities. In fact, protocol rules are not set unilaterally; they must necessarily fit the particularities of the concerned parties. In this context, globalisation must not erase differences and specificities, but rather exploit them to enrich political life and communication between officials.

To achieve this, it is indispensable to resort to a specialised team with multiple practical skills, from proficiency in applying protocol fundamentals to competency in political, social, and cultural backgrounds for the activities and meetings that it has the duty to organise. We have always been keen on keeping up with current developments, especially at the level of work technology and the computerisation of the work's daily mechanisms.

After all, international protocol consists of drawing the platform on which international relations grow and preserving mutual respect, no matter how big or small the countries may be.

HM King Abdullah II welcomes HH Pope Benedict XVI to Jordan

9. Guest and host

Role of host

Whether you are welcoming numerous dignitaries from around the world for a high-level event or hosting an intimate dinner for a couple of close business partners, the importance of being authentic is key. Being a gracious host who makes sure that people feel comfortable in the presence of everyone around will ensure an atmosphere of mutual understanding and encourage genuine interest in others. Try not to struggle with too much fuss and strict protocol during meetings or encounters that do not necessarily require it.

In the previous chapter the role of the protocol officer was described in achieving the goals of an event and making sure that those goals are aligned with the mission and strategy of the organisation by managing hospitality and meaningful encounters. However, it is the host who has the overall responsibility for an event, so his/her role is of vital importance for a good final result. The role of a host is to give his/her guests the right amount of attention. As discussed in the previous chapter, all guests deserve a certain amount of attention and engagement, which is normally based on the echelon they fit in. Co-hosts might assist in making sure that all guests are looked after in a proper manner.

Mutual interest

Either hosting or attending a social diplomatic occasion can often feel like a part of the job. This is of course because it is not just an opportunity to eat and drink well, but a part of a diplomat's or politician's core work to represent their country. While the purpose of the actual event is often to celebrate a holiday or diplomatic ties between countries or with an organisation, the purpose of an invitee attending the event should be aligned with his/her organisation's mandate and interests.

The website of the U.S. State Department indicates how the United States, as host country, shows how meaningful events with mutual benefit can contribute to completing the work of foreign diplomats as 'guests' in the country:

> *The Diplomatic Partnerships division is the newest addition to the Office of the Chief of Protocol. The division was founded on the idea that through the exchange of ideas, cultures and traditions we can build upon the*

Administration's efforts to foster international goodwill and provide the Diplomatic Corps greater insight and understanding of our people, customs and institutions. The Diplomatic Partnerships division pursues this goal by organizing new events with the Diplomatic Corps, offering diverse types of exchanges as a means to foster lasting relationships, enhance our mutual understanding and ultimately assist the Diplomatic Corps in completing their work while here in the United States.

As mentioned earlier, social occasions contribute to completing the work of diplomats as well. In this respect, Richard Sennett refers to Sir Ernest Satow (who wrote Satow's Diplomatic Practice as a bible for professional diplomats in 1917) when he discusses protocol of an ambiguous sort that shapes seemingly social occasions:

Diplomatic receptions and cocktail parties are occasions for the relentless exchange of non-controversial observations about sports or pets; in the flow of these inanities, the diplomat will 'casually' drop into the conversation something meaty about a government's plans or personnel, knowing that the conversation will be minutely dissected, if it hasn't actually been covertly recorded; the casual comment will later be fished out and acted on. The diplomatic craft, for the speaker, requires making sure the message gets through without too obviously dropping the hint; the skill of the listener lies in seeming not to notice. This ritual of casualness is, so professional diplomats say, very hard to get right, a demanding form of light touch; it is most often used for issues too explosive to be put on paper. Satow rightly views these cocktail-and-canapé occasions as meetings in disguise.

These 'meetings in disguise' on the other hand are also more than relevant to provide a transparent answer to the question related to the goals of such events: 'What would I like to achieve for my guests as well as myself?' And afterwards: 'How do I achieve this?' A good and interesting event with well-prepared content and policy background notes can be very helpful, but personal encounters arranged by the host 'off the record' might be even more successful. According to McCaffree, Innis, and Sand (2002), hospitality and

entertainment (are) an indispensable tool for developing satisfactory relationships with the Diplomatic and Consular Corps and the cultural, political, economic, and social communities. A friendly conversation at a dinner party may do more to resolve difference of viewpoints between nations and officials than weeks at a conference table.

HM King Abdullah II of Jordan (2011) reflects on the impact of 'off the record' personal relations as follows:

> *A difference between politics in the Middle East on the one hand, and Europe and the United States on the other, is that the first one is very personal. In the West, international relations are often regulated by institutions and permanent civil service frameworks, which ensure the political continuity while political leaders come and go. Personal relations seem less important than the right choice of conversation topics. In my region we rather prefer to talk to each other personally. We are proud of our culture of hospitality, which often results in eating together and informal gatherings. In the West it is very acceptable to do business with a Head of State for twenty minutes and then leave. In the Arab world it is considered rude to stay for such a short while. The correct way to host honoured guests is to offer them a lavish dinner. The real work is done during informal one-on-one get-togethers after the meal, instead of during official meetings.*

Making a shift from diplomacy to the corporate world, LoCicero (2008) refers to the goal of a specific SME business event and the role of its host as follows:

> *Many times business owners, in launching a business or in their excitement over its growth, decide to have a grand opening event. Unfortunately, the entire effort sometimes seems to be directed toward having a party. While a party is certainly warranted, particularly given the effort and energy expended in starting an enterprise, a grand opening should be a multilayered event that favorably impacts future sales, initiates valuable contact, sustains relationships, and attracts favorable media coverage. Don't be satisfied with a grand opening that's simply a three-hour wine-and-cheese affair, a ribbon-cutting ceremony, or a one-day sale. Use your grand opening as a platform that extends far beyond a single event.*
> *To maintain a jovial atmosphere during the grand opening you must consider yourself the host or hostess of the event. Be outgoing and greet all guests. Remember as many names as possible. If the event has many needs to tend to, delegate those or hire others to handle aspects that might take you away from the matter at hand: promoting your business with this audience. If you're behind the scenes arranging flowers and carting out food, you're missing prime opportunities for meeting future customers and thanking supporters.*

The examples above can only be successful if the host and guest share a mutual interest and on top of that the organisation should be able and willing to facilitate the encounters. In her book *Leap of Faith – Memoirs of an Unexpected Life*, HM Queen Noor of Jordan described a situation related to this (seen from her American background) in the mid- 1980's:

> *I got criticized because I broke with a certain tradition. Every year, a couple of official Iftars – the meal during Ramadan after sunset – were organized at the royal court, but only a few of them were accessible for women. I decided to organize a couple of Iftars on which influential women from various parts of the country would be welcome. In this way information could be exchanged and this ritual could be experienced together. It would be a good opportunity for women to 'network', just like men had been doing for ages. But the royal court did not agree. Women were supposed to stay at home, preparing the Iftar for their husbands. I thought that was ridiculous. The Ramadan takes an entire month, so other members of the family could prepare the Iftar once in a while as well. However, I did not want to have the royal court against me, before knowing how other women thought of it. Most women I shared my plan with, were so enthusiastic, that I decided to persevere. But the court did not give up easily. At a certain moment my husband was put under so much pressure, that he asked me to get rid of the plan. He was quite surprised when I did not object, but I knew what would happen. There were that many women who protested loudly against abandoning the Iftars, that I continued organizing them again a year later. Over the years, my Iftars expanded towards meals which included diplomats, students, orphans and representatives from all kinds of organizations, both male and female.*

Such a broad mixture of guests and stakeholders is also more than relevant in the cultural and corporate world, as is explained by Mr Axel Rüger, Director of the Van Gogh Museum in Amsterdam, the Netherlands, in the Dutch magazine Winq (January / February 2015). He stresses that the cultural and creative sector should wield a greater deal of influence. At trade missions of the municipality of Amsterdam, he mentions that a delegation of the cultural sector is always present, together with the mayor and representatives of the corporate sector. He indicates that that is much less so with state visits. If he can join, he often only hears that he can talk to the cultural organisations, but nothing more. Rüger believes that one should progress towards a more integrated approach, also in a broader perspective. Many CEOs of multinationals are member of supervisory boards of cultural institutions in the Netherlands, but hardly any leading person from the cultural sector has a commissioner's position at large or mid-sized enterprises. According to Rüger, the Van

Gogh Museum manages a world brand and does an enormous amount of market research, has visitors from all over the world, monitors its consumer's behaviour and works closely with the travel industry. The museum manages a very broad group of stakeholders, much broader than many commercial organisations will. If he mentions this to one of those CEOs, there is a minute of silence and then they say that he is actually right and that they never thought of that. Rüger's conclusion is that this is what should be given a start; much more cross-fertilisation and much more exchange.

Guest list

This cross-fertilisation and exchange should be one of the objectives of actually the majority of events, both diplomatic and corporate. One should therefore make sure that a guest list should be interesting for host as well as guest. Try to find a balance between government officials and business representatives, current clients and potential clients, young and old guests, men and women, and include a couple of 'beautiful people' like distinguished personalities in the arts, literature, academia, media, or society. Last but not least, personal friends of the host and guest of honour could be added to the guest list as well. In case one is planning to distribute a guest list to the invitees, it is wise to compose the list in alphabetical order in order to prevent possible discussions about precedence.

For recurring events it might be convenient to have an 'Iron List', a list of guests who should always participate in that particular event. This list prevents you from re-inventing the wheel all the time when composing a guest list. It is possible to have more than one Iron List since every event has a different focus. Concentration and accuracy in compiling an Iron List is essential; do not forget anyone who is important enough to belong on the list to avoid sensitivities and embarrassments.

Example of an Iron List for American citizens at a State Banquet at the White House (all with partner), based on reviewing several guest lists from the past:
– *President of the United States*
– *Vice-President of the United States*
– *Speaker of the House of Representatives*
– *Chief Justice of the United States*
– *Secretary of State*
– *(Deputy Secretary of State for specific region)*

- *(Secretary of Defense)*
- *(Secretary of Energy)*
- *(Other relevant Secretary)*
- *Assistant to the President and Chief of Staff*
- *Assistant to the President for National Security Affairs*
- *Assistant to the President and Chief of Staff to the First Lady*
- *Assistant to the President and Press Secretary*
- *Chief of Protocol, State Department*
- *Chairman of the Joint Chiefs of Staff*
- *United States Ambassador to the guest country*
- *1-2 United States Senators*
- *1-2 United States Representatives*
- *1-2 Associate Judges of the Supreme Court*
- *Mayor of a relevant city (not necessarily Washington, D.C.)*
- *5-10 Business men*
- *+/- 5 representatives of IOs / NGOs*
- *+/- 5 musicians and/or athletes*
- *1-2 White House Correspondents*

Prior to and during the event, the host needs to be appropriately briefed and assisted by a protocol officer in order to ensure the success of the function. Good preparation affects the role of the host as well as that of the guest in a positive way. Below one will find a couple of guidelines for a guest to take into account in order to make the most out of attending an event (some of the guidelines are based on La Red's, *EHBN: Eerste Hulp Bij Netwerken*).

Guest's checklist in order to facilitate strategic networking

Planning & Preparation

- Before the event takes place, ask for the guest list or predict who will attend and consider whom you would like to meet.
- Do your research: what are personal preferences of your host and guests and what kind of cultural differences should be taken into consideration? Check relevant backgrounds, curriculum vitaes, pictures, preferences, and interests of the people you want to meet.
- Set your goal in advance; when can you call the event successful?

Engagements upon arrival and welcome

- Be on time; also walk-in time is network time.
- Greet the host/hostess and thank them for the invitation.
- Tips regarding gifts and/or flowers are included in Chapter 6.

Introductions during reception

- A man is always presented to a woman, with the exception of the president of any country, a king, a dignitary of the church, or when a junior female officer is 'officially' presented to a senior male officer.
- The higher-ranking person's name is stated first, then the name of the person being presented.
- Young people are presented to older people of the same gender.
- A single person is introduced to a group.
- Observe the audience and decide where you are going to introduce yourself and mingle.
- Remain sincere during conversations and treat your conversation partner with respect.
- Change conversation partner once in a while.

Engagements during farewell and on departure

- Do not leave too late; try to avoid being the last remaining guest.
- Do not leave the event without saying goodbye to your conversation partner(s).
- Do not leave the event without saying goodbye to the host/hostess or at least a co-host.

Evaluation & Follow-up

- It is not necessary to send a letter or thank you note to the host/hostess after an official reception or formal gathering, but it is appropriate to do so if you particularly enjoyed the event.
- After the event write down whom you have spoken to and what about.
- Decide whom you would like to meet again.
- Take action; make an appointment, send an email, link on LinkedIn, etc.
- Evaluate the goal you have set in advance; can you call the event successful?

Once more, protocol and strategic networking are essential tools for the success of any diplomat or business person. As professor Erik Goldstein concludes his 2009 article on *Developments in Protocol*:

> *As times change so do customs generally. In diplomacy protocol too changes and develops, mirroring broader societal norms. Protocol is often considered to be synonymous with formality, but for diplomacy protocol provides the commonly accepted norms of behaviour for the conduct of relations between states. As informality becomes the norm in diplomacy, so diplomatic protocol will help systemise and therefore stabilize these new forms in the communication and negotiation between states.*

And even though protocol used to be reserved for governments and diplomats, in his 1994 article *'Global Quality Leadership: A protocol Perspective – International Business'*, John Hayes makes reference to Sondra Snowdon's ten principles of protocol as imperative in the corporate world as well. Five of them are worth mentioning here as a final note:

– *A strong understanding of protocol is the absolute basis for effective communications between strangers, both verbal and non-verbal communications.*
– *Personal protocol in the era of instantaneous communications. In the information age, every face-to-face meeting becomes a vital opportunity.*
– *In any negotiation, knowledge is power. The more you know about the other party's motivation and needs from their cultural perspective, the stronger your negotiating position becomes.*
– *In today's global markets, the most compelling demand is the demand for quality.*
– *Protocol is the golden key that unlocks the door to mutual respect between people of different cultures. From that respect comes understanding, from understanding comes the resolution of mutual interest, and from mutual interest comes the relationship that will assist you in 'gaining the global edge'.*

Mr Martin van Pernis, former President of the Board of Siemens, the Netherlands

After his study in Electronics, Martin van Pernis started his career at Siemens A.G. in Munich, Germany. After positions at several divisions of the company he retired in January 2010 as CEO of Siemens Netherlands and president of the Siemens Group in the Netherlands. The group had in 2009 3,300 employees and a turnover of 1.6 billion Euro. From 2002 to 2010 he also was the speaker of the North West European companies of Siemens. After his retirement he started his own company Vapecon B.V. for which he performs several functions. Van Pernis was and still is also active in a number of social functions as chairman of the supervisory board of the Rotterdam Philharmonic Orchestra (until 9/2020), chairman of the Austrian Culture Foundation in the Netherlands, founder and chairman of the Ambassadors Club Nederland, chairman of the board of Habitat for Humanity Netherlands, and member of the advisory board of the Foundation Theatre Walhalla. In the past, he held various board positions, including supervisory board leadership of Airbus Defence and Space Netherlands, Dutch Space, EADS, Feyenoord, SACON BV, Protocolbureau, Batenburg Techniek, the Royal Institute of Engineers KIVI, and the Commission 'Adviespunt Klokkenluiders' (Advisory Council for Whistleblowers). He has also held various board positions at the employers' organisations VNO-NCW and FME. He currently holds various supervisory and advisory roles at the Koning Willem I Foundation, Business Club TEN, the Expert Committee SME Innovation Stimulation Top Sectors South Holland, Aalberts NV in Utrecht, Rabobank Nederland, ASM International in Almere, NSR (Nomination, Selection and Remuneration) Committee, CM.com and CM Payments in Breda, and G4S Nederland. Van Pernis has been decorated as an Officer of the Dutch Order of Orange-Nassau and was awarded the Bundesverdienstkreuz Erster Klasse der Bundesrepubliek Deutschland.

Interview with Mr Martin van Pernis

Mr Van Pernis, first we would like to thank you for your willingness to have this interview with us. We are extremely grateful. You spent the greater part of your career working at Siemens the Netherlands. Immediately after your technical study in 1971 you began work at Siemens and held many different roles there. In 1987, you were appointed to the board and later in 1996 you became a member of the board of directors and president of the Siemens Group, a company with some 3,300 employees, a job that you held until you retired on 1 January 2010. At what moment in your career did you realise that international protocol plays an important role in a multinational corporation like Siemens?

Actually, quite quickly. I began in Munich and immediately came into contact with the sales division. I had to submit a proposal, and as enthusiastic as I was, I signed it personally. That was wrong – as I discovered almost immediately through various channels in the organisation – I was not to put my own signature on things. It then became clear to me that there were business protocols in place that I had to bear in mind. But most important was that I immediately came into contact with the outside world. Approximately 80 percent of what Siemens produces and supplies goes to government bodies and ministries, such as defence, as well as to public companies, such as telecoms and energy companies. It was always in the government sphere that you had to be careful. To whom are you speaking? Who are you talking about, and who is it you are talking to, and how should you address that person? I soon arrived at NATO in Brussels for an international tender and met all the delegates. I learned a lot about protocol there, including its negative aspects. But if your business depends on it, you soon learn the rules. I should however also mention that the Germans are quite a bit more formal than the Dutch, and in that sense they have much better manners in the hierarchical model – sometimes taken to the extreme. I will also never forget that when I was in Austria I noticed that it was even more pronounced there. Even when I met Austrians later as board chairman, they always addressed me extremely formally, calling me 'Herr General Direktor.' I always had to say 'Just call me Martin.'

While we are on the subject of the more formal manners in Germany than in the Netherlands, in the context of a German company like Siemens, is it then also so that conduct in the Dutch company is based on the German standard, or is the Dutch culture more reflected in the company here?

I think I can say the following about that: in Germany, the company has to deal with all the aspects of a company, from sales to research and development. If you work in a national organisation, you're much closer to the market and much closer to the client, and the world outside the company is what's most important for you. Certainly, as director and chairman, I always had to take great care. I realised only too well that if someone makes a mistake, people will remember that even ten years later – especially when it comes to dealing with people. If something goes well, it is soon forgotten, but missteps and mistakes always follow you. In that sense, I've introduced a number of practical things. I'll give you a couple of examples. Under no circumstances would we allow invitations to be sent out with a printed signature, something that was customary in the past and which didn't change for us with automation. I always wanted to sign invitations personally, not only for the benefit of the client, but also because then I had an opportunity to check the invitation itself – are the titles correct, is it correctly addressed, does it make sense, are there any spelling mistakes? The same applies when receiving important guests. You can't leave that to your secretaries. When you invite someone, then you should be at the door on time to greet your guest yourself. This sometimes requires good coordination between your secretary and your driver to get it all organised. Similarly, if I was invited somewhere, I would always take a critical look at the invitation and the respect that was shown. My wife was even more critical than me about that. Personally, sometimes I thought it would do, but she had her own opinion about it. One way or another, she always had clear insight into these sorts of situations. I always tried to train my staff well in this, both by giving personal instruction and having them take courses. Ultimately, it all comes down to how you approach the outside world, and deal with your customers. Managing your address book and list of contacts is also extremely important. There are companies where, when someone retires, that person is immediately removed from the database, without considering whether or not that same person might soon be back as a supervisory director of a company, chairman of a supervisory board, or a mediator. It may seem like something small, but it is a huge mistake to take that person out of your address book right away. It is one of those simple things, which can enable a company to stand out. I've always been very irritated by the number of spelling and grammar mistakes that people make and the wrong forms of address, how often people are incorrectly seated in seating arrangements. One person might be very upset, while another might not be much bothered, but either way, it still makes a bad impression. You can do simple things like keeping a place free in the front row if someone is delayed – you have to understand that the person concerned is not deliberately absent. They may still arrive, and in the meantime you can place one of your own staff in the seat. Nothing is more disconcerting for an important guest than to be told that their place has been given to someone else and they must sit in the third row. For this reason, Siemens developed a system for placing important guests at client dinners.

During the course of your working life did you find protocol to be an important instrument for customer relations? If so, can you give us some examples?

Yes, definitely! I think I can say that during my time at Siemens we built up a broad network, although building a network is very different from maintaining one. That can only happen if you show respect for one another and are interested in other people. When receiving a large party, there are always people who remain somewhat aloof, they stand alone, often because they're new. You need to give them extra attention. I always said to my own people: 'Keep your eyes open and pay attention to our guests; don't stand around talking to each other. Think of our guests, we invited them, they are our clients.' Regardless of whether you are a director or a colleague, pay attention to our guests! These are all just practical things, but the same applies in the exchange of letters or communication by email. A different approach is often taken with email, but it's nonsense. An email should be written with as much care as a letter, and should also show respect. I would never want to send an invitation by email. You can make an announcement by email, but not send the invitation itself. That shows a lack of respect and I always maintained that right up until my retirement. In my present role as supervisory director I have tried to maintain that too, although I realise that my role now is different than when I was a director. However, I continue to believe that an invitation should be sent on paper and give every appearance of having been prepared with care and attention to detail.

So you say that everyone in your organisation from high to low who is concerned with external affairs should give greater priority to correct customer relations and tolerate no mistakes.

Indeed, it should never be the case that you invite people who have died, moved, or changed jobs. Maintaining an up-to-date database is a 'hell of a job' but vital for your customer relations. Even when we were sending out around 700 invitations, I went through the stack personally and where I had my doubts, I had it checked again. I cannot say that it never went wrong, but I always did my best to avoid mistakes.

Were you also involved with ceremonial events like a product launch during your time as chairman of the board? And what role does the chairman play in that?

In various ways. I took part in the 125th anniversary jubilee celebration of Siemens Nederland and the 150th anniversary of Siemens Germany. These are, of course, important events attended by many dignitaries from other business sectors in Germany and high-ranking government representatives. I have also led several trade missions to the Middle East and Northwest Europe, which I was also responsible for in my last five years. The role of chairman of the board at these sorts of celebrations or events is crucial, because you represent the company, and you want no protocol mistakes to be made. On my trips to Northwest Europe, of course, protocol was often an important part of it and I also observed that things often turn out differently from what you had expected and that it is not the same everywhere in the world. It's not the same in Western Europe and Asia, for example. I can still clearly remember when I visited China with a Dutch minister of Transport and Water Management. Upon arrival at the airport in Beijing, where I disembarked with the CEO of Philips and other colleagues, along with the minister, we were immediately separated from the minister and her public officials because we were private sector. They were led through a special corridor to the exit, while we had to follow the same route as all the normal passengers. After this, all the government representatives were transported in stately cars, while we had to follow them in a bus. This was fine until the bus could not drive under a viaduct, and we spent half an hour wandering about in Beijing before we could reach our hotel. The minister then urgently requested that this arrangement be changed, in the sense that she would prefer it if the government officials rode in the bus, and the business representatives in the comfortable cars, but to no avail! This is where you see how differently one can think about protocol. But I also remember a visit with another minister to Shanghai where they proudly showed us how they had brought the traffic to a halt to allow our motorcade to pass smoothly through the city. They were very proud of this despite the traffic chaos they had created as a result.

Mr Van Pernis, Siemens is known for its very well-organised client dinners. I understand that you initiated this. We can assume that you therefore had the necessary expertise in-house. How important was it for you to have a good head of protocol in your organisation?

Yes, I should mention that I did not initiate this, rather it was one of my distant predecessors who began the tradition. He considered it important to receive his most important clients in his own home. But at that time we had only about thirty customers. With each successor these events became larger. In my time, the number had risen to around 400 guests. It was difficult to arrange something of this nature in our own company restaurant, but we managed it in the end. It was important, for my own people as well. Such an evening begins with a reception, which provides an ideal opportunity to talk to your clients, especially for directors. All of them enjoyed this. It was an enormous undertaking, as was the security, and with my people in the kitchen. I know that we couldn't have managed a task like this alone, so we always brought expertise in from outside. They helped with receiving guests, with serving, and most particularly, with the logistics surrounding the preparations for an evening such as this. Because they had to make sure that everyone seated at the round tables was served more or less at the same time. For these logistical reasons, I often hired my own top chefs to make sure that everything ran smoothly. I had the incredible good luck to have a head of communications who had a clear sense of protocol, and who could also give a good presentation on such an evening to ensure that everything went without a hitch. He led his team with enthusiasm to make sure that everything was perfect. As you probably know, we used a computer programme to make the seating plan, but there were also some charming hostesses at the door to inform the guests where they were to sit. Everyone was given a table number and a place setting card with their name on it, based on what the computer had printed out. To start with, the guests did not understand this but in the end it led to surprising and interesting seating arrangements, as there were never two doctors or two people from the energy sector at any one table, for example. That took a little while to get used to because people from the same discipline have a tendency to seek one another out and stand together, and because they already know one another they want to sit together. However, our system made sure that we had well-mixed tables, and in the end, the guests were also very excited by this arrangement. Very different kinds of conversations took place, and the guests met new and interesting people. There are always people who complain of course, either that they didn't like where they were sitting, or

> they thought they were placed too far back. I had to make sure that my most important guests, such as a government minister, a king's commissioner, a mayor, a speaker or a guest of honour were seated with me on the head table, and my table was never bigger than the other tables. If I had too many head table guests, I would have to spread them among my chairman of the supervisory board or chief financial officer. My successor does it differently, and now has a bigger table placed in the middle. Everyone has their own criteria, of course, but the aim is always to focus on the guests.

It is only natural that the seating plan for the head tables should be done carefully and in accordance with protocol. Did you attend to the seating arrangements yourself? If so, what general principles did you apply to that?

> In response I can say that the head table should, of course, always be set up perfectly, nothing less will do. You really need to attend to your most important guests, they simply cannot be seated by the computer. The head table was always pre-arranged and, in my time, so were the tables of the chairman of the supervisory board and the CFO. Although the aim was to make everyone comfortable and have the arrangement be functional, protocol always came first, especially if you had presidents of parliament, ministers and other government officials at the table. In this case, protocol always prevailed. At least one of my directors or deputy directors would act as co-host at every other table. They could submit two preferences for their tables, but did not have to – it was up to them. Some did and some didn't. In any event, it could not be more than two people from their own area of work. The system that we developed automatically placed these people at these tables and they could choose their own seat at the table. My own people were always very enthusiastic about this, particularly about the diversity of the people seated round the tables.

It was striking that you, as president of the board of directors, always greeted your guests in person and introduced yourself to them, even though you were hosting an event with more than 400 guests. That must require some preparation – can you say anything about that?

> Indeed, I greeted everyone on arrival. That meant that the flow of guests had to progress smoothly, and you have a steering role in that yourself. You know that your own people are standing by to make sure that the guests don't spend too long in conversation and can direct them on to the reception area.

Welcoming guests by name requires some preparation, while on the other hand, you should never invite people you do not know. This is taken care of in the process leading up to it beforehand. Actually I knew everyone well, but there were, of course, newcomers who had just taken on a certain position to whom I had to give extra attention. I learned about their background and briefly looked at their photo. I did that also for our Christmas Concert in the Nieuwe Kerk in The Hague, where my wife and I received the guests together with my CFO and his wife.

That was about your time at Siemens, but you still have been very active since your departure. You made yourself available for a great number of public functions and supervisory directorships at a number of companies. To start with the most recent one, it is interesting to note that you are chairman of the supervisory board of the Dutch company *Protocolbureau*, and the Institute of Protocol The Hague. What led you to do this? Was this based on your experience and particular interest in protocol?

I would first like to mention that I had already started to get involved in these kinds of activities while I was still at Siemens. I did that very deliberately, because there is more to life than just technology, and I felt that I wanted to do more in civic roles. So, while I was at Siemens I became a supervisory director for Feyenoord Football Club, as well as a supervisory director of the Institute of Protocol The Hague.
Why the Protocolbureau and the Protocol Institute? It was more because of my frustration in cases where it is not done properly. I had often seen the students of the Protocolbureau in action in The Hague – ushers, as they're known – and I was always pleased to see them at an event giving the guests care and attention. I knew then that everything would run smoothly, and I could also say to my wife 'look how well it is being run.' You can definitely tell the difference when they are not at an event. You are left by yourself, for example, you are not led to your table, and you have to look yourself up on a list to see where you are seated; that's not what you are there for. That was why the Protocolbureau appealed to me. I like it when people are cared for. It makes good business sense too – if you want to do business, you need to treat your customers as you would like to be treated yourself, and that's with respect. These ushers have a good sense of how to deal with certain situations and understand protocol, and for those reasons the Protocolbureau particularly interested me. When I became chairman of the supervisory board at the Protocolbureau, I always said that the different disciplines were well represented on the board. It

includes people from across the entire spectrum who can help set up and guide such matters. We had someone there from defence, Gilbert was there, we had someone from education, someone from the entertainment industry, someone financial, which is always important. As a supervisory board, you are also responsible for the running of the company. I found it important that every aspect of protocol should be included.

Did you also see protocol playing a part in other businesses where you served as member of a supervisory board?

Yes, I see it with many businesses, although in some it is entirely lacking. It has to do with the nature of the company, of course. I'm also chairman of the Rotterdam Philharmonic Orchestra, and a lot of thought goes into the way that clients should be approached and treated. There is always room for improvement in such matters. I was recently at a performance of the orchestra as part of a big production at a large external venue, when regrettably I noticed that the coffee stands were already closing while the intermission was not yet over. This simply cannot be; the hospitality then falls short.

Do I understand you correctly that you think protocol has just as important a role at cultural events as it does in the business world?

Absolutely! It can often be done much better. People do not sufficiently understand the importance of protocol. The customer has paid for a ticket, and apart from the concert, expects to be treated with care and concern. The management is too often more interested in creating a good music programme, and too little concerned with what goes on around it. Consideration and respect are what it's all about when it comes to dealing with people.

It's often said that protocol is something for the public sector and less so for the private sector. Do you share that opinion? And do you think that a book on international protocol could also play an important supporting role in the business world?

Geographically, the Netherlands is a small country, which means that other countries are not very far away. You need to learn about the cultural differences, which there certainly are, even with neighbouring countries. You approach a German in a completely different way than you do a Dutchman, the same goes for a Belgian or a Briton. It doesn't really matter whether that is an official contact or a private one. But if you do this, you need to know what you are doing and what's expected of you, and what the culture is. It is important that you follow the rules that everyone observes. It's quite simple really. The same goes for attire. Make sure you know what's expected of you. It's as wrong to appear in a dinner jacket as it is to show up in jeans, if that's not the prescribed dress code. It's also important to know someone's name, certainly if you've met them before. Nothing is less respectful than having to introduce yourself to someone again or ask for their business card. At big events I always look through the guest list to see if there's anyone I know and their name. You look really foolish if you call someone Peter when his name is Robert. These are all simple but very important things. I very much believe that such a book could be extremely useful in the private sector. Business people travel a lot and also have to deal with cultural differences and the prevailing protocol, where the ultimate goal is to create an environment in which you can do business together.

A book like this is then also extremely important for the business world in the sense that anyone who comes into contact with the outside world needs to know the rules, and this can help enormously, especially today. In the past, you often learned about all of this at home, as part of your upbringing, but times have changed and the world is more complex now. We become independent at a younger age and have much more responsibility. So we need to make sure that the younger generation is trained and learns what to do. This book would definitely help to do that.

Mr Van Pernis, we would like to thank you once more for your excellent contribution to the book with this interview, and your forthright answers to our questions.

Dancers of New Zealand dance company Black Grace

Mr Samuel Wuersten, Artistic Director Holland Dance, former Member of the Executive Board of Codarts Rotterdam

Samuel Wuersten's life in dance is multifaceted. He enjoyed a diversified career as a contemporary repertory dancer, created self-produced as well as commissioned work as a choreographer, and is a sought-after teacher of contemporary dance around the world. He is the artistic and general director of the renowned Holland Dance Festival, former executive co-director of Codarts Arts University Rotterdam, as well as the artistic director of the Bachelor Dance programme at Zurich Arts University in Switzerland. He regularly serves as a jury member and consultant to various dance and arts organisations. For over a decade, he was the artistic co-director of the Steps International Dance Festival in Switzerland as well as a member of the artistic committee of the Prix de Lausanne. Since 2013, Samuel Wuersten has curated the international CONTEXT festival for Russian ballerina Diana Vishneva.

Samuel Wuersten was born and raised in Gstaad, Switzerland. He had his formal dance training at the Hamburg Ballet School and at Codarts Arts University Rotterdam (formerly Rotterdam Dance Academy). He is currently based in the Netherlands. In 2011 he was honoured with a knighthood in the Dutch order of Orange-Nassau. In the same year he was admitted to the French Order of Arts and Letters and given the title *Chevalier dans l'ordre des Arts et des Lettres*.

Protocol and Dance by Mr Samuel Wuersten

As in every other professional field, there is also a form of protocol applied and followed in dance. Possibly the best known aspect of dance protocol may be the etiquette of applauding and bowing in a live performance. There is more to it than meets the eye when it comes to the way one applauds, how applause is received and acknowledged. As an audience we have several choices of how we applaud. We can reveal and share our enthusiasm and appreciation by politely clapping our hands or raise the level of intensity to clapping frenetically and loudly. We can even go as far as standing up to clap our hands accompanied by screams and shouts of admiration and joy. If displeased with the performance, we can sit in stony silence or even shout 'boos' to give voice to our discontent. Throwing the infamous tomatoes or rotten eggs has luckily gone out of fashion. It has become myth instead of custom.

On the receiving end, dancers are expected to acknowledge the applause with elegance and grace. Experienced performers develop their bows to perfection in a clever mix of self-confidence and pride, throwing in a disarming dash of humility and surprise. Watching a dancer take a good bow is a true delight for the audience. Sometimes it is almost as exciting as the actual performance, or at least very much the cherry on top of the cake. As a presenter and organiser of various dance events such as festivals, galas, and benefit performances, I became acquainted with protocol on various occasions. I found it fascinating to learn about the ins and outs of protocol when confronted with official visits of invited guests who attended one of our events in their formal function. Who sits where and next to whom? Protocol provides very clear guidelines for this. However, there is also the strategic point of view when hosting official guests. Events of this nature, where a dance performance forms the framework, is also a golden opportunity to create encounters between people that might not be possible otherwise. We have very diligently used the planning of such evenings with two and three acts and their necessary intervals to create a variety of arranged meetings. For example, we would seat one guest next to an official guest during one act of the programme and another guest during the second act of the programme. While preparing and exploring these options and possibilities, I found it very helpful to be able to refer to protocol for guidance. I would be dishonest if I claimed I understood all of it and that everything made sense. But over the years I have become more familiar with the way protocol works in our context. Once I got the hang of it, I found myself back on familiar territory. It became evident to me that the way an evening with official guests at the opening of the Holland Dance Festival works has a strong resemblance to choreography. The entire evening is mapped out beforehand. From the moment of the arrival of the official guests until their departure, everything is thought through and planned. At first I found it almost suffocating. I felt that the preparations created tension and fear of doing the 'wrong' thing. But to my surprise, quite the opposite happened. Depending on the official guests and their ability to handle their visit, I experienced that the detailed preparation in fact created a lot of space for spontaneous interaction. I found that the preparation according to the rules of protocol allowed the official guests to feel at ease and to open up to their surroundings. As a result, everyone involved in such an official moment was able to relax into the situation.

I am by no means deeply knowledgeable about protocol, but I detect elements of protocol in so many daily actions we all take. It all comes down to courtesy and respect for the people around us. The good news is that we do not have to be kings and queens to observe those rules to enjoy the benefits of protocol on a daily basis.

You never walk alone
A tribute to Captain Sir Thomas Moore (30 April 1920 – 2 February 2021)

Captain Sir Thomas Moore was a British war veteran known for his achievement raising money for National Health Service charities in the run-up to his 100th birthday during the COVID-19 pandemic. On 6 April 2020, at the age of 99, he began to walk laps of his garden with the goal of raising £1,000 by his birthday 24 days later. In the course of his fundraising, the media's growing interest made him popular throughout the United Kingdom. On his birthday, the total raised by his walk passed £32 million from more than 1.5 million supporters. In a statement, Prime Minister Boris Johnson said the centenarian's 'fantastic fundraising broke records' and provided the country with 'a beacon of light through the fog of coronavirus'. His birthday was further marked in a number of ways, including a flypast by the Royal Air Force. He received over 140,000 cards and was given the honorary title of colonel.[18] On 17 July 2020, after a nomination from the prime minister, he was invested by Queen Elizabeth II as a Knight Bachelor at Windsor Castle in the open air, socially distanced, with a very limited number of guests, while keeping the most important element of the long-lasting tradition of the investiture ceremony in place—the accolade. On 2 February 2021, Captain Tom passed away due to complications related to the coronavirus. His death was marked all over the country as football players, the prime minister, and countless others stood in a minute of silence to pay tribute to him.

https://www.bbc.com/news/uk-england-beds-bucks-herts-52732300

10. Protocol and stakeholder engagement during and after the COVID-19 pandemic

Introduction

Face-to-face multilateral meetings, overseas business trips, state visits, public events, and ceremonial occasions: on a global scale they have all been heavily affected by the circumstances related to the COVID-19 pandemic. International protocol and strategic networking had to adapt to a 'new normal' throughout 2020. But that has not been a novelty. Developments in protocol have taken place over the centuries, as is described in chapter 1. And creativity, technology, political reality, and common sense have all contributed to keeping protocol relevant in modern days.

While citizens around the world were urged to avoid 'the three Cs' (crowded places, close-contact settings, and confined and enclosed spaces), diplomats and global business leaders—accustomed to flying from one international hub to the next—found themselves stuck at home negotiating via videoconferences. The United Nations, the G20, the European Union, and the World Economic Forum, among many others, have all been meeting online or in hybrid settings. The Davos Agenda in January 2021 was themed 'the Great Reset'. And indeed, the pandemic has reminded us just how fragile and complex humankind is and that, despite all our technological progress, humanity remains vulnerable to catastrophes that shake the world. However, as in every dramatic event of our history, many people have proved that these unfortunate occasions are also a rich breeding ground to reveal their resilience, innovation, and retrofitting skills. And as Toby Ord, senior research fellow at the Future of Humanity Institute at Oxford University, put it in *The Economist* on 13 November 2020:

> *2021 will be our best chance to do so, when we have recovered just enough to be able to raise our eyes to the future, but while the shock of the past still stings.*

COVID-19 will mark our generation forever, and we will only defeat it if we learn some valuable lessons from these challenging times. This renaissance creates numerous opportunities but also requires continuous creativity, adaptability, and flexibility, since the unpredictability of various mutations remains and the next pandemic might be around the corner. At the same time, the situation in numerous countries is almost back to pre-COVID times, although the economic consequences remain catastrophic and mental health along with other issues have deteriorated on an unprecedented scale. The hardest thing for many people is to keep up their spirits during this pandemic, since it has an emotional impact on almost all of us.

Protocol and stakeholder engagement will inevitably be affected even once we are all vaccinated. Social distancing remains important, as do frequent handwashing and wearing facial masks. And we have all learned a lot about virtual event productions and have experienced their advantages, such as reduced costs, a larger reach of audiences, and more environmentally friendly ways of doing business. These new technological behaviours adopted during the pandemic will most certainly outlast it.

'Please mute your microphone!'

In addition to the endless possibilities with virtual meetings and events, there will be an increasing demand for exclusive, intimate gatherings to provide the highest level of personal attention to one's most valuable stakeholders. A lot of small-scale is the new large-scale!

To be able to explore the best ways to pivot during this unprecedented period, international cooperation and the sharing of experiences are more essential than ever. Whatever our language or culture, this pandemic has helped remind us that what we have in common far outweighs our differences and that we truly live in a 'small world'. This pandemic has opened our eyes to the fact that 'we are all in this together'. But due to the fact that restrictive measures have varied tremendously in time and in place, a 'one-size-fits-all' approach has not been possible. For example, the presentation of credentials of new ambassadors to receiving heads of state differed from one country to another in 2020. In some cases, facial masks were worn; in other situations, a high table was placed in between the officials to avoid physically handing over the document; and in other countries, these ceremonies took place virtually. The inauguration of President Joe Biden at Capitol Hill in Washington, D.C. had only a select number of dignitaries and personal friends present, while nearly 200,000 flags on the National Mall represented those who could not attend. And three weeks later on the other side of the world, 30,000 spectators per day were initially allowed at the Australian Open in Melbourne, until a five-day lockdown was in place halfway the tournament after which an audience of around 7,500 was able to be present again at the (semi-)finals. In the near future, the opening and closing ceremonies of the postponed Tokyo Olympic Games are expected to be carried out with a 'simpler, more restrained approach', as announced by the Organising Committee at the end of December 2020. The ceremonies will be designed to 'reflect the overall simplification of the Games'. The committee hopes that the iconic opening and closing include 'symbols of the unity and symbiosis of humankind in its overcoming of the COVID-19 pandemic'.[19]

The first year of this pandemic showed that what worked in for example Estonia may not be perfect for the United Arab Emirates but might inspire a local solution. It also taught us that the strategies implemented in Canada may not work in India but might spark a light that illuminates the way. For that reason, in this chapter more than 30 professionals from around the world will share their best practices and struggles related to the past year. They have been asked to fill out the questionnaire reproduced on the following page, and their respective contributions are placed in alphabetical order by country. The chapter concludes with an overall **Top 40** lessons learned, along with predictions and recommendations for the (near) future. Get inspired!

---

19   https://edition.cnn.com/2020/12/23/sport/tokyo-olympic-games-opening-closing-ceremonies-spt-intl/index.html

To what extent did the restrictive measures due to the COVID-19 pandemic affect your work related to protocol, high-level event management, and/or stakeholder engagement?

 Please provide your most creative or successful example of how you were still able to organise (or attend) an event, ceremony, or international business trip?

 Please provide your most creative or successful example of how you organised (or attended) an online or hybrid event?

 What necessary one-off adjustments that you (or your team) were forced to make could actually remain in the future, even after COVID-19?

 Please provide any additional relevant information if you wish to do so.

Contributions from around the world

Francisco Caligiuri, Cristian Baquero, Diego Monasterio, and Lisandro Montero, Organising Committee, World Forum on Protocol, Communication and Image 2020, *Buenos Aires & Córdoba, Argentina*

The measures imposed in Argentina prevented us from organising events with the physical presence of participants. Consequently, all scheduled programmes were postponed. Due to this, communication was focused through different digital platforms, maintaining the usual channels and incorporating interaction alternatives that would facilitate closeness with the public. This is how our team concentrated its efforts on organising large-scale training events related to 'A New World: A New Protocol' that allowed the interaction of participants from all continents.

Our team devised, organised, and coordinated two online events in the second half of 2020: 'World Forum on Protocol, Communication and Image' and 'Post World Forum on Protocol, Communication and Image'. In addition, we did the same with a hybrid event known under the name 'International Seminar on Protocol, Communication and Image'. The three mentioned events had 120 speakers from 52 countries on five continents and accommodated more than 8,000 participants. There were over 70 hours of training that were offered in two virtual conference rooms simultaneously, and we offered simultaneous translation into Spanish, Portuguese, and English. At the end of the conferences, an informal interaction took place in which participants and speakers were encouraged to convene in a digital networking space in order to foster professional relationships and contacts.

We think it would be very valuable to keep the hybrid event format in order to facilitate immediate interaction as well as to achieve greater numbers of attendance by the public through online participation. From our estimates, different alternatives emerge that could turn event proposals into very attractive options for the participants who choose to be present but also for the host cities of the proposed events.

The spin-off of our virtual events was the establishment of the World Protocol Organization, which aims to become a space for everyone interested in the field of protocol, communication, and image—not based on the fact that we are all the same but rather on the fact that we are all different.

Stephen Brady AO CVO, former Ambassador to France, the Netherlands, and Sweden as well as former Chief of Staff to the Governor-General of Australia, *Sydney, Australia*

COVID-19 prevented me from delivering public speeches and attending any in-person board meetings or official gatherings. Instead, these were moved to Zoom or Microsoft Team meetings. My work year was seriously impacted, but technology allowed work to continue to a large extent.

Each year, Advance Australia (which is directed to the promotion of Australia's diaspora of 1 million people) organises a glittering black tie dinner in Sydney with notable Australians singled out for their achievements. In 2020, the award ceremony was conducted virtually across multiple time zones and was judged to be a success.

As international travel will continue to be curtailed in 2021 and many reluctant to place themselves in large gatherings, I believe there will be a need for organisers to be pro-active in assuring invitees to an event that all reasonable precautions (even if not legally mandated) have been taken. For that reason, more effort and consideration needs to go into event planning and management to ensure the safety of all guests and staff present. Temperature checking at events, the compulsory provision and registration by attendees of contact details before events, limits on numbers and enforced social distancing (by seating guests), no sharing of lecterns or handling of microphones, strict monitoring of numbers in elevators, staff wearing masks and sending out details of health measures to all attendees with invitations will need to continue until the pandemic is over. Ventilation is also going to be a big issue for indoor events. For the foreseeable future, it would be irresponsible to proceed with crowded sit down or stand up affairs. Buffet style food service is not feasible and waiting staff should wear masks (as was the case in Australia in 2020). I attended an event hosted by the Embassy of Sweden at the Australian National Maritime Museum in Sydney where guest numbers were restricted; guests were seated at tables and socially distanced; canapes were served on individual plates and drinks also served individually to guests. Receiving lines are unlikely to be wanted until we are in a post-COVID environment.

Patricia Butera, Director, 60ZONE Pty Ltd, *Sydney, Australia*

As a trainer and consultant in leveraging cultural intelligence for global strategic engagement, I found the pandemic had an immediate impact on the programmes I was able to facilitate in person. Scheduling in-person client meetings was no longer a question of 'when' they could take place but 'if' they should or could take place at all. There was a sharp shift in focus on their staff's health and well-being rather than training and development needs. Stakeholder engagement took on a different focus—the need to engage to ensure everyone's safety rather than to nurture interest.

As a cross-cultural specialist, I couldn't help but look at these changes through the lens of culture. I posted a piece on LinkedIn a month into the escalating seriousness of the pandemic titled *'Is the Australian attitude "She'll be right" being tested?'*. The term, 'she'll be right' refers to the Australian laid back but positive attitude towards any problem. It means that no matter what goes wrong, it will right itself again; whatever goal or objective you're striving towards will be achieved. But, a few months down the track, I do believe that the premise of 'she'll be right' has been duly challenged and continues to be so.

A regular user of the Zoom platform well before COVID, my pivot was not so much to do with the use of the technology. Instead, it was to calibrate the juxtaposition presented by the overload of virtual engagement with the growing feeling of being disconnected at the human level. The adjustments required a redesign of strategic engagement which, pre-COVID, may have only been looked at through the prism of a guest list, seating chart, or order of events.

This redesign revealed other cultural differences to manage. Of note, the disparate pandemic experience at the local level impacted engagement in the new virtual dynamic. Participants were often unaware of the COVID reality on the other side of the screen. Each person's local experience coloured the lens through which they perceived, experienced and contributed within the virtual training context. It became a noticeable barrier and one that has forced a reframing of the rules of engagement in these virtual settings. Offline, increasing the touchpoints, check-ins, and even adapting the language that forms part of the virtual engagement vernacular has been an important consideration.

Above all, cultural sensitivity has played a critical role in stakeholder engagement. In a post-pandemic world, I believe it will be even more relevant.

Pedro Amorim, CEO & Founder, "Gestão Diamante Consulting" for Strategic Protocol, *Rio de Janeiro, Brazil*

A national survey conducted by the SEBRAE, the Brazilian Service of Support for Micro and Small Enterprises, detected that 98% of the events sector in Brazil was directly affected by the pandemic in April 2020, one month after the quarantine started in our country. All events had to be postponed or cancelled, and the government passed a law on how professionals should proceed at that time. The law gave guidance on the rescheduling of services, reservations, and postponed events as well as the provision of discounts or credit for use in the purchase of other services and events available. Protocol offices in the public sector were also affected, as face-to-face events had to be cancelled and new technologies had to be studied and used as alternative options.

Brazilian professionals have had to rely on their creativity throughout the pandemic. The good news was that even the high-level executives were enthusiastic about the innovation in events and protocol. I think the most successful examples of creativity were the use of technology to compose backgrounds, digital frames, auditoriums, and tables of honour during virtual events. Resources like animated entrances, virtual flags, websites developed for registering attendance, and the audience attending with their personal web cameras helped to make the virtual events more interesting, dynamic, and personal. Perhaps the most famous and most creative events in Brazil were the drive-in weddings, where the guests arrived in a big parking space inside their cars and watched their friends getting married on a big stage like a rock concert in a new old-style way.

I organised several webinars using videoconference platforms. The most creative moment for me was when I created a virtual avatar of myself that was able to dance and perform a song in a virtual classroom during one of my webinars (something I would never do live in a face-to-face event). The avatar was named AmorimX, and his dance and participation has been a great success with the audience.

The sanitary measures are very severe, but I think most of these health-related measures will remain for the future, as it is becoming a part of a cultural behaviour-changing movement. Another important adjustment that will remain is the hybridisation of events. Speakers do not need to travel 10,000 km anymore to attend an event, for example, as the use of videoconferences has been widely tested and approved by audiences, contractors, and sponsors on many occasions, also with a great positive effect on the general budget of the event.

Stewart Wheeler, Chief of Protocol of Canada, Global Affairs Canada, *Ottawa, Canada*

Overnight, official travel by VVIPs was grounded; high level visits were cancelled, ceremonies and events postponed. At the same time there was an increased need for stakeholder engagement and clear, consistent communication with the diplomatic corps in order to continue offering the full range of services, but all in new ways – online, over the telephone and through virtual methods. Initially, I was quite worried about the future of the protocol role, but as the world of diplomacy moved online and found all sorts of new ways to engage, it became clear that the role of protocol expertise and experienced event management was going to be more important than ever.

Not long after we were all working from home, holding virtual town hall meetings and info sessions, video meetings and conference calls, it became clear to me that all the virtual work would not replace one-on-one in-person interaction. Virtual engagement may get part of the job done, but diplomacy and international relations is much more than that. I was reminded that the relationships we build and nurture through our protocol and diplomatic work are personal relationships. In my role as Chief of Protocol, I serve as a de-facto Ambassador to the Ambassadors in Ottawa. So I realized that I needed to do what so many people were doing with their friends and neighbours during COVID: I needed to reach out personally. I needed to make sure that my diplomatic friends were okay, that they had what they needed to persevere. So as the weather started improving in the spring I jumped on my bicycle and started doing house calls. It was my version of bicycle diplomacy. It wasn't about in-depth formal meetings, it was about stopping by and knocking on people's doors to make a human connection and see how they were. And it really took off from there, I have been tweeting about it on social media and other chiefs of protocol have started doing similar things internationally. In times of crisis, we need to be creative to find safe and healthy ways to continue to engage.

Stewart Wheeler on one of his bicycle diplomacy visits

One of the nicest things we do as a foreign ministry is to offer a formal farewell lunch for departing Ambassadors ending long time postings in Canada. With no more in-person events, I felt it was important that we not abandon our traditions of honouring the relationships that had been built and expressing thanks for dedicated collaboration. So we developed a new Virtual Farewell Tea event for departing heads of mission. It includes a separate VIP virtual tête-à-tête with a Deputy Minister, the delivery of chef prepared hospitality and a parting gift to remember their time in Canada – all while providing a group opportunity for cherished colleagues to come together virtually to bid a fond farewell.

Dr Jiali Zhou, Associate Professor, China Foreign Affairs University (CFAU), *Beijing, China*

The biggest impact for us was that foreign scholars could not come to China to provide guest lectures at our university. In a more generic way, greetings between persons changed dramatically from the start of the pandemic. The normal way of greeting in China is handshaking, and obviously that was not encouraged anymore. Around the country, various alternative, nonphysical ways of greeting came back from former days, such as waving, bowing, the fist & palm salute, the hold fist salute, and the *Namasté* gesture.

CFAU held a memorable hybrid graduation ceremony in July 2020. Some students attended the on-spot graduation ceremony, while many others joined the graduation ceremony through a live broadcast. University leaders, the representatives of teachers, some emotional students, overseas students, and proud parents spoke respectively. University leaders awarded the degree certificates and set the academic caps for graduates in order to keep as many of the traditional ceremonial elements in place.

CFAU is organising a virtual lecture series about international protocol. Five senior experts have been invited to deliver online classes to a couple of hundred students of our university between November 2020 and May 2021. Even though the foreign speaker and the students cannot see each other face to face, this format greatly increases the students' skills as well as mutual understanding. One of the experts, for example, talked about face masks as part of a dress code or to boost bilateral ties. When placing two country flags on them during a bilateral visit—or the logo of a conference, a presidency of a multilateral organisation, or a presidential / royal seal—it can have an added impact on the conveyed message or image of the person / visit / event involved. Personally, I would consider it appropriate to indicate wearing face masks on an invitation card under 'dress code' if needed under the health circumstances at the time. Wearing face masks at outdoor events should be encouraged much more as well.

As part of dining etiquette, additional public chopsticks and spoons for taking food from joint platters and bowls in restaurants and during official meals should be used, instead of your own chopsticks to pick food from these shared dishes. While eating, one can use their own chopsticks and spoon. This approach is more hygienic and in my opinion should remain in the future.

Anu Mõtsla, Chief of Protocol, Riigikogu (Parliament of Estonia), *Tallinn, Estonia*

At the beginning of the pandemic, the influence of the restrictive measures was very strong. One day we were planning big events and visits, and the next day everything was gone. We tried to switch over to virtual events/meetings as fast as possible, but it took time as the world was under shock and the situation unknown. We were very grateful to the parliament's ICT department, which quickly organised several seminars on how to manage and secure the 'meeting systems'. For live events, which were very small and mostly took place in the open air in the summer, we followed the restrictions as foreseen by our Health Board. The second important thing was to 'stay in the picture' by letting our stakeholders know that we still exist even when working from home and asking how they are doing health- and business-wise.

We organised two official visits in October 2020, which were quite challenging concerning the restrictions. At first, we had to follow the new rules of procedure regarding entry into the country. As the rules were new to the authorities as well, the applications took more time. The delegation members and meeting participants were obliged to wear masks for the whole time. We provided delegations with hygiene kits (including the medical masks and disinfection gel) and briefed the drivers, personal protection officers, and hotel and restaurant staff on the conditions that needed to be applied when welcoming the delegation (wearing masks and gloves, contactless check-in/checkout, minimising contacts, doing safe-as-possible setups, etc.). During the meals, for example, we used the zigzag seating, which meant that no one was sitting opposite to another person, only diagonally. The diameter of the table was around two meters. We also used the 'speed-dating' dinner format: we split the delegation into groups of four, all with the same professional background, and each table had one guest of honour from Estonia. The delegation was pleased that they could hold the discussions in smaller groups and get answers to their burning questions.

As Estonia was chairing the Baltic Assembly in 2020, we had to organise the annual session of the Assembly (around 100 participants) in the beginning of November. Until the end of August, we had hopes that it could be a live event in a smaller format; however, the board of the Baltic Assembly decided it would be a virtual event on the KUDO multilingual web conferencing platform, with all the delegations going on air or live from their home country. Due to proper planning and rehearsing with the support of some external logistical and technical expertise, it was a success after all!

Thomas Vitart, Protocol & Visits Manager, Australian Embassy, *Paris, France*

It has had a very big impact on our direct diplomacy and visit activities. Given that we have had to limit movements and group gatherings, all large events have been either cancelled/postponed or done on digital platforms.

We had a senior visitor for about a week, which required us to assess the risk factors ahead of the visit and then to organise carefully with respect to anti-COVID measures. For example, we limited the number of people travelling in vehicles and the number of people attending face to face meetings, and we respected social distancing. We also checked measures in place at the hotel. The visitor and his party were tested prior to the visit and before their departure.

 In April last year at our Anzac Day commemoration ceremonies in the Somme, attendance was limited to the Ambassador and the Defence Attaché, with limited local authorities. The main elements of the ceremonies remained the same, but it was reduced to the essentials, and all the events organised around the ceremonies were cancelled.

To continue engagement between diplomats and embassy staff, we use the Webex online platform to share videos and PowerPoint presentations with an MC and several speakers, generally followed by an open discussion.

An interesting virtual high-level event that some colleagues attended was the Paris Peace Forum 2020 edition in November. Our Ambassador participated in the online debates and the Australian Foreign Minister sent a video contribution.

> *Third Paris Peace Forum, 11-13 November 2020*
> *Over the course of three days, this edition allowed 12,000+ participants from more than 150 countries each day to have a virtual experience on the event's interactive platform, which was broadcast live on Facebook and YouTube. The Forum included prerecorded speeches or the online presence of 50+ heads of state and government, 12 international organisations, over 400 speakers and presentations related to 100 projects. The virtual opening session contained an interview with the Mayor of Paris and on the second day a live session was streamed from the Elysée Palace, with contributions from the French and Senegalese Presidents, the International Monetary Fund Managing Director, and the European Council President. Even though the organising committee had to change the entire format of the Forum, they successfully managed to stick to their original approach and content.*

Afua Obeng, Lead Consultant, Perfect Manners Consultancy, *Accra, Ghana*

My organisation transitioned to online interactions. This opened up an even wider clientele nationwide for us, also in different fields and perhaps outside the mainstream target audiences when one thinks of protocol and stakeholder engagement.

We were invited to deliver a training programme for a premier Market Women Foundation on the topic of 'Business Etiquette for Managing and Sustaining my Business during COVID-19'. I was able to deliver these sessions via Zoom to participants from all over the country. The goal for this

training was to help them understand how to use etiquette and manners for business growth during the pandemic. We discussed the following subjects:
- Importance of etiquette,
- Good and polite attitude,
- Good hygiene/cleanliness (COVID-19 protocols),
- Appropriate grooming,
- Considerations,
- Great customer service: going above and beyond for a customer.

We delivered the modules with visual examples. This allowed individuals working in the informal sector to quickly grab the concepts we wanted to teach. For example, we used photographs to explain basic etiquette, which helped them to understand the importance and role that social manners play in sustaining their businesses during the pandemic. For instance, on the importance of grooming, we showed pictures of an unkempt seller versus a neatly dressed seller. The subject of 'first impressions' and the power of a smile was depicted through images of sellers with different non-verbal characteristics. In addition, one of the key elements was related to the fact that social distancing guidelines must be followed at all times.

Manoj Kumar, Founder & Principal, Cosmentum Advisory Services Pvt Ltd., *Bangalore, India*

Like most places, the news of the pandemic preceded the lockdown in India by four to six weeks. In the beginning, this was a news item during meetings and interactions. Slowly, it gained importance as an item with possible impact on travel to start with, impacting international and then intra-state and finally inter-city travel. All kinds of events, client meetings, and key stakeholder engagements came to a grinding halt as restrictions got stricter. The organisations that had had practice with online meetings were able to quickly switch over to the new scenario with minimal disruption. These were typically organisations and businesses in the IT sector. A large spectrum outside this sector was unfamiliar with online meetings and initially tried to make it up with voice calls. But soon it became clear that the situation was far from being temporary, therefore video conferencing was explored as a trial option. Zoom, Google Meet, and Webex were the most popular platforms used; however, Zoom ran into issues following security breach concerns. Indian platforms like Milan Setu and Jio Meet were launched and have been growing gradually.

One of my clients was in the business of organising and hosting exclusive events to promote its business that required hands-on experience to be provided to its target of niche customers. Several events were planned in different cities across India, and these had to be shelved overnight after the lockdown announcement. The initial month was a period of watching and waiting. But when the extended lockdown became a reality, the management started looking at alternative strategies. The possibility of a 60 to 90-day lockdown followed by travel and event restrictions was seen as a core business problem. The only opportunity it presented was that restrictions would make it easier to get attention and engage participants digitally. Online events were choreographed and practiced before launch, mimicking the content and flow of the physical event with added protocols applicable to the digital medium. This provided a level of continuity to the events planned and helped maintain customer engagement.

After the initial set of events which were heavy on speaking, it was noticed that participants were feeling disinterested and missing the experience aspect of an event attended in person. And since participants were mostly off camera and off audio as well, maintaining constant engagement was key. This led to the creation of a product bouquet that would be provided to participants in a live event to be home delivered. The events were re-choreographed to include ceremonial aspects of a live event, and attendees were encouraged to communicate and interact through texting to create a 'live-like' experience with speakers keeping an eye or regularly skimming the text on their screens, including being prompted by the MC. Additionally, competitions and promotions with giveaways were planned to create 'curiosity', 'information', and 'excitement'. This met with considerable success and generated positive reviews from the participants.

Giovanni Battista Borgiani, National Delegate for Training, Events and International Relations, Associazione Nazionale Cerimonialisti Enti Pubblici (ANCEP), *Genoa, Italy*

For this publication, the Italian Association of Protocol Officers surveyed 60 employees of protocol departments from all over the country regarding the impact of the COVID-19 restrictive measures on the professional organisation of ceremonies and events. Almost half of the respondents work for public entities, while the others are engaged as professionals at companies or as protocol consultants, students, or interested individuals.

On a 10-point Likert rating scale, 40.3% of the respondents were greatly affected (10) by the restrictive measures, 42% were very much affected (values between 8 and 9), while the rest of the respondents stated they were less affected (values between 1 and 6). From the recorded values, it shows that those involved in protocol at public entities have noticed the most major changes; many events had to be canceled or adapted to online mode.

The quantitative reduction in the number of authorities and guests, cleaning and disinfection procedures, as well as social distancing are the most common features specified by all the respondents involved in events and ceremonies. Some compensated with creative and decorative elements (e.g. coloured cubes instead of normal chairs) or sent texts of liturgical celebrations via social networks to avoid physical contact with booklets and paper. Others organised new spaces with tents outside the institutional premises to accommodate a larger audience and changed 'placements': people involved in the ceremony were placed along the central aisles to facilitate access to the stage. For awarding ceremonies or exchange of materials, special tables were used to avoid physical contact. Many events were repeated several times over several days. To reduce the number of people, on many occasions the national anthem was broadcast pre-recorded and not performed in person.

In general, Italy has shown a good level of adaptability of institutional events to new forms of interaction: what was lost in terms of form was achieved through the substance. By expanding the spaces for audiences, facilitating accessibility, bridging physical distances, and readapting events to the virtual environment, we managed to achieve greater involvement of foreign guests/speakers, adjusting the types and styles of intervention employing technology. An example of a successful hybrid event was the Ceremony of the Rosa Camuna 2020 Award in Lombardy, with the authorities in attendance and the winners participating through streaming, each introduced by a video presentation.

Almost all of the respondents pay a lot of attention (values between 8 and 10) to the formal aspects of ceremonies and events they attend, even if they are not directly organised by them (streamed online or reported through images on social networks).

Janine D'Angelo, Head, Ceremonial Protocol, Executive Board Secretariat, UN World Food Programme (WFP), *Rome, Italy*

The COVID-19 pandemic has accelerated changes and innovation worldwide, and WFP was no exception. Against this backdrop, our organisation has been facing multiple challenges that encompass a broad range of elements including access to adequate technology, the re-shaping of communication protocols, and the need to continue our work in virtual negotiation settings. The impossibility to meet face to face given the confinement, social-distancing, and other sanitary measures has demanded an overnight transformation of the traditions of diplomatic business as we know it. Visits and bilateral meetings can only be organised if very rigid COVID protocols are followed and a medical pre-screening questionnaire is submitted by the visiting delegation 24 hours prior to the visit.

Probably one of the biggest ways in which WFP suffered from COVID-related restrictions was linked to WFP being awarded the Nobel Peace Prize 2020. Due to the pandemic and worldwide travel restrictions, WFP did not get the honour to travel to Norway (for now) to attend the traditional Nobel Peace Prize ceremony and gala event. Instead, the Nobel Medal and certificate was received at our Rome headquarters in a 100% virtual ceremony lasting over two hours. It was a very laborious and complex process involving multiple internal stakeholders in WFP working hand-in-hand with the Nobel Bureau's protocol lead and external communications expert. A celebratory ceremony bound to longstanding traditional protocol was successfully orchestrated 100% virtually.

WFP Headquarters, Rome, Italy, 10 December 2020
Mr. David Beasley, Executive Director of the United Nations World Food Programme, received the Nobel Peace Prize awarded to WFP in 2020. Ms. Lisa Pelletti Clark, Co-President, International Peace Bureau Nobel Peace Laureate 1910, delivered the prize on behalf of the Nobel Peace Prize Committee.

One of the first diplomatic duties of incoming Ambassadors is to present credentials to the Head of State of the host government and thereafter to present credentials to other entities, such as UN organisations. The COVID-19 pandemic has required a fast adaptation, hence, those meetings are now being managed virtually, replacing the traditional in-person credential ceremony. In order to replicate similar protocol parameters in the virtual ceremony, we designed a specific run of show that is being managed by a master of ceremonies online, including simultaneous interpretation and an official photo opportunity. The formula was very well received by the diplomatic community, and we are satisfied with this rather unique solution for now. Capitals receive appropriate feedback from their diplomatic representative in real time, allowing for swift social media coverage.

In general, WFP was one of the first UN agencies whose Executive Board adapted to a virtual platform, which greatly facilitated governance processes. WFP has also very quickly adapted to the new digital environment, particularly our Executive Director, and used new virtual platforms to reach wider audiences more efficiently and effectively—and in so doing, we have

Marcel P. van Aelst, Chairman of the Board of Directors, Okura Nikko Hotel Management Co. Ltd Japan, *Amsterdam, the Netherlands*

The mandatory lockdown and the extended closure of restaurant outlets in hotels and the cancellation of conferences, meetings, and incentives had an unheard-of financial effect on the hotel industry. The uncertainty about the duration of the various government-enforced regulations and frequent last-minute changes resulted in a re-thinking of our modus operandi. Priorities shifted.

In order to accommodate a national soccer team playing the Dutch national team, all hotel team members that possibly might have contact with anyone of the national team were tested for COVID on a voluntary basis. Any staff member not tested was not allowed to enter guestroom floors and/or the banquet space of the national team. The Hotel Okura Amsterdam was able to accommodate the group of about 80 persons in this way. In addition, this same hotel built a setup for hybrid meetings where speakers with a maximum of 100 guests can gather in the hotel and the event can be broadcast to more attendees worldwide.

One hotel organised a meeting for a local company during which a maximum of 30 participants were allowed to attend in one meeting room, keeping a distance of 1.5 meters. Other participants attended online. In order not to break with tradition, where possible the hotel delivered some treats during the webinar at the home address or office of those participants.

In a recent PKF survey (Pannell Kerr and Forster), the question was asked: 'What will matter more in the future?' While for decades, hoteliers and asset managers listed 'location' as the most important factor for the success of a hotel, today 'hygiene' was rated as the most important factor, followed by 'past experience'; location only came in third. Next to food safety (HACCP) and the introduction of the European GDPR (General Data Protection Regulation) resulting in the appointment of a Data Protection Officer, the industry now will introduce Hygiene Officers (and in some cases already has). On a corporate level, we have teamed up with experts from the field of medicine and public health. Within weeks after the COVID outbreak, our company introduced a manual that outlined tasks such as more frequent deep cleaning of public areas, providing disinfection wipes, the installation of plexiglass screens between workstations and guest contact areas such as the front desk, using mobile technology for more connection but less physical contact, and replacing self-service buffets with prepacked food items.

I think it is important that Hotel Management Schools include in their curriculum how to deal with a pandemic and the impact on the operation of a hotel. It is wishful thinking to assume there will be no more pandemics.

Olivier Monod de Froideville, Chief Commercial Officer (CCO), Unlimited Productions, *Breda, the Netherlands*

With the market virtually closed and with little perspective in prospect, the very core of the event industry has been affected. For us, a major festival in Thailand and a large corporate event in Seoul were canceled in January and February 2020, respectively. Then we really took the helm. We immediately sent all our relations a memo stating that there is a virus in the world that may affect the Netherlands. It brought awareness to our customers, which meant that a number of them could still arrange for insurance to cover any related costs. It sparked a bit of discussion about possible cancellations at a later stage when it would be difficult to invoke force majeure.

It is interesting to see how relationships with customers and suppliers evolve. It is like when you win the lottery or end up in hospital: only then do you know who your real friends are—or from a business point of view, who your real partners are—in this crisis. Because we moved along, many customers have committed themselves to us for a preferred partnership or a long-term connection. The same is happening on the supplier side. We have to do this together, and then it is nice to see who you want to continue doing that with in the long term.

It is now important to find alternative business models and to develop initiatives. When we saw the emergence of drive-in concepts in Denmark and Germany, we responded to this, but the Dutch government never acknowledged that it was safe to attend large-scale events in a car. We then shifted our focus to online events. We entered into discussions with a number of parties to create digital propositions, and we are particularly strong in building customized studios for large corporates. In addition, our streaming kits travel all over the world so that high-quality discussions can be set up without having to rely on home WiFi.

The online element will never go away and will always be part of major events. However, I do not believe in the standard combination of online and offline at business events. In my opinion, staging an event half online and half live ends up being two halves and never becomes more than one. You should either focus on online or focus on a live event. In my view, there should always be one of the two in the lead and the other considered as a supplement.

We will still have to deal with the social distancing rules, health testing, and possible contamination risks in larger groups in the (near) future. As a result, we introduced the 'Corona Toolkit' for events. In collaboration with various renowned companies, three tools have been developed that will make it possible to organise live events again. The first tool relates to people flow monitoring and capacity optimisation simulation, the second one is a proximity monitor app / smart bracelet, and the third is a user-friendly COVID-19 quick test.

Ehsan Turabaz, International Relations Leader, Inter IKEA Systems Group B.V., *Delft, the Netherlands*

In fact, due to COVID-19, both high-level management and stakeholder engagement which are important parts of my daily work have been affected. We have established pandemic-specific policies and procedures, capabilities for employee communications, telecommuting, and personal and family leave to minimise disruptions. The first priority was the safety and well-being of our co-workers. Therefore, we invested in tools to enable personnel to work remotely and collaborate virtually.

Proactively create a mutually beneficial relationship with local and foreign government institutions, business associations, civil society, and the diplomatic community for the purpose of supporting and promoting the development of the IKEA franchise business and the protection of the IKEA brand. I have tried to call and actively approach my network personally, taking into account the corona protocol, while exposing this actively on social media.

I had face-to-face meetings with ambassadors, relevant governmental authorities, and private sector decision-makers. I have also used all kinds of communication instruments like Team, Zoom, Facetime, and LinkedIn in order to keep my network in good shape.

Traveling less to existing and new IKEA countries. We have tried to maintain the contacts and organise meetings through multiple channels. We must continue to do so and reinforce their interests as priorities.

Working from home and business traveling will be a major challenge for all multinationals. Sustainability has been a main priority for IKEA, even before COVID-19. Ideally, investing more and more in sustainable ways of working should be top of mind for any organisation.

Gilana Mikhailova, Director, Russian Academy for National Economy and Public Administration, Center for International Protocol, *Moscow, Russian Federation*

2020 was a year of changes in the work approach of protocol officers. The number of events at all levels has decreased. Some of them have acquired new formats, while others have ceased to exist. Of course, we can't say that all events went online; some remained in-person or became hybrid. How protocol works today: government agencies moved the majority of meetings and events to the online format. The number of people invited to in-person events has halved. This trend was evident from the Russian President's press conferences: journalists were admitted in two different places, and their number was limited. Managers of commercial organisations continue to conduct part of their meetings in-person while observing health safety measures: before each event, each participant's body temperature is necessarily measured and a blood test is performed. Of course, this increases the meeting time because the test results are available after 15 to 20 minutes. Representatives of companies working in offices take weekly COVID tests. I hope that the pandemic has taught colleagues to take responsibility for their own health and the health of others, since often people tend to neglect health issues until they end up in a hospital.

Some colleagues participated in one of the rounds of the international championship of vocational skills (WorldSkills Russia) throughout the country—from Sakhalin to Sochi. Three championship management centres were established, and the jury members were accommodated in several venues. The participants of the competition were at their workplaces. What could not be assessed online was previously sent by email. The grand opening and closing of the championship took place in a hybrid format, simultaneously across the country, with only 50 distinguished guests present in-person.

Conducting online meetings and joint discussions. We started a training on practical skills and launched a YouTube channel 'Protocol Pro' where we touch on the most relevant protocol issues. This provides an opportunity for continuous learning and professional growth for everyone, regardless of their location. We should avoid a situation where people who for whatever reason find it difficult to adapt to the new realities get left out of the workflow.

Increase creativity. In 2020, we had to solve a lot of issues that were not relevant before. This made it possible for anyone to showcase their own creative skills.

Andrea Miliccia, Head of Protocol & VIP Management, Saudi Aramco, King Abdulaziz Center for World Culture (Ithra), *Dhahran, Saudi Arabia*

We obviously were heavily affected by the restrictive measures implemented to contain the spread of the COVID-19 virus. During the spring of 2020, at the time of the first global lockdown, all VIP visits and events were cancelled. Slowly, they did resume at the beginning of the summer and ramped up during the last quarter of the year, with figures almost in line with the 2019 ones. Over the course of the past months, what really changed is the interaction with the guests—less physical yet warm, and a whole series of precautions needed to comply with the safety measures in place (i.e. temperature check and hand sanitising upon entrance, social distancing for seating arrangements, guided tours, limited number of people in elevators). What did not change is the level of service provided to our VIPs and the commitment of the team in delivering a memorable experience to all our guests.

In compliance with the COVID-19 safety measures implemented, we did organise various events during the past few months. We were able to do so successfully because both staff and guests were open to accepting new procedures and ways of behaving. From a protocol point of view, the most meaningful example is related to the review of the seating capacity in the VIP lounge and other components such as the Theater and Cinema. Social distancing has had a huge impact on seating arrangements. When planning for an event, we would recommend inviting a lower yet relevant number of guests to ensure safety is maintained at all times. Our experience says that the revised seating capacity may drop to one-third or one-fourth of the original one, depending on the setting.

As a team, we decided to replace the handshake greeting with the no-contact *salaam* (right hand on heart) one, out of respect for personal boundaries and to comply with the health safety measures. Because the gesture is deeply rooted in Islamic culture, we may decide to keep it, especially when receiving Muslim dignitaries and guests.

In terms of gift presentation, to avoid the selected gift being physically handed over by the host to the guest of honour—and therefore being touched by three people at least (protocol officer, host, guest)—we decided to display it on a table for presentation. With the right backdrop, it can be a tremendous photo opportunity with or without the guests!

When it comes to photo opportunities, our preference is for our guests not to wear their masks but to keep a safe distance instead (1.5 m at least). This usually works well when we have a group picture with no more than five guests.

Marina Fernández, Secretary General, Organización Internacional de Ceremonial y Protocolo (OICP), *Madrid, Spain*

Protocol officials live their professional lives according to a strict schedule. Everything is planned down to the minute. However, a good protocol professional needs to be flexible, always be ready to react, and always have a plan B up its sleeve. Although we are used to facing many storms, a pandemic putting the world as we know it upside down was not something we were ready for. Back in March 2020, things were not looking pretty in the European events circuit. Huge landmarks such as the Milan Fashion Week or the Barcelona World Mobile Congress were being cancelled. And the rest of the world was only to follow into this doomsday scenario. Being OICP, an international organisation that hosts more than 20 protocol associations from around the world, the impact of travel restrictions was brutal to our activity. At the very core of the OICP is the networking amongst international protocol professionals, with an annual conference that, after almost 20 editions, has become one of the most prestigious events in the protocol arena. And it was not only OICP that had to put aside its 'business as usual'; also all of its members were cancelling their face-to-face events and workshops.

It really is a good thing that creativity and imagination lie at the core of protocol officials. Despite the picture that is often painted, thinking outside the box is what we do best. Hence the quick response that enabled OICP not only to survive these difficult times but also to strive amidst the tragedy. I cannot begin to imagine how it would have been if COVID had hit 15 years ago, but in 2020 the internet and social networks came to the rescue, and we used them to our advantage. Refusing to see the bottle half empty, we welcomed new people into our activities who had not been able to join us before due to a hectic work schedule, family responsibilities, or a tight budget situation. YouTube, Facebook, and Instagram became the OICP's open window to the world. From the comfort of your own house, you could attend online seminars and workshops by some of the top international professionals and get in touch with likeminded individuals from around the world. Experiences were shared, professional advice was given. We were apart, but we felt closer than ever.

COVID-19 means change and adjustments. It is very likely that some of the changes that we had to come up with during the pandemic are here to stay. And this does not have to be a bad thing. In the midst of every crisis lies great opportunity. We had to be creative and design solutions for problems that, at first, felt like a bad sci-fi movie. And in the process of doing so, the science of protocol and the art of event planning have grown.

David Chikvaidze, Chef de Cabinet of the Director-General, United Nations Office at Geneva (UNOG), *Geneva, Switzerland*

All meetings at UNOG conference facilities had to be suspended on 16 March 2020 due to preventive measures taken by the Host Country and following the World Health Organization's guidance. Upon the easing of the restrictions by the Host Country, and responding to the wishes of the Member States, UNOG ensured a safe, controlled, and gradual resumption in truncated form of the meetings of intergovernmental and expert bodies included in the official General Assembly calendar. UNOG did so in three ways: a very limited number of physical meetings, with simultaneous interpreting in selected conference rooms in strict compliance with hygiene and social distancing rules; and virtual or hybrid meetings with or without simultaneous interpreting.

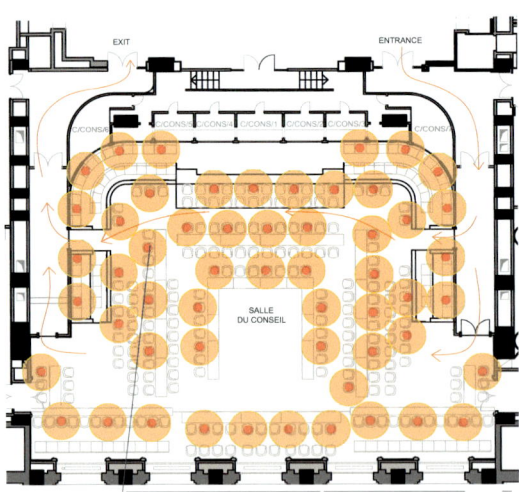

Setup of Council Chamber at Palais des Nations, using a socially distanced seating arrangement

From the resumption of conferencing activities in June through December 2020, 2,915 in-person meetings (of which 685 with simultaneous interpreting) and 1,359 virtual and hybrid meetings (of which 572 hybrid meetings with simultaneous interpreting) were held; far less than the 10,000 or so meetings usually held annually at the Palais des Nations, but a significant number nonetheless under the circumstances.

UN Geneva remained the location of choice for UN-led mediation processes such as the signing of the complete and permanent Ceasefire Agreement by the Libyan Joint Military Commission, meetings of the Syrian Constitutional Committee, and the 2020 Afghanistan Conference. UNOG proceeded with high-level meetings at the Palais des Nations, including visits of the UN Deputy Secretary-General, the President of Switzerland, the President of the Senate of Uzbekistan, and ceremonies of the presentation of the Letters of Credence by new Ambassadors and Permanent Representatives.

UNOG managed to mark 100 years of multilateralism and 75 years of the UN in various ways:
– Commemorations were officially launched with the annual Model UN at UNOG.
– Three virtual dialogues took place with youth on multilateralism during and beyond COVID-19, contributing to the global discussion launched by the UN Secretary-General.
– The centenary flags were raised on the Mont-Blanc Bridge in August.
– On UN75 Day (24 October), the Palais des Nations and Geneva's Jet d'Eau were lit in blue.
– Simultaneous play chess tournament on twenty boards were conducted by the 16th World Chess Champion Anatoly Karpov on the occasion of UN75 (won 19, drew one).

A major high-level hybrid conference on 'Global Leadership for the 21st Century' planned by UNOG and the World Academy of Art and Science for September had to be rescheduled to November and was ultimately held in December. When it became clear that it would have to be virtual, things were quickly changed around and the event was nevertheless a success.

The COVID crisis will entail changes to how conferences and events are organised. Smaller Member States, NGOs, persons with disabilities, etc. will likely continue to request hybrid conferences with simultaneous interpreting beyond the lifting of COVID-related restrictions.

Rubén Ortiz Pamplin, Events & Office Assistant, IndustriALL Global Union, *Geneva, Switzerland*

The pandemic accelerated the process of a change that many had envisioned for the distant future. The restrictive measures stripped us of all our established *savoir-faire* and forced many to start literally from scratch. Everything was diminished to a screen, a microphone, a headset, and internet connection; and we all know how frustrating it can be when there is no perfect harmony between those four components. Our social skills had to be adjusted. That involved a significant investment in equipment as well as in time learning social skills from *YouTubers* and *Bloggers*! Event managers had to 'let go' of some of the interpersonal skills required to organize presence-based events to adapt to a new situation where they were required to be experts in videoconferencing systems, remote interpretation management, and health & safety, to name a few. It also meant having to work from home. Working surrounded by toddlers running up and down the house did make the task quite a challenge. To tackle those challenges, I readapted one of my walk-in wardrobes, converting it into a mini studio with isolation and some audio and video equipment. If somebody had seen the result some years ago, they would have presumed that I was a YouTuber, which is far from the truth: I am a specialist in event management, but this is our reality today!

Virtual and hybrid events are here to stay based on three facts:

    1. The implementation of 5G, which will further develop possibilities, including attendance in meetings with Virtual Reality glasses where one can see the holographic image of guests from their places. I would not be surprised if that ends up being a convenient alternative, not a replacement, for real attendance to events in the future.

    2. The necessity of tackling climate change and readapting our activities around the principle of reducing our environmental impact. Today there are very few—if not zero—restrictions on events causing a substantial impact on the environment. I think, however, that sanctions and limitations will gradually appear. The event industry and the protocol sector, for example with state visits, will very possibly develop their activities

around such environmental restrictions in the years to come. There are some initiatives in Switzerland already, for example the guidelines by the Swiss Federal Institute of Technology and the University of Zurich (2018)[20] and the International Standardization Organisation with ISO 20121:2012.[21]

3. Presence-based events are more expensive and have a bigger environmental impact than virtual events.

For one of our virtual meetings, we recreated a television studio in one of our conference rooms. Each official was seated in compliance with the social distancing regulations. The room had several cameras installed, which were pointed to the speakers. An additional camera freely hoovered all around the room with a system of cables. With ten interpreted languages plus three passive languages, our main objective was to bring in that human side to 'close the gap' between speakers and attendees.

Giovanni Criscione, Head of Protocol for International Visits, Expo 2020 Dubai, *United Arab Emirates*

To the question: 'What is Protocol?' my mentor, Prof. Massimo Sgrelli, former Head of Protocol in the Italian Prime Minister's office, used to say, 'Protocol is the particular art or science that when it works nobody really notices it, but when there is a problem—such as an upside-down flag or a wrong order of precedence—it can become a major obstacle to conquer, but at the same time it can be a useful challenge to learn from.'

Well, with the COVID-19 pandemic, this art or science has inevitably resulted in everyone having to adapt to many unprecedented and unforeseen challenges. In Expo 2020, we had a significant increase in virtual meetings and conference calls at all levels, which allowed us to be even more productive. One of my favourite quotes is from His Highness Sheikh Mohammed bin Rashid Al Maktoum, Vice President and Prime Minister of the UAE and Ruler of Dubai, 'We don't wait for opportunities, we create them.'

I think that in every circumstance we experience, even the most difficult ones such as those we are experiencing now with COVID-19, there is always space to create opportunities to be better, and this is what we do at Expo 2020 Dubai.

---

20 www.sustainability.uzh.ch/dam/jcr:162bc47e-435f-4dd6-9dc1-ed101dfe5547/2018 06_Guideline%20Sustainable%20Events_UZH.pdf
21 www.iso.org/obp/ui/#iso:std:iso:20121:ed-1:v1:en

Expo 2020 Dubai is an opportunity to bring the world together in a spirit of hope and optimism and to help shape a better, post-pandemic future by inspiring new and exciting solutions to overcome some of the world's most challenging issues. The COVID-19 pandemic certainly created restrictions, but as we look forward, Expo 2020 Dubai's theme of 'Connecting Minds, Creating the Future' is exceedingly apt, as now, more than ever, humanity needs to come together to remember what unites us.

Al Wasl Plaza at Expo 2020 Dubai site

Never give up and continually look ahead. There is always a suitable solution even in the most challenging situation. I like to paraphrase Pythagoras and Giacomo Leopardi: we should in no way stop where we have reached but we should constantly go, move, and look beyond.

Always keep your protocol eyes, heart, and mind open and be ready to act or react constructively. When you receive and greet visiting guests, whether they are Heads of State or the drivers of their cars, smile with your eyes and be confident and humble at the same time. In that moment, please remember that all the protocol elements you are managing will make that visit memorable for everybody alike whether they be Heads of State or their drivers.

Continually exercise courage and patience. Augustine of Hippo used to say that patience is the companion of wisdom. Even if this current pandemic has tested our patience strongly, we should look at it as an opportunity to sharpen our skills.

Finally, I would like to share the five values of Expo 2020: integrity, humility, respect, cooperation, and excellence. They should always be part of everyone's life, especially for those who exercise protocol.

Patricia Kenneth-Divine, Principal Consultant at Synergy Systems Consults (UK) Ltd as well as President of the Association of Certified Protocol Practitioners in Nigeria, *London, United Kingdom / Lagos, Nigeria*

My work for both organisations has been impacted to a large extent, especially in the areas of advisory in logistics, travel, and event management. Many protocol officers in my network mainly operate as 'field workers' on a logistical and operational level, but due to the pandemic I and my colleagues felt the urgency to increase their knowledge of policies, digital transformation, and cultural intelligence in order to be able to redistribute responsibilities and to become more inclusive.

To appraise the impact of the pandemic, a global virtual conference was organised in July 2020 with a diversity of participants from across the African continent as well as professionals from other parts of the world. We discussed new practices, such as the need for virtual leadership for a protocol professional, e-protocol regulations (e.g. agreeing on the speaking order during digital multilateral meetings or the consistent positioning of flags behind the officials), how to enhance your network through technology (by proactively engaging with your stakeholders and empathizing with them wherever they are), what changes you can bring to your teams/organisations, as well as how to amend traditional rituals and customs like diplomatic meet-and-greet occasions in times of social distancing. Since many events and international visits had to be canceled in the first months of the pandemic, we also emphasised relevant insurance policies in the industry.

Also, the restrictive measures around the world differed greatly from one place to another, so a travel and airport app was launched, indicating the numbers of COVID-19 infections per country, travel restrictions, additional visa procedures, etc. By means of the networking components of the conference, we raised the level of awareness on the use of digital activities and tools in the new fields of protocol and global travel. We can see the impact of the pandemic as a revolution in doing business, and by increasing the ability of field workers to become more creative, innovative, and knowledgeable, we can maximize the power of the wide range of virtual opportunities.

Overall, orientation and training in the applications of digital transformation, performance, networking, and management are key!

Leslie Lautenslager, 2016 – 2020 President, Protocol & Diplomacy International – Protocol Officers Association, *Alexandria, United States of America*

Unfortunately, the COVID-19 pandemic necessitated our having to cancel our in-person annual International Protocol Education Forum that had been scheduled to take place in Montreal in July of 2020. This was heartbreaking for many of us who look forward each year to being able to gather in person with colleagues from around the world.

Canceling the annual Forum was a difficult decision to make, although we know it was the right one. We were able to plan a virtual abbreviated Forum though and surprised everyone—ourselves included—with how well we were all able to adapt and develop an interesting and engaging virtual program, as we had never done anything like this before. The proverbial genie is now out of the bottle, and we will now always and forever include some sort of virtual presence or opportunity whenever we 'gather' for an in-person event.

If our in-person Forums have at best welcomed as many as 170 attendees in the past, we were thrilled, delighted, and surprised to have 300 guests sign up to attend our virtual Forum.

All our gatherings going forward will be hybrids to allow both in-person and virtual participation. We have always been sensitive to the fact that not everyone from within our membership can travel across the globe each year for our annual Forums. Ours is an international organization, and though we try and cater to the interests of our members from all the various countries and cultures represented, we know that some locations are more easily accessible than others, and some locations are more appealing than others. By adding a virtual component each year to our annual gathering,

I feel certain that we will be able to serve our global members better and be able to encourage greater participation.

Although by no means would I ever wish on anyone this heartbreaking period we are all experiencing, I would encourage everyone to try and pay close attention to the things we have had to change or practices we have had to embrace that may in fact be beneficial going forward. No doubt we all look forward to that day when we can travel and gather and simply share the human touch of a greeting again. But until that day, may we all be ever so careful to be extra kind, extra encouraging, and extra comforting in our interactions, virtual though they may be.

Deanna Tryon, Chief of Protocol, Silicon Valley Office of Protocol, *Los Altos, United States of America*

One of the issues my office faced during the pandemic was the use of (now-standard) video conferencing apps to conduct meetings. We had difficulty in the beginning organizing around platforms that were secure. We had been cautioned about certain video conferencing apps with regard to sensitive government communications, and it took weeks and extensive coordination with several agencies to assure safety and privacy. As U.S. government agencies were verifying the security of these platforms, sometimes meetings would have to be postponed until all parties had verified security issues. There are still so many options for video conferencing, many based here in Silicon Valley, that we had to be diplomatic while arranging meetings with stakeholders at certain companies while we were, in fact, vetting and clearing their software. Many of our local tech companies use their own systems, but those systems had to be agreed upon by the missions of other countries as well.

I have discovered that many of our colleagues—myself included—pride ourselves on our ability to 'read a room' or anticipate the feelings and needs of our principals. With video conferencing, there have literally been 'walls' up in some interactions between participants. Even after everyone became more comfortable with the medium, issues that could have been hammered out in one meeting took several, and the interaction lost the valuable 'personal touch' from which we benefit in face-to-face contact.

On a positive note, we have learned that in an emergency, people can pivot effectively, and we can take lessons from these adaptations. Also, the whole world has learned how to more effectively communicate by 'face on camera', so perhaps more diplomats will soon be increasingly comfortable in media appearances.

Eva Oskam, *Rijkstrainee* **/ Third Secretary, Permanent Representation of the Kingdom of the Netherlands to the United Nations,** *New York City, United States of America*

The pandemic has in many ways affected diplomacy, of which shifting our work to online settings is the most prominent. Diplomacy is a field where personal contact, building relationships, informal chats, and special contact are at the core of its work. Fortunately, digital technologies provide a variety of new means to do so, but it must also be said that such connections are more distant. Whereas the atmosphere in the negotiation room often affects diplomatic efforts, a Zoom room allows for more anonymity and distance, which makes it harder to create alliances or persuade other parties. The diplomatic community is still trying to find the most appropriate 'online protocol'. Physical protocol is fairly ingrained, but you cannot take over everything one-on-one in the virtual world. It is a constant search for how to politely ask for the floor or respond to an intervention. You can often sense this during physical meetings, but online it works differently. And catching up with a colleague in the corridors after such meetings is now only possible by picking up the phone in a much less organic way. It is often during such informal moments that you are able to gain new insights, personally thank that colleague for something that recently happened, or touch upon tomorrow's discussion. These moments have not become impossible, but by lacking their organic nature it is noticeable that they have become less fruitful.

At the same time, going digital allows for a quick exchange of position and views. It has become more common to share documents while at the negotiation table. Digital possibilities can contribute to building stronger alliances and can increase the participation of non-usual stakeholders in the discussion, such as civil society organizations and think tanks. Instead of flying in people, they are now able to join discussions from their homes. This is very cost-effective, which means that organizations/persons can join who otherwise would not have had the means to do so.

I believe it is also important to mention the environmental impact that has been created. We have become more aware of our footprint and were forced to become innovative and resilient. Diplomacy needs in-person meetings and contact, and we should be willing to invest in that, but we can become more selective with attending events in person in the future.

I was privileged to experience these developments among others during the 'High-level meeting' week of the United Nations General Assembly in September, while being present at UN Headquarters with a limited audience. Under normal circumstances, world leaders from around the globe would gather in New York then, but this was obviously not the case in 2020. Their speeches were prerecorded and streamed online. Afterwards, I followed all negotiations of the Third Committee on Social, Humanitarian, and Cultural Issues virtually as well. The procedural meetings, like official adoptions of resolutions or occasional votings, took place on site.

Hopefully, we can all adapt to this 'new normal' in good health!

Maryse Larche Mele, Executive Officer, Protocol, NATO's Supreme Allied Commander Transformation, *Norfolk, United States of America*

Considering we are the only strategic NATO headquarters on this side of the Atlantic, travel restrictions had a big impact on protocol, while work in HQ continued via virtual meetings, webinars, or just simple email. While local visits to HQ continued, my dilemma was how to facilitate events and create relationships virtually. During our conference preparation, protocol officers needed to be more engaged in the registration process, really getting to know the audience and what they wanted to achieve. The focus was therefore on creating a virtual 'experience' rather than a simple presentation. Some forced changes actually facilitated the relationship building.

I initially put too much effort in trying to establish formal ways of greeting to replace the handshake. I quickly realized that people bond over common issues, and when my principal met guests who quickly offered an elbow bump as a greeting, it was an immediate icebreaker. Both parties relaxed and bonded over being forced into a situation outside of their comfort zone.

The military are used to dealing with crises. HQ quickly adapted in order to ensure work could continue while keeping people safe. Most of our events continued with adaptation. Military ceremonies continued with social distancing measures. During a retirement ceremony, we allowed families to sit grouped together but socially distanced from the next person or family unit while wearing masks. The setup on stage was still very much the same as it would have been before COVID; we just needed more space.

I attended a site visit in Europe during this time frame. Before the trip we connected by email, each one of us ensuring that signature blocks contained all contact information. However, once we started meetings, new people were joining the team. Business card exchanges were still a necessary part of business. Each person was prepared and presented an open cardholder requesting the recipient to help themselves to a business card. Hand sanitizer was also available around the table. However, Protocol of the hosting team may have wanted to get permission in advance to email the contact information of each attendee to all players in order to avoid business card exchanges.

Our HQ hosts an annual event that brings together the Chiefs of Transformation from NATO nations to improve the coherence of warfare development work in the Alliance. In preparation for the event, this year we hosted a virtual workshop in September, and in October our Commander hosted a virtual meeting with the Chiefs of Transformation. These preparations meant that all attendees were better prepared when they met virtually by VTC in December. The event was successful. Protocol ensured that all participants would see their national flag represented at the top end of the conference rooms from where our Commander was running the meeting. People respond to personal touches, and it is Protocol's responsibility to ensure that even virtual events provide a simple personal touch like the display of participants' national flags.

Deborah K. Rodday, Director, Advancement Protocol and Visits, Carnegie Mellon University, *Pittsburgh, United States of America*

Like most of the world, the government and our own organizational restrictions impacted our work immensely. An American idiom came to life—we had to turn on a dime. We had to reimagine interactions. How do you maintain vital levels of engagement and protocol? We, like many, explored virtual experiences.

Prior to the pandemic and subsequent restrictions, we mainly organized events on campus or in domestic and international locations where large amounts of alumni and donors resided. In-person attendance and engagement met our expectations for those onsite events. After the restrictions were enforced, we hosted similar virtual events with similar content (e.g., faculty dialogue programs). The response was phenomenal; attendance exceeded our expectations. We had alumni and donors from around the world attending the virtual events. We were reaching members of our audience that weren't previously engaged. Planning for the virtual event was similar to an in-person event, although all interactions were virtual. Video communication platforms allowed us to successfully plan and execute our events.

In addition to the now-conventional virtual events, we successfully organized and implemented a cross-campus and community conference. This particular conference was an annual event, so it needed to match if not exceed expectations. It included standard plenary sessions, panel discussions, product demos, sponsor booths, resources, and networking opportunities. We decided to partner with a virtual platform for this conference. Fearful of video and screen fatigue of conference attendees, we transitioned the two-day conference into a four-week series with video networking immediately available after the sessions.

As we had several high-level, in-demand keynote speakers and panelists, we introduced a virtual green room that our platform had not considered. This allowed us to meet and greet the speakers, provide the appropriate level of care to nurture our guests prior to the live-streaming event, and most importantly reinforce that it was our event and not the platform's.

We cannot ignore the 'wins' of this last year. We expanded our engagement with live-streaming and other video events. They should continue. We should also continue to reexamine traditional options. If a plenary speaker is not able to travel to a location, could we record the session and have the speaker live for the question/answer session? Yes!

There have been numerous gifts that have emerged during these trying times. But I must say one of the most surprising gifts was written correspondence; it was welcomed like an old friend. Letters were once again treasured and provided a much-needed respite from the blue light of our computer screens while warming our hearts.

Maureen Sweeney, Principle, Maureen Sweeney Consulting, as well as Founding Partner, Tiller Language Services, *Salt Lake City, United States of America*

It affected all aspects of my work. The 2020 Olympics in Tokyo were postponed one year, which resulted in the cancellation and re-negotiation of my separate contracts (all related to language services and interpreting with the Tokyo Olympic Organizing Committee). As a result, I had to cancel contracts with the 70+ interpreters and technicians I had hired. The International Olympic Committee, one of my larger clients for protocol services, cut back my contracts for protocol-related work with the Tokyo and Beijing Olympic Games, resulting in far fewer days of work for 2020. In addition, all the training sessions related to protocol that I was supposed to deliver in person in Tokyo and Beijing were held online. I delivered five training courses on various aspects of protocol online for these Olympic Organizing Committees. These sessions were around two hours each and included simultaneous interpreting. The Bill and Melinda Gates Foundation, another of my larger clients, cancelled—or moved to online platforms—all live events and trips for 2020.

All meetings that ended up taking place were conducted via online meeting platforms. These meetings have had varying levels of success online. Making this transition from real life to online meetings takes creativity in general. Trying to make a two to three-day event that usually includes a lot of social interaction and 'fun' into something interesting online isn't easy. Many of our events got a bit shorter and included less entertainment/socializing elements. People are far less likely want to attend an online event than a live one (in my experience), so trying to find ways to make them more appealing takes creativity. Higher level speakers can be a draw, as can the opportunity to interact with people who might broaden your network in some important way. People have varying reactions to games and performances as part of an online event. While some find them interesting, others will see them as a waste of time.

Tiller Language Services provided online interpreting for 50+ different online events for the Biden/Harris campaign from July to October 2020. These online events allowed the campaign to utilize simultaneous interpreting for large-scale events that have not had interpreting in the past due to their large size and the resulting prohibitive cost. Being able to offer simultaneous interpreting for this type of political campaign event was something that has not been done much in the past (in the USA) but could be adopted by other campaigns in the future—regardless of whether the event is live or virtual. Innovations in remote interpreting could be a game-changer for future political campaigns. The platforms have improved greatly due to the innovations spurred by the pandemic and offer opportunities that can be taken advantage of once we return to more 'live' events taking place in real life.

Barbara Wellink, Social Secretary & Protocol Officer, Delegation of the European Union to the United States of America, *Washington, D.C., United States of America*

In Washington, D.C., the spouses of the EU Member State Ambassadors hold monthly gatherings hosted by one of the spouses. On November 24, 2020, the spouse of the EU Ambassador hosted a lunch in the garden of the EU Residence. Biodegradable lunch boxes with name cards on them (related to dietary restrictions) were preplaced on the tables as a main course, while the dessert was presented on plates, which the guests could collect at the bar together with coffee or tea. The date of the event coincided with the 25th anniversary of the *American Visionary Art Museum* in Baltimore, Maryland. We had invited its founder/director to give brief remarks on a selection of art pieces from the museum's collection on display in the EU Residence dining room from November 2020 until May 2022. The spouses especially appreciated the opportunity of a personal art tour (in small groups with face masks on).

For each event at the EU Residence, the following *Coronavirus Safety Protocol* is sent together with the invitation:
– The Residence public spaces and kitchen are thoroughly cleaned on a daily basis following the guidelines from the (local) authorities.
– Guests who have been in contact with someone who has tested positive for COVID-19, who are feeling cold/flu-like symptoms, or who belong to high-risk groups are kindly asked to stay home.
– All participants will wash their hands upon arrival and in addition, hand sanitizer will be available. Guests will not shake hands.

- Seating arrangements will take social-distance guidelines into account. Guests are respectfully asked to maintain a 6-feet distance from the Residence staff and other guests whenever possible.
- All Residence staff will be wearing masks and gloves and will wash their hands regularly.

As long as the social distancing measures are in place, indoor lunches or dinners have a maximum of eight guests. Examples of possible seating arrangements are shown below (please find the abbreviations on page 60).

Seating with host and guest of honour   Seating with couples, including guest of honour

The most creative and successful online event I helped organize was our annual Holiday staff party, which usually takes place at the Ambassador's Residence. The one-hour event (joined by approximately 75 colleagues) took place via Webex and was hosted by the Ambassador from his Residence (joined by his spouse and daughter). We had organized a trivia quiz (in teams), an *Ugly Sweater Contest*, a segment in which colleagues shared a treasured Christmas ornament/tradition, and—as a special surprise—three personalized Christmas carols sung by choristers of *The Washington Chorus*. The event was a highlight in which colleagues actually had fun (afterwards, prizes in the form of a bottle of Prosecco for the winner of the contest and cookies baked by the Residence Chef for the winners of the quiz were delivered).

75 years of freedom in the Netherlands by Mark Verheul

In 2019 and 2020, the Netherlands celebrated the 75th anniversary of its liberation and the fact that we have enjoyed living in freedom since then. In addition to existing commemorations and celebrations, a wide range of large-scale events were planned throughout the country. The overall coordination of the jubilee activities was the responsibility of the National

Committee for 4 and 5 May, where I am involved as a strategic adviser of stakeholder management. One of the committee's main tasks is to organise the national observance of Remembrance Day on 4 May and the national celebration of Liberation Day on 5 May.

Normally, the national observance of Remembrance Day takes place on 4 May at 8 pm, when two minutes of silence are observed throughout the country to commemorate Dutch victims of war. A major commemoration ceremony is normally held on Dam Square in Amsterdam in front of the Royal Palace in the presence of the King and Queen and various representatives of both the Council of Ministers and the Dutch Parliament as well as tens of thousands of citizens. This national observance is held simultaneously with local commemoration ceremonies in nearly every town and city in the Netherlands. At 8 pm, the entire country is silent for two minutes. In this commemorative year, for the first time in history, our head of state was supposed to give an address at the ceremony in Amsterdam on a packed Dam Square. And then there was corona...

Stay home! Social distancing. Intelligent lockdown. No public gatherings.

Despite the extraordinary and difficult circumstances, we wanted to make it possible for the entire Dutch population to commemorate and reflect on the end of the Second World War 75 years ago in a dignified and interconnected manner. We wanted to draw special attention to our veterans and all those fellow citizens who experienced the horrors of this war but who are also more vulnerable to the COVID-19 virus.

Obviously, quite some logistical and protocol aspects of the commemoration ceremony had to be adjusted in the light of the restrictive measures. First of all, it was decided that the ceremony would proceed without the public, so the entire square in front of the palace had to be blocked off as well as all the streets leading towards it. Normally, two lines of honour guards are positioned from the main entrance of the palace towards the National Monument, through which the royal procession takes place. But not this time, since it would have involved too many soldiers and veterans. To still pay respect to their personal stories, a special website was designed by the Veterans Institute to highlight some of their experiences.

The royal procession normally consists of 10 persons, which had to be cut down to six. It was decided that the chairperson of the National Committee (as host) and the King and Queen would walk in the first line of the procession, with the King as head of state in the centre, the Queen to his right and the chairperson to his left (so the chairperson had the royal couple as guests of honour to her right). Behind the King, the chief of the Military

House of His Majesty was positioned with the prime minister to his right and the mayor of Amsterdam to his left. All of them kept a distance of 1.5 meters. Two aides-de-camp, a lady-in-waiting, and the King's commissioner in the province of Noord-Holland were not included, in order to keep it a compact procession.

4 May 2013

4 May 2020

The two aides-de-camp were positioned next to the wreath on the side of the National Monument. Under normal circumstances, they would have handed over the wreath to the King and Queen so they could position it on the standard in front of the monument. But in times of social distancing, this handover would have been a breach of the regulations because four people would be standing approximately one square meter from each other. It was decided that the aides-de-camp would lay the wreath on behalf of the King and Queen, after which the royal couple would come forward to arrange the ribbons and pay their respect.

After the military signal 'Taptoe' (the Dutch version of The Last Post), two minutes of silence were observed, followed by the first stanza of the national anthem, played by ten military band musicians. Again, all of them kept a distance of 1.5 meters.

Afterwards, under normal circumstances, nine other wreaths would have been laid by representatives of first generations survivors, veterans, the Senate and House of Representatives, the Council of Ministers, the Armed Forces, and the City of Amsterdam. However, since we were not able to have all these persons in attendance at the ceremony, a teenage brother and sister, both of them in their Scouts uniform, were asked to lay these wreaths on their behalf, preceded by short video messages of the representatives who were supposed to take part in the ceremony. In this way, respect could still be paid to all the stakeholders involved.

As you can imagine, it was a very surreal ceremony with a speech by the King on an empty square, while the entire nation was watching it on television. And since all the local ceremonies were cancelled, we encouraged people to pay their respect at local monuments on an individual basis spread out over the day on their way to do their groceries or to lay flowers virtually through our website. Since the flag protocol on 4 May prescribes that the national flag is flown at half-staff only from 6 pm until sunset, the National Committee and the Council of Ministers decided to amend the regulations for this year, officially allowing the flag to be flown at half-staff from sunrise to sunset. On 5 May, Liberation Day, the flags are flown the entire day at full-staff every year.

The Federal Chancellor of Germany was supposed to deliver the 5th of May Lecture in The Hague this year at the invitation of the Dutch Prime Minister and in the presence of many dignitaries, diplomats, and students. This event, underlining the re-establishment of good bilateral relationships in the past seven and a half decades, had to be cancelled and postponed to a later date. Despite the fact that we could not come together physically, I was extremely grateful for a sincere online message to the citizens of the

Netherlands on the occasion of 75 years of freedom by the Ambassadors of Australia, Belgium, Canada, France, Germany, New Zealand, Norway, Poland, the United Kingdom, and the United States.

The yearly closure of Liberation Day is an open-air concert along the famous Amsterdam canals and bridges but took place this year in an amended format in a nearby theater with a live broadcast on national television, but again without the public. So, the traditional finale of the concert could not have been more appropriate in this unprecedented time of the pandemic: Dame Vera Lynn's famous song during the Second World War: *We'll Meet Again!*

Overall Top 40 lessons learned as well as predictions and recommendations for the (near) future

1. Embrace the new world of virtual and hybrid events. That new world is not going to disappear with the end of the pandemic. Protocol is a frame of mind. It is the way we meticulously approach our work: the way we negotiate every detail and clarify expectations between visitors and hosts, the way we are able to step back from the substance of a meeting to focus on the overall run of show, the look and feel, the interstitial moments where relationships are built. Applying all those concepts to making one's organisation's virtual events shine is where we will find a new niche.
2. Take care of the visual form of online events (scenography, furnishings, appropriate appearance, flag display, correct light sources). Entrust the backstage of online events to professionals.
3. Test systems extensively to be sure they work for everyone. For example, is your online meeting platform accessible and stable in all the countries where participants come from? Ensure reliable internet connections to avoid screens from 'freezing'.
4. The camera does not lie. Make sure colleagues are aware of the nuances captured on screen that may be overlooked. The subtle roll of the eyes or texting when someone else is talking can possibly offend stakeholders and damage relationships.
5. This pandemic has led organisations to update and increase IT skills and tools, to reduce bureaucracy, and to focus more on event objectives. Learn to be a digital communicator to an audience that you often do not see and do not know if they are really there. Not everyone has the same level of technical expertise. Online platforms may seem simple to

you but may still be incredibly challenging for others. Make sure that instructions are simple and that colleagues are on stand-by to provide technical support.
6. Keep investing in and researching how to make online events an unforgettable experience for your attendees. They could include such elements as break-out rooms, voting systems, virtual reality glasses for brainstorms, polls, text chats, pre-recorded messages, exhibitions, remote interpreting in various languages, games, simulations, videos, avatars, networking rooms, and reception halls. These approaches can ensure good engagement with your audience. Include some warmth and find ways to personalise experiences to show that an online event can be as soulful as a traditional one.
7. Speeches during online events could be reduced in length to keep the span of attention of your audience.
8. The COVID crisis has triggered long-term changes to how conferences are organised. Participants—especially those from less-developed countries and NGOs as well as persons with disabilities—will continue to request hybrid conferences beyond the loosening of COVID-related travel restrictions.
9. Hybrid and virtual meetings boost the attendance and quality of participants. Your chances of securing high-level guests for a hybrid meeting can be considerably greater now than in the past. In this, cutting on travel time is key.
10. The world will need to adjust to and adopt the best of both worlds: a new 'hybrid diplomacy' that combines face-to-face and online meetings. Highly delicate negotiations will continue to require the gathering of real people in actual rooms, but many other more routine meetings can and should shift to online formats.
11. Quite some public and private organisations have realised that many meetings that previously required budgeting flights, accommodation, visa fees, and tedious and tiring travels can be spared and replaced by 'comfortable' online meetings that one can do from anywhere in the world. After seeing how much cheaper it is at the end of the financial year, they established rules that numerous events with, for example, less than 40 or so participants will remain virtual (with strategic exceptions, of course). So, travel for non-essential face-to-face meetings is likely to be reduced significantly.
12. Protocol has 'suffered' from the casual approach of videoconferences, so do not overlook the details and dress codes, especially when hybrid and virtual meetings/events continue to be the rule.

13. Preparation is key to maintaining levels of quality. During the pandemic, errors in production were often overlooked as the audience was more forgiving than before. Once a level of normalcy returns, the forgiveness may not be there or last long.
14. Having a strict agenda for virtual events is key to respecting people's time.
15. Practicing with all speakers and panelists prior to virtual occasions has become more important than before, since if someone does not know when to speak or what to do, it is more difficult to 'quietly' intervene as would be the case at physical events.
16. Online events can also include an 'in-person touch', for example by sending a food & beverage box beforehand or a handwritten thank-you note via post afterwards.
17. For in-person events, more effort and consideration need to go into planning and management to ensure the safety and health of all guests and staff present.
18. Be prepared for a 'Plan B', no matter what your plans are. Always have alternatives in place just in case new insights arise that force last-minute changes and adjustments.
19. Choose non-physical-contact ways of greeting each other. Also, avoid as much physical contact between staff and guests as possible. For example, pre-place plates already at a table and let guests serve themselves. Upon entering a venue, provide guests with an antiseptic gel to clean their hands.
20. Comply with health regulations given by authorities, follow the advice of professionals, and ensure safety measures. Ensure clear and sufficient signage and sanitising options are in place. Follow social distancing guidelines and wear masks when appropriate.
21. Depending on the setting of your venue, the new maximum capacity might be only half, one-third, one-fourth, or even one-tenth of your regular seating matrix. Create wider aisles as well. Allow 1.5 to 1.8 meters (five to six feet) between guests. Classroom-type seating for conferences can create forced barriers to ensure social distancing. Seating for four people to a 12 top round table could be seen as a norm. For regular receptions, approximately three persons can be accommodated per square meter: with social distancing, three persons per 7.5 square meters could be used as a guideline.
22. While preparing for events, use for example three different scenarios related to numbers of attendees and start planning for the maximum capacity scenario, since downscaling is easier in the process than upscaling.

23. While adjusting your guest list to smaller numbers, determine the most appropriate reflection of the traditional version, perhaps using specific percentages per guest category or prioritising certain groups specifically for the purpose of the event.
24. Host small-scale meetings for your most valuable stakeholders to give them high-level personal attention. A lot of small-scale is the new large-scale!
25. Stay positive, be kind, keep calm, and just follow protocol! To organise a successful high-level event, the focus should still be on the guidelines described on page 235.
26. To ensure a safe and proper flow of events, you might need to increase the staff-to-guest ratio.
27. Let this not be the flavour of the month. Hygiene regulations should be the new normal. Better safe than sorry. Do not take any health risk: be open and honest to your guests or clients in case of an infection among your staff. Temporarily close the venue or cancel the event to ensure safety for all. That is a short-term pain for a long term-gain.
28. Business continues with possible temperature checking at events, the use of health apps, or requesting a negative *PCR* test or proof of vaccination. Even after the pandemic is over, it is advised that you continue with compulsory registration of contact details before events; limits on guest numbers; no sharing of microphones; cleaning lecterns between each speaker; wiping all chairs, door handles, extension cords, etc. before and after each event; using a sanitised pen for each person during a signing ceremony; avoiding buffet lines; strict monitoring of numbers in elevators; staff wearing masks and gloves; opening windows and doors for ventilation; and sending out details of health measures to all guests with invitations.
29. Quite some anti-virus transmission measures will remain in place for a while. Try to be able to quickly implement them again in the event of other possible pandemics.
30. Our planet needed a break. Climate is an issue that event planners have been dealing with for quite a while now, and the pandemic has given us a move in the right direction. We were forced to organise online events, which have a very low carbon footprint. Not only that, but the planning stage was also through virtual advance meetings and so proved to have zero to none impact on the environment. It was possible to design events without the need for hardcopy invitations or printed programmes, for instance. No paper was wasted. Keep working in this direction; the goal could be zero paper waste in events through the use of QR codes, online documents, etc.

31. Adapt and align rites, ceremonial elements, and processes that were established decades or centuries ago. This brand-new moment requires other methods and procedures for protocol rituals, but try to maintain the essence and purpose of them as much as possible.
32. Think through the various objectives of events and come up with a feasible, safe, alternative way of achieving it. Be creative and adaptive and go back to the basics to reimagine different ways of achieving goals. 'Thinking outside the box' and using common sense was never more vital than it was during this year of uncertainty.
33. Make sure the right speakers and participants are involved. Try to 'right-size' events to be sure they are not too long, and do not waste people's time. Have a clear goal or objective for meetings so people have a good reason to attend.
34. While technology continues to advance at the speed of light, we are losing the art of good living. The in-person service-oriented industry is becoming somewhat of a much-desired luxury. Being 'human' will always be sought after. People enjoy being around those of us who know how to make them feel comfortable while setting parameters for success. To stay in the game, we have to focus on these human skills.
35. Maintain regular contact with current stakeholders, even if there is no immediate need to communicate—so that when you do need something, the chance of a response is more likely. Possibly send them a small token of appreciation.
36. Reach out to potential new stakeholders by giving them a phone call, which is more personal than only contacting them by email.
37. Keep your social media networks relevant and regularly reach out to your most important contacts with individual messages.
38. Home office practices are likely to remain a common practice when physical presence is not required. However, deskless workers make up to 80 percent of the hospitality workforce, so make sure they do not feel disconnected from the rest of the organisation. They should not be ignored when it comes to the digital transformation.
39. Do not forget students, trainees, and fresh graduates, either. They are the future, and it is our duty to care for this profession—pandemic or not.
40. Protocol is more important than ever. It is difficult to say when life will return to normal. There may never be a full return to normalcy as we knew it before—certainly not if effective vaccines are not universally accessible and shared across the world. Our job as protocol officers in this kind of global crisis is to be as creative as we always have been,

applying that creativity to a constant re-imagining of the methods we use to achieve our organisation's goals. It falls to us, then, to apply our meticulous event planning skills to these new scenarios and to the new adapted methods of connecting so that our organisations can continue to build relationships and advance their agendas across cultural and international lines.

Authors' biographies

Mr Gilbert Monod de Froideville, Honorary Chamberlain and former Master of Ceremonies of Queen Beatrix of the Netherlands, founder of Protocol International, master trainer, consultant, lecturer and author

Having joined the professional army as a cavalry officer he occupied various posts in the operational sector. He was appointed instructor at the Cavalry Reserve Officer Cadet School in 1968. In 1973, he was posted to the Federal Republic of Germany where he served as squadron commander in a tank battalion.

He returned to the Netherlands and was appointed aide-de-camp to the commander-in-chief of the Royal Netherlands Army (also chief of the Royal Netherlands Army staff) from 1977 until 1981, when he was transferred to the RNLA personnel department. After several years in this department he was appointed aide-de-camp to the chairman of the NATO Military Committee in Brussels. He worked for more than three years in the office of the chairman taking care of the meetings and tours of the Military Committee and the military protocol.

On 1 December 1986 Gilbert Monod de Froideville was appointed aide-de-camp to HM Queen Beatrix of the Netherlands.

On 1 January 1988, he was appointed master of ceremonies to Queen Beatrix. On this date he left active military service and was appointed reserve lieutenant colonel.

During his time at the royal court he was responsible for:
- The organisation of all palace events, receptions, and presentation of honours and awards.
- All protocol affairs within the royal court, including the welcome and departure ceremonies for visiting heads of state, presentation of credentials, and wreath-laying ceremonies.
- All of the outgoing and incoming state visits.
- The implementation of protocol and training of staff at the royal household.

With almost nine years of service in the royal household Gilbert Monod de Froideville was posted to the protocol department of the ministry of Foreign Affairs and on 1 January 1997 was appointed head of the aspect management team, in charge of organising the Dutch presidency of the European Union.

Gilbert Monod de Froideville assumed his assignment as consul general of the Netherlands in Chicago in September 1997.

On 1 May 2001, Queen Beatrix re-appointed him master of ceremonies. During this time he organised all of the family celebrations, such as wedding anniversaries, three royal weddings, three state funerals and two baptisms.

He retired on 1 June 2007 and was appointed honorary chamberlain of Queen Beatrix of the Netherlands (now Princess Beatrix).

After his retirement in June 2007 he established his own consultancy 'Protocol International'.

As a specialist in the field of protocol, ceremonies, and project management, he advises and assists governments, international and private organisations in the preparation of national and international events and the organisation of ceremonies.

Moreover he teaches both individuals and groups in all matters concerning protocol and ceremonies such as cultural awareness, dining etiquette and seating arrangements, and provides specific training for young Dutch and foreign diplomats in the Netherlands and in other countries. In addition he delivers lectures on specific subjects.

Between September 2007 and the end of February 2009, he had the privilege and honour to work, together with Mark Verheul, in the Middle East as consultant and trainer for a royal court, an experience which provided him with valuable insights into the Middle Eastern culture.

He looked into the standard procedures of royal ceremonies, palace events and state visits, making assessments and advising the chief of royal protocol how to improve these procedures and implementations and trained the protocol department in international protocol.

In 2010, he was in charge of the organisation of the wedding of Their Royal Highnesses The Duke and The Duchess of Parma, Prince Carlos and Princess Annemarie de Bourbon de Parme in Brussels.

As director of his company, Protocol International, he has for many years performed as master trainer and advisor at the Institute of Protocol in The Hague and at the Protocol School of Washington. He delivers lectures on specific subjects in training courses for government agencies, international organisations, and corporations in the Netherlands and abroad.

During the COVID-19 pandemic, he acted as subject matter expert for different consultants in the Middle East.

He is also the co-author of *Nederlandse Titulatuur*, a practical handbook of forms of address in the Netherlands (2012).

Gilbert Monod de Froideville has been the recipient of a plethora of state honours (orders of chivalry) awarded to him by Austria, Belgium, Chile,

Finland, France, Iceland, Indonesia, Japan, Jordan, Lithuania, Luxembourg, the Netherlands, Norway, Portugal, Spain, Sweden, Thailand, and Venezuela.

Group picture with Gilbert Monod de Froideville and Mark Verheul after a three-day training programme in Thimphu, Bhutan, April 2017

Mr Mark Verheul, former Head of Protocol, City of The Hague, and founder of Mark Verheul - International Protocol & Strategic Networking

For more than 1.5 decade Mark Verheul's career has been focused on protocol, diplomacy, event management, and strategic networking on local, national and international levels and has brought him to five continents. In different occupational capacities he has been involved in coordinating state and official visits, conferences with foreign dignitaries, royal weddings and christening ceremonies, round table discussions and high-level one-on-one meetings, (inter-) national commemorations and celebrations, receptions, dinners and concerts, social, cultural and sports events as well as numerous business forums and university visits. Mark Verheul's expertise is combining content with logistics and hospitality.

In 2016 Mark Verheul established his own company: *Mark Verheul – International Protocol & Strategic Networking*. This training and consultancy firm delivers training programmes and professional consultancy to governments, international organisations, educational institutes and corporations as well as private training courses on international protocol and strategic networking. Projects have taken place in such cities as New York, Chicago, San Diego, Moscow, Kathmandu, Thimphu, Doha, Abu Dhabi, Riyadh, Lagos, Geneva, Madrid, Dublin, Brussels, Amsterdam, and The Hague.

In addition, Mark is active as a strategic adviser of stakeholder management for the National Committee for 4 and 5 May in Amsterdam. The National Committee helps determine how meaning is given to commemorating and celebrating the end of the Second World War and how to keep the memory of the Second World War alive. It organises the national observance of Remembrance Day on 4 May and the Liberation Day activities on 5 May. In 2019 and 2020, the Netherlands marked 75 years of freedom with a multitude of additional and virtual events.

In his most recent position as head of protocol of the City of The Hague (2010-2018), Mark Verheul was responsible for the external relations of the city executive with a wide variety of stakeholders in the governmental, diplomatic, social, corporate and academic world, and was advisor for all internal parties on matters related to protocol, intercultural communication, ceremonies, conferences and high-profile events. He also represented the city executive on a wide range of diplomatic events in order to strengthen the image of The Hague as international city of peace and justice.

Mark Verheul has previously worked as project coordinator in the office of the chief of royal protocol at the Royal Hashemite Court in Jordan (2008-2009), project assistant to the master of ceremonies at the royal household of the Netherlands (2005-2007) and was involved in many events and visits of the related royal families at home as well as abroad. From mid-2002 to early 2004 Mark was project manager at the *Protocolbureau* in The Hague. The Protocolbureau plans and develops official events, events with VIPs, and award ceremonies for companies and governmental organisations.

Mark Verheul studied at the Hotelschool The Hague (1999-2003) and obtained his Master's degrees in International Relations & International Communication at the Macquarie University in Sydney, Australia (2004-2005). He had internships at the front desk of Cliveden, a luxury country house hotel in the Thames Valley, United Kingdom (2000) and as public information assistant to the desk officer for EU institutions and Benelux countries at the United Nations Regional Information Centre for Western Europe in Brussels, Belgium (2005).

Mark Verheul was co-founder and first secretary of the Macquarie United Nations Society (MUNS) in Sydney, Australia (2004-2005). MUNS was founded to bring all facets of the UN to the attention of university students. On a regular basis, the board organised presentations by professors as well as prominent domestic and foreign guest speakers.

Mark Verheul has composed a remarkable number of manuals, reports and training programmes (including an on-line course for a world-renowned hotel consortium). He has given numerous lectures on intercultural communication, protocol and relationship management to colleagues, external clients and university students. Besides, Mark Verheul was member of the advisory board of the Institute of Strategic Relationship Management (2012–2017). The institute trains students and course participants to become professionals in relationship management. The courses combine an understanding of strategic networking with applied diplomacy, contemporary protocol management and modern organisational methods. Participants are diplomats, event organisers, protocol officers, and external relations managers.

In 2017 Mark Verheul joined the Supervisory Board of Holland Dance. The team of Holland Dance connects people worldwide through dance for over 30 years already. Its most important product is the world renowned Holland Dance Festival. During three weeks around 50 performances of internationally distinguished dance companies are presented. Variety, uniqueness and quality are guiding principles in the programming.

Mark Verheul has a strong interest in experiencing different cultures and nature, modern dance, wine tastings and culinary discoveries, classical concerts, contemporary art, visiting family and friends, and travelling (he has visited some 75 countries around the world).

Mark Verheul has been the recipient of state honours (orders of chivalry) awarded to him by Germany, Luxembourg, and the Netherlands.

Bibliography

Berman, M. & Sok, J. (2009). *Welkom! Gastvrijheid, de sleutel tot success.* Baarn: Tirion.

Clinton, H.R. (2000). *An Invitation to the White House: At Home with History.* New York: Simon & Schuster.

Encyclopedia *Grote Winkler Prins* (1968). Amsterdam / Brussel: Elsevier, 7th edition.

Federal Foreign Office (2003). *Visits to Germany by State Guests.* Berlin: Federal Foreign Office – Protocol.

Fernandez, F. (2004). *Ceremonial y protocolo: Guia complete.* Madrid: Oberon.

French, M.M. (2010). *United States Protocol, The Guide to Official Diplomatic Etiquette.* Lanlam: Rowman & Littlefield Publishers, Inc.

Groot, de, H. (2013). *Protocol, Handboek voor de ceremoniemeester.* Den Haag: Sdu Uitgevers.

Groskamp-ten Have, A. (2000) (geheel herzien door Reinildis van Ditzhuyzen). *Hoe hoort het Eigenlijk?* Bloemendaal: Becht.

Guyot, P.C.G. (1858). *Bijdragen voor vaderlandsche geschiedenis en oudheidkunde, Xe deel.*

Hardman, R. (2007). *A Year with the Queen.* New York: Simon & Schuster.

Hartmann, J. (2007). *Staatszeremoniell.* Berlin: Carl Heymanns Verlag.

Hayes, John G. (1994). Global quality leadership: A protocol perspective. *Business America, Vol. 115 Issue 10.* ATE

Heert, C. baron van (1965). *Nederlandse en buitenlandse Ridderorden en Onderscheidingen.* Amsterdam: Agon Elsevier.

Hickey, R. (2008). *The Protocol School of Washington's Honor & Respect: The Official Guide to Names, Titles, and Forms of Address.* Columbia, South Carolina: The Protocol School of Washington.

Jarrett, M. (2014). *The Congress of Vienna and its Legacy, War and Great Power Diplomacy after Napoleon.* New York: I.B. Tauris & Co. Ltd.

Jehaes, B. & Panneels, Y. (2002). *Protocol praktisch, De kunst van het hoffelijk aanspreken, corresponderen en organiseren.* Antwerpen: The House of Books.

King Abdullah II of Jordan (2011). *Our Last Best Chance, A Story of War and Peace.* New York: Viking.

Makarczyk, J. and others (1984). *Essays in International Law in Honour of Judge Manfred Lachs.* The Hague: Martinus Nijhoff Publishers.

La Red, *EHBN: Eerste Hulp Bij Netwerken.* Taiko 2008-2012, 2015.

LoCicero, J. (2008). *Meeting and Event Planning.* Avon: Adams Media.

Lovette, L.P. (1960), *Naval Customs Traditions and Usages, 4th ed.* Menasha, Wisconsin: Banta Co.

McCaffree, M.J. & Innis, P. & Sand, R.M. (2002). *Protocol 25th Anniversary Edition: The Complete Handbook of Diplomatic, Official and Social Usage.* Washington, D.C.: Devon Publishing Company, Inc.

Muller, D.G. (1862). *De oorsprong der Nederlandsche vlag, opnieuw geschiedkundig onderzocht en nagespeurd.* Amsterdam.

Nickson, D. & Siddons, S. (2006). *Project Management Disasters & how to survive them.* London: Kogan Page.

Plischke, E. (1958). *Summit diplomacy; personal diplomacy of the President of the United States.* College Park: University of Maryland.

Protocol and Liaison Service United Nations Office at Geneva (2004). *Guidelines on Diplomatic Courtesy in Geneva.* Geneva.

Queen Noor of Jordan (2003). *Leap of Faith, Memoirs of an Unexpected Life.* New York: Talk Miramax Books.

Queensland Government, Department of the Premier and Cabinet (2009). *Protocol Handbook, A Guide for the Queensland Government Officers.* Queensland.

Radde Ph.D., P.O. (2009). *Seating Matters, State of the Art Seating Arrangements.* Longmont: Thriving Publications.

Sennett, R. (2013). *Together, the rituals, pleasures & politics of cooperation.* London: Penguin Books.

Serres, J. (1992). *Manuel Pratique de Protocole, Nouvelle Édition.* Courbevoie: Éditions de la Bièvre.

Shevchenko, V.N. and others (2000). *Protocol of the Russian Federation.* Moscow: Vagrius Publishers.

Sierksma, K.L. (1963). *Vlaggen, symbool-traditie-protocol.* Bussum: C.A.J. van Dishoek Publisher.

The Economist, *The World in 2021*, edition of 13 November 2020. London: The Economist Group

Transition Center Foreign Service Institute U.S. Department of State (2005). *Protocol for the Modern Diplomat.* Washington, DC.

United Nations Institute for Training and Research (2014). *Course Syllabus United Nations Protocol.* New York, November–December 2014.

Visser, D. (1995). *De Nederlandse vlag in heden en verleden.* Amsterdam: De Bataafse Leeuw.

Winq, January / February 2015 edition. Amsterdam: Winq Media BV.

Zamoyski, A. (2011). *De ondergang van Napoleon en het Congres van Wenen.* Amsterdam: Uitgeverij Balans.

Websites

21-gun salutes: www.en.wikipedia.org/wiki/21-gun_salute
Arlington National Cemetery: www.arlingtoncemetery.mil
British Monarchy: www.royal.gov.uk
Coronavirus: Captain Tom Moore awarded knighthood for NHS fundraising: www.bbc.com/news/uk-england-beds-bucks-herts-52732300
Developments in Protocol: www.diplomacy.edu/books/mdiplomacy_book/goldstein/goldstein.htm
Diplomatic Partnerships: www.state.gov/s/cpr/c35648.htm
Event sustainability management systems — Requirements with guidance for use by ISO: www.iso.org/obp/ui/#iso:std:iso:20121:ed-1:v1:en
Flags and flag etiquette: www.everything2.com/user/Kallen/writeups/Flags+and+flag+etiquette
Flags half mast: www.nl.wikipedia.org/wiki/halfstok
Flags of the world: www.nl.wikipedia.org/wiki/vlaggen_van_de_wereld
Flying Flags in the United Kingdom: A Guide to Britain's Flag Protocol: www.flaginstitute.org
Guideline Sustainable Events by University of Zurich and Swiss Federal Institute of Technology Zurich: www.sustainability.uzh.ch/dam/jcr:162bc47e-435f-4dd6-9dc1-ed101dfe5547/201806_Guideline%20Sustainable%20Events_UZH.pdf
Official Dutch flag instruction: www.rijksoverheid.nl/onderwerpen/grondwet-en-statuut/vraag-en-antwoord/wanneer-kan-ik-de-vlag-uithangen-en-wat-is-de-vlaginstructie
Orders of precedence: www.en.wikipedia.org/wiki/Order_of_precedence
Precedence of representatives to the United Nations: note by the secretary-general: www.un.org/law/ilc/index.htm
Regalia: www.en.wikipedia.org/wiki/Regalia
Tokyo Olympic Games: Opening and closing ceremonies to be pared back: www.edition.cnn.com/2020/12/23/sport/tokyo-olympic-games-opening-closing-ceremonies-spt-intl/index.html
United Nations Correspondence Manual, A guide to the drafting, processing and dispatch of official United Nations communications: www.archive.unu.edu/hq/library/resource/UN-correspondence-manual.pdf

Illustrations and photographs

Page 9: HRH Prince Carlos de Bourbon de Parme / photograph by Jeroen van der Meyde
Page 16: *Le congrès de Vienne,* Jean-Baptiste Isabey / www.knaw.nl/nl/actueel/nieuws/tweehonderd-jaar-goede-internationale-omgangsvormen-de-betekenis-van-het-congres-van-wenen-1814-1815
Page 28: Professor Jaap G. de Hoop Scheffer / private collection of professor De Hoop Scheffer
Page 40: Order of precedence of Portugal / authors' private collection
Page 53: Dame Rosalyn Higgins, DBE, QC / www.balzan.org/en/prizewinners/rosalyn-higgins
Page 58: Ushers of the Protocolbureau / private collection of Protocolbureau
Page 60: English seating according to precedence, with gender differentiation / designed by Elmer Dumlao
Page 60: English seating with only a host / designed by Elmer Dumlao
Page 60: French seating according to precedence; with gender specification / designed by Elmer Dumlao
Page 60: French seating with only a host / designed by Elmer Dumlao
Page 61: English seating with head of state / designed by Elmer Dumlao
Page 61: English seating with host and co-host / designed by Elmer Dumlao
Page 62: French seating with host and guest of honour / designed by Elmer Dumlao
Page 62: Round table with couples, including guest of honour, opposite to each other / designed by Elmer Dumlao
Page 62: French seating with couples, including guest of honour / designed by Elmer Dumlao
Page 63: Two round tables with couples spread / designed by Elmer Dumlao
Page 64: French seating with host and hostess, with option for no women on end of table / designed by Elmer Dumlao
Page 64: English seating with couples, host and male 1 on head of table / designed by Elmer Dumlao
Page 64: Round table with couples, host and male 1 opposite each other / designed by Elmer Dumlao
Page 65: U-shape table with couples only on one side of the table / designed by Elmer Dumlao
Page 65: U-shape table with couples next to each other on all sides of the table / designed by Elmer Dumlao
Page 65: Horseshoe table with couples / designed by Elmer Dumlao
Page 66: State banquet with one long main table and four other long tables / designed by Elmer Dumlao
Page 66: Official delegation meeting, parties opposite each other / designed by Elmer Dumlao
Page 68: Overview room lay-out with tables numbered / designed by Elmer Dumlao
Page 69: Round table with couples, including guest of honour / designed by Elmer Dumlao
Page 70: Front row conference seating / designed by Elmer Dumlao
Page 71: Two blocks conference seating, centred / designed by Elmer Dumlao
Page 71: Two blocks conference seating, towards sidelines / designed by Elmer Dumlao
Page 72: Three blocks conference seating, centred / designed by Elmer Dumlao
Page 72: Three blocks conference seating, towards sidelines / designed by Elmer Dumlao
Page 72: Four blocks / designed by Elmer Dumlao
Page 75: Receiving line / designed by Elmer Dumlao

Page 76:	Procession order (number 1 is the host) / designed by Elmer Dumlao
Page 76:	Seating car driving right / designed by Elmer Dumlao
Page 76:	Seating car driving left / designed by Elmer Dumlao
Page 77:	Dr Abiodun Williams / private collection The Hague Institute for Global Justice
Page 86:	UN flag parade in the International Zone of The Hague / www.merkdenhaag.nl
Page 89:	Royal Standard of HM Queen Elizabeth II / www.wikipedia.org, *Royal Standard of the United Kingdom*
Page 89:	Personal flag of the president of the United States of America / www.wikipedia.org, *Flag of the President of the United States*
Page 89:	Mediaeval Banner / designed by Elmer Dumlao
Page 89:	Mediaeval Banner / designed by Elmer Dumlao
Page 90:	State banner of the Netherlands / www.koningsfan.dse.nl/troonswisseling.html, *Koninklijk Huisarchief, Ben Grishaaver* (*Universiteit Leiden*)
Page 91:	Flag elements / designed by Elmer Dumlao
Page 92:	Flag of Ethiopia / authors' private collection
Page 92:	Flag of the Arab Revolt / authors' private collection
Page 93:	Flag of the Arab Liberation / authors' private collection
Page 93:	Flag of Egypt / authors' private collection
Page 93:	Flag of the Czech Republic / authors' private collection
Page 94:	Flag of the Netherlands / authors' private collection
Page 96:	Dutch flag and orange pennant / authors' private collection
Page 100:	Flag of host country the Netherlands and flag of guest country Belgium / designed by Elmer Dumlao
Page 101:	Double sets of flags / designed by Elmer Dumlao
Page 101:	Flag of the Netherlands with the European flag / designed by Elmer Dumlao
Page 102:	Flag of guest country Canada and the flag of the host country United Arab Emirates / designed by Elmer Dumlao
Page 102:	Two flags crossed, Spain and Portugal / designed by Elmer Dumlao
Page 103:	Three flags, the Netherlands host country, second flag Belgium and third flag Spain / designed by Elmer Dumlao
Page 104:	Three flags, United States host country, followed by the flag of France and the flag of Germany / designed by Elmer Dumlao
Page 104:	Flying more than three flags in an uneven quantity, United Arab Emirates host country and centre position, other flags in alphabetical alternating right and left / designed by Elmer Dumlao
Page 105:	Flying more than three flags in an uneven quantity, United Arab Emirates host country followed by the other countries in alphabetical order / designed by Elmer Dumlao
Page 106:	Flying more than three flags in an even quantity, United Kingdom host country, other flags follow in alphabetical order / designed by Elmer Dumlao
Page 106:	Flying two or more flags on the left side of the forecourt of a building at an angle to the main entrance / designed by Elmer Dumlao
Page 107:	Flying two or more flags on the right side of the forecourt of a building at an angle to the main entrance / designed by Elmer Dumlao
Page 108:	Flags in a semicircle / designed by Elmer Dumlao
Page 108:	Flags in a full circle / designed by Elmer Dumlao
Page 109:	Flags in a full circle, clockwise / designed by Elmer Dumlao
Page 110:	American flag vertically against a wall / authors' private collection

ILLUSTRATIONS AND PHOTOGRAPHS 335

Page 110: Union Jack vertically against a wall / authors' private collection
Page 111: Flags on a podium, speaker's platform, example 1 / designed by Elmer Dumlao
Page 111: Flags on a podium, speaker's platform, example 2 / designed by Elmer Dumlao
Page 113: Vehicle of the president of the United States of America with U.S. flag and personal flag of the president / www.autoblog.nl
Page 113: Vehicle of HM Queen Elizabeth II with Royal Standard on top / www.autobody-fremont.com, photograph by S. Foskett
Page 113: Royal Standard of HM Queen Elizabeth II flying outside a cockpit / www.inpho.ie, *Morgan Tracy, 513062*
Page 114: Royal Standard of former Queen Beatrix of the Netherlands with black pennant / designed by Elmer Dumlao
Page 117: Flag of the Netherlands with backpack / authors' private collection
Page 117: Mr François Brunagel / private collection of Mr Brunagel
Page 124: Composition of invitations / authors' private collection
Page 132: American invitation (dating from 2010) for a reception hosted by President Obama / https://naglrep.files.wordpress.com/2013/06/wh-pride-invite.jpg
Page 137: British invitation (dating from 2014) for a garden party hosted by Queen Elizabeth II / http://sandyman.tv/adminlogin/images/omega_423118.jpg
Page 137: German invitation (dating from 2012) for a garden party hosted by Federal President and Mrs Schadt / http://ein-letzter-wunsch.de/buergerfest-des-bundspraesidenten/
Page 138: French invitation (dating from 2014) for a reception hosted by President Hollande / www.genealogie22.org/fr/IMG/jpg/invitation_elysee.jpg
Page 139: British invitation (dating from 2011) for the marriage of HRH Prince William of Wales with Miss Catherine Middleton / http://img2.timeinc.net/people/i/2011/news/110228/prince-william-invitation-320.jpg
Page 141: White Tie / designed by Elmer Dumlao
Page 142: Ball Gown / designed by Elmer Dumlao
Page 143: Black Tie / designed by Elmer Dumlao
Page 144: Short Evening Dress / designed by Elmer Dumlao
Page 145: Morning Dress, Jacquet, Cut-away / designed by Elmer Dumlao
Page 146: Formal Day Wear, Morning Dress, Afternoon Dress / designed by Elmer Dumlao
Page 147: Informal, Dark Suit, Business Suit, Lounge Suit, Tenue de Ville / designed by Elmer Dumlao
Page 148: Cocktail Dress, Long Skirt / designed by Elmer Dumlao
Page 149: Ladies Business Suit / designed by Elmer Dumlao
Page 150: Business Casual, Smart Casual / designed by Elmer Dumlao
Page 151: Ladies Smart Casual, Business Casual / designed by Elmer Dumlao
Page 152: Professor Olivier Arifon / private collection of professor Arifon
Page 164: Composition of state decorations / authors' private collection
Page 169: Exchange of honours between HM Queen Beatrix of the Netherlands and the late Sultan of Oman, HM Qaboos bin Said Al Said / photograph by Robin Utrecht, ANP
Page 172: White tie with full decorations / designed by Elmer Dumlao
Page 174: Example of miniatures on white tie / authors' private collection
Page 175: Buttonhole decoration, grade of officer / authors' private collection
Page 175: Example of batons on uniform / authors' private collection
Page 176: HE Mr José de Bouza Serrano / private collection of HE Mr De Bouza Serrano
Page 182: Torchbearer arrives at Opening Ceremony Olympic Games London 1948 / private collection of Mr Andrea Miliccia

Page 201:	Presentation of Credentials at Noordeinde Palace / photograph by Frank van Beek, Rotapool
Page 217:	Mr Andrea Miliccia / private collection of Mr Miliccia
Page 224:	Ushers preparing for an event / private collection of *Protocolbureau*
Page 236:	Jeroen Koks, Ruben Nederpel and Ivo van Vliet / photograph by David de Haan
Page 239:	Mr Jean Paul Wijers / private collection of *Protocolbureau*
Page 244:	Inspection of the guard of honour by the former President of the Republic of Lebanon, HE Mr Michel Sleiman, at his state visit to the President of Brazil / private collection of Mr Lahoud
Page 245:	Mr Lahoud Lahoud / private collection of Mr Lahoud
Page 248:	HM King Abdullah II welcomes HH Pope Benedict XVI to Jordan / photograph by Stefano Spaziani, Vatican Pool
Page 257:	Mr Martin van Pernis / private collection Mr Van Pernis
Page 268:	Dancers of New Zealand dance company Black Grace / private collection Mr Samuel Wuersten
Page 269:	Mr Samuel Wuersten / private collection Mr Wuersten
Page 272:	The Queen confers the honour of Knighthood on Captain Sir Thomas Moore / photograph by Chris Jackson, Getty Images
Page 274:	G20 Summit in Riyadh, 21-22 November 2020 / Anadolu Agency, Getty Images
Page 281:	Stewart Wheeler on one of his bicycle diplomacy visits / private collection of Stewart Wheeler
Page 290:	WFP Headquarters, Rome, Italy, 10 December 2020. Mr. David Beasley, Executive Director of the United Nations World Food Programme, received the Nobel Peace Prize awarded to WFP in 2020. Ms. Lisa Pelletti Clark, Co-President, International Peace Bureau Nobel Peace Laureate 1910, delivered the prize on behalf of the Nobel Peace Prize Committee. / photograph by Rein Skullerud, WFP
Page 298:	Setup of Council Chamber at Palais des Nations, using a socially distanced seating arrangement / private collection of David Chikvaidze
Page 302:	Al Wasl Plaza at Expo 2020 Dubai site / photograph by Dany Eid, private collection of Expo 2020 Dubai
Page 312:	Seating with host and guest of honour / designed by Elmer Dumlao
Page 312:	Seating with couples, including guest of honour / designed by Elmer Dumlao
Page 314:	National observance of Remembrance Day, Amsterdam, 4 May 2013 / photograph by Koen van Weel, ANP
Page 314:	National observance of Remembrance Day, Amsterdam, 4 May 2020 / photograph by Patrick van Emst, ANP
Page 322:	Mr Gilbert Monod de Froideville and Mr Mark Verheul / authors' private collection
Page 325:	Group picture with Gilbert Monod de Froideville and Mark Verheul after a three-day training programme in Thimphu, Bhutan, April 2017 / authors' private collection

In case one feels that the authors did not give attention to certain resources, the authors would welcome input, comments, and suggestions for inclusion in future editions. Please mail to: gilbert@protocol-int.com or info@markverheul.com.

Index

1984 154
3zProtocol 12
55 Days at Peking 156

Aachen 49
Abbasid's 93
Abdullah II, HM King 248, 251
Abu Dhabi 198, 326
Accession to the throne 48, 207
Accolade 272
Account manager 67, 226, 228, 241-242
Accra 29, 285
Accreditation date 41, 52
ADC 216
Admission card 129, 140
Advisory Commission 34-35
Aelst, Marcel P. van 291
Afghanistan 34, 299
Africa 25, 68, 92, 303
African culture 24
African-American 216
Afternoon dress 146
Age 23, 48-49, 59, 67, 119
Aide-de-camp 200-201, 216, 323
Air Force One 114
Airplane 112, 192
Ajuda Palace 178
Al Maktoum, Mohammed bin Rashid 301
Albania 30-31
All Souls' day 167
Allies 41, 161
Alphabet 31, 49, 51
Alphabetical order 13, 31, 44, 49-51, 73, 99, 104-109, 174, 219, 253, 275
Alternate 49, 71, 88, 107
Alumni 308-309
Ambassador 13-14, 19, 23, 41-42, 44-47, 50, 56, 67, 81, 117, 127, 131, 138, 156, 160, 171, 176-177, 186-189, 192-193, 198-203, 214, 225, 254, 275, 277, 281-282, 284-285, 290, 294, 299, 311-31, 316
Ambassador-at-large 50
Ambiguity 153, 155, 158-159
Amorim, Pedro 279-280
Amsterdam 28, 197-198, 207, 212, 218, 252, 291, 313-316, 326
Angelo, Janine D' 289
Anglo-German 120
Anglo-Saxon 153
Ankara 198
Annan, Kofi 77-78
Anniversary 118, 138, 261, 311-312
Announcement 125-126, 233, 260, 287
Annual meeting 70, 79, 214

Ante-room 79
Anthem 22, 27, 30, 32, 119, 121, 179, 183, 193-195, 200, 209, 219, 288, 315
Anthropological perspective 152
Antwerp 218
Applause 270
Arab League 51, 99
Arab Liberation, flag of 93
Arab Revolt, flag of 92-93
Arab states 246
Arabic 12, 99, 110
Arafat, Yasser 118-119
Archbishop 48, 206
Argentina 44-48, 51, 63, 212, 276
Arifon, Olivier 13, 152
Aristocracy 125
Arlington National Cemetery 197-198, 208
Armed forces 46-47, 90, 183, 193, 197, 203, 213-214, 315
Armoured car 37, 196
Arrival ceremony 185-187, 190-193, 195-196, 198, 208
Arrival 23, 30, 42, 56, 75, 88, 98, 129, 177, 183, 186, 191-193, 199, 205, 215, 219, 221, 226-230, 233-234, 238, 255, 261, 263, 270, 311
Arthur, King 59
ASEAN 51
Asia 21-22, 24, 63, 68, 152, 165, 245, 261
Assembly 45, 49-51, 53, 73, 78-80, 118, 135, 178, 184, 188, 195, 207, 215, 245, 284, 298, 307
Athens 218
Atmosphere 81, 187, 229, 231, 234-235, 246, 249, 251, 306
Attendee 19, 59, 67, 71, 73-75, 196, 198, 241, 245, 278, 287, 291, 301, 304, 308-309, 317-318
Attitude 156, 278, 286
Audience 22, 59, 74, 78, 111, 136, 154, 168, 191, 200-202, 209, 214, 226, 231-232, 245-246, 251, 255, 270, 274-275, 280, 285, 288, 290, 307, 309, 316-318
Australia 25, 33, 44-48, 51, 110, 126, 151, 277-278, 316, 326-327
Austria 41, 258, 324
Authentic 225, 249
Authorities 9, 17, 23, 41, 46, 73, 79, 101, 118, 165, 170, 188, 190, 192-193, 196, 198, 205-206, 216, 222, 239, 283-284, 288, 294, 311, 318
Authority 87, 95, 109, 184, 187, 197, 206, 208, 215, 219-220
Autonomy 51
Aux Morts, bugle call 198
Avennes Émile Prisse d' 18
Award 35, 89, 167-168, 170, 173, 184, 240, 277, 288, 323-324

Backstage 316
Ball gown 142
Baltic States 33, 36
Ban, Ki-moon 77-78, 121
Banners 87, 89-90, 115, 168, 195
Banquet 59, 66, 69, 134, 140, 171-174, 178-179, 187, 253, 291
Baron 42, 47
Baronets 47
Bath, Order of the 47
Batik 151
Battery 210, 213
Battlefield 87
Bearers of high honours 47
Beatrix of the Netherlands, HM Queen 21, 97, 114, 121, 169, 239, 323-324
Beijing 213, 217, 261, 282, 310
Belgium 34, 44-47, 50, 63, 100, 103, 119, 167, 204, 207, 215, 245, 316, 324
Bends, flag element 91
Benedict XVI, HH Pope 248
Beneficiary 55
Benefit performance 270
Berlin 200, 212, 218
Berline carriage 200
Bharat Ratna 47
Bicameral legislature 45
Bicycle diplomacy 281
Biden, Joe 275, 310
Black pennant 91, 114
Black tie 133, 139, 143-146, 172, 191
Block 59, 71-74
Board of directors 171, 228, 257, 263, 291
Body language 24
Border, flag element 91
Borgiani, Giovanni Battista 287
Bosnia 77-78
Bourbon de Parme, HRH Prince Carlos de 9, 13
Bouza Serrano, José de 176-177
Brady, Stephen 277
Branches of government 45
Brazil 44-48, 63, 79, 104, 213, 217, 279-280
Breaking the flag 98
Break-out rooms 317
Brielle 94
British Empire, Order of the 47
Brunagel, Francois Joseph 117
Brussels 37, 99, 152, 176, 180, 202, 217, 258, 323-324, 326
Buckingham Palace 69, 114, 134, 168, 220
Bundesländer 46
Burial 112, 204-205
Bush shirt 151
Bush, George 32, 71
Business casual 150-151
Business suit 147, 149-150, 172
Business 11, 17-18, 23-25, 36, 48, 67, 77, 81, 166-167, 186, 226, 239, 264-266, 273-274, 276, 283, 285-287, 289, 292-294, 297, 304, 308, 319, 325

Butera, Patricia 278
Buttonhole decoration 172, 175

Cabinet 43, 46-47, 96, 117-118
Caligiuri, Francisco 276
Caliphate 93
Calling card 75
Canada 22, 44-48, 51, 63, 88, 102, 104, 209, 275, 280, 282, 316
Cannon 208
Canterbury 48, 206
Canton 46
Canton, flag element 91, 109-110
Capital 47, 51, 170-171, 190, 202, 205, 213, 290
Car convoys 178-179
Car standard 112
Carabinieri 192, 215
Carbone, Dr 125
Cardinal 20, 48
Caste system 48
Cathcart, British representative 41-42
Catholic Church 41, 118, 167, 183
Celebration 71, 128, 131, 138, 184, 186-187, 209, 218, 261, 288, 312-313, 324-325
CEO 36, 48, 67, 237, 242, 252-253, 257, 261, 279
Ceremonial funeral 205
Ceremonial guard 212, 214
Ceremony 11, 21-23, 25-26, 30, 32-33, 35, 43, 75, 97, 112, 118-121, 129, 138, 165, 167, 171, 177-178, 182-188, 190-202, 204-210, 213-215, 217-220, 239, 251, 272, 276-277, 282, 288-290, 307, 313, 315, 319
CFO 263-264
Chairman of Government 193-194
Chairman of the Civil Honours Advisory Commission 34
Chairman of the High Council of Nobility 47
Chairperson-in-office 28
Chamber of commerce 48
Chamberlain 200-201
Championship 295
Chancellor of the Netherlands Orders of Knighthood 35, 47
Chancellor 48
Chargé d'affaires 199
Charles, HRH Prince 121
Charlie Hebdo 216
Charter of the United Nations 50, 54, 57
Chatham House rule 82
Checklist 232, 254
Chevron, flag element 91
Chief financial officer 263
Chief justice 46, 253
Chief of protocol 14, 133, 176, 192-193, 203, 217, 245, 249, 254, 280-281, 283
Chief of the Military House 43, 204
Chief rabbi 48
Chikvaidze, David 298
China 25, 33, 165-166, 184, 209, 213, 245, 261, 282

INDEX
339

Chi-Rho emblem 87
Chivalric orders 167-168
Chopsticks 283
Choreography 179, 270
Christian representative 47
Chronological order 51
Church of England 206
Churchill, Sir Winston 26, 205
CIA 46
City flag 98-99, 103, 107, 112
City hall 136, 178
Civil and Military Houses of the President of the Republic 177-179
Civil service 43, 245, 251
Civil society 82, 152, 294, 306
Class system 42
Classic protocol 240
Claus, HRH Prince 22
Client 52, 67, 73, 220, 226, 242, 253, 258-262, 265, 278, 285-287, 310, 319, 327
Clinton, Hillary 121, 133
Coats of arms 41, 87
Cocktail dress 148
Codes of conduct 17-18
Coffin 112, 204-205
Cogan, Charles 160-161
Cognitive 158
Co-host 60-63, 68, 228-229, 231, 234, 249, 255, 263
College of Arms 88
Colours 89-94, 144-146, 148-149, 151, 166
Colours, the 90, 195
Columbus, Christopher 9
Comb plan 65
Comillas Pontifical University 12
Comitas 19
Commander of the armed forces 46-47
Commander of the Honour Guard 170, 195, 200
Commission for Precedence According to Protocol
Commonwealth 50, 110, 209
Company flag 98
Comparable rank 54-55, 66
Computer screen 309
Conference call 281, 301
Conference 11, 29-30, 33, 52, 70-72, 83, 137, 225, 232, 234, 245-246, 276, 282, 291, 297-301, 303, 307-309, 317-318, 325-326
Confirmation 128-129, 169, 232-233
Conflict prevention 77-78
Congo 49
Congress of Aix-la-Chapelle 49
Congress of Vienna 41, 73, 199
Constantine, Roman emperor 87
Constitutional monarch 190
Contactless 284
Convention on Privileges and Immunities of the United Nations 53-55
Cordon 172
Corona toolkit 293

Corona 272, 294, 311, 313
Corporate world 9, 229, 251-252, 256
Cortege 75-76
Coucher 20
Council of Europe 28, 44, 117
Council of Ministers 49, 217, 313, 315
Counsellor 54
Count of Barcelona 180
Counts of Holland 93-94
County of Holland 93
Court etiquette 19
Court of Justice of the European Union 45, 120
Court of Louis XIV 59, 78, 152
Courtesy 18-19, 42, 52, 63, 76, 121, 176, 179, 186-187, 189-191, 271
Courtier 19-20, 155
Couturier 73
COVID-19 12, 14, 26, 60, 272-321
Cravat 146
Cravate blanche 141, 171
Cravate noir 143
Creative sector 252
Creativity 12, 14, 122, 217, 273-274, 279, 295, 297, 310, 321
Credentials, presentation of 23, 41-42, 49, 131, 145, 184, 186-188, 199-203, 275, 290, 323
Criscione, Giovanni 301
Croatia 30, 152
Crossbeam 89
Crown Equerry 204
Crowned head of state 48-49
Crowning 51, 188, 206
Cultural awareness 246, 324
Cultural differences 23-24, 235, 254, 266, 279
Cultural intelligence 278, 303
Cultural return event 22
Cultural sector 17, 36, 136, 252
Culture 10-11, 17-18, 20, 22-24, 26, 32, 34, 36, 82, 151, 155, 158, 165-166, 183-185, 197, 221, 226, 237, 249, 251, 256, 258, 266, 275, 278, 295-296, 304, 324, 327
Curalia 19
Curriculum vitae 254
Customer 251, 259-262, 264-265, 286-287, 292
Cut-away 141, 145
Czech Republic 93, 135, 204

Dame 53
Dance event 237-238, 270
Dance festival 238, 269-270, 327
Dark suit 147
Database 259-260
Dean of the diplomatic corps 41, 44, 56
Debriefing 234
Deceased 112, 115, 204-205
Decentralisation 83
Decision-maker 82-83, 294
Decorations 11, 23, 134, 141-143, 164, 166, 169, 171-172, 174-175, 178-179, 183, 187, 190-191

Defence 46, 258, 264
Delaware 50
Delegation 22, 28-30, 32-33, 66, 69, 74, 80, 83, 109, 119, 165-166, 179, 185, 187, 189, 191, 194, 196, 198-199, 207, 217, 252, 283-284, 289, 311
Delft 205, 210, 293
Denmark 63, 116, 168, 173, 176, 199-200, 206, 209, 292
Departure ceremonies 23, 183, 187, 190-191, 193, 195, 323
Departure 56, 73, 88, 178, 185-186, 195, 219, 221, 227, 230, 234, 255, 264, 270, 284
Deputy-registrar 54
Diana, Princess of Wales 114
Dies Natalis 138
Dietary restrictions 129, 311
Digital environment 290
Digital transformation 303-304, 320
Dignitary 80, 83, 177, 206, 255
Dining hall 229
Dinner jacket 143, 266
Dinner 19, 22-25, 33, 37, 61, 63, 65-69, 74-75, 81, 133-134, 140, 150, 166, 187, 190-191, 227, 229-231, 243, 249-251, 259, 261, 266, 277, 284, 317, 325
Diplomacy 10, 26-29, 31, 33-34, 49, 53, 78, 81-82, 84, 129, 152-155, 157-162, 217, 245, 251, 256, 280-281, 284, 304, 306, 317, 325, 327
Diplomat 21, 26, 34, 37, 41, 50, 56, 67, 78, 81-84, 152-153, 155-160, 162, 165, 171, 179, 187, 194, 240, 249-250, 252, 256, 273, 285, 315, 324, 327
Diplomatic attaché 179
Diplomatic community 126, 290, 294, 306
Diplomatic corps 41, 44, 56, 59, 73, 75, 127, 228, 250, 280
Diplomatic discourse 17, 33, 153, 158, 160, 162
Diplomatic etiquette 21
Diplomatic immunities 54
Diplomatic language 152-155, 158, 161-162
Diplomatic mission 54
Diplomatic partnerships 249-250
Diplomatic practice 153, 250
Diplomatic privileges 54
Diplomatic relations 9, 11, 17, 22-23, 26, 29, 55
Diplomatic skills 235
Diplomatic world 20, 29, 41, 165, 221
Director of state protocol 193-194, 202
Discourse 17, 33, 130, 153-155, 158-160, 162
Disinfection 283-284, 311
Display of flags 17, 23, 27, 95-98, 101, 105, 110-112, 114-115, 203, 221
Dispute 59
Dissimulation 155
Diversification 83
Doha 116, 326
Doors open 192
Double flagging 112
Doublespeak 152, 154-155, 158, 160, 162
Doyen 41

Dress code 11, 81, 125-129, 140-151, 171-173, 178, 266
Drive-in 280, 292
Drum rolls 200-201
Duchess 125, 324
Duke of Cambridge 167
Duke of Edinburgh 69, 134, 211-212
Duke 18, 41-42, 47, 69, 125, 134, 167, 211-212, 324
Dukedom 41
Dynasty 18, 42

East European countries 33
Eastern Europe 22
Echelon 226-229, 237-238, 249
Economic and Social Council 50
Economic mission 189
Edge of a flag 88-90
Edward III, HM King 168
Egeland, Jan 240
Egypt 21, 93, 200
Electronic invitation 126
Elephant, Order of the 173
Elias, Norbert 155-156
Elite 125, 218
Elizabeth II, HM Queen 89, 113-114, 137, 177, 205-206, 272
Eloquence 156, 161
Élysée Palace 285
Email 126, 128-130, 140, 255, 260, 295, 307-308, 320
Emblem 87-88, 128
Emeritus 28
Empire, Mongol 9
Encounter 225, 232, 234, 240, 249-250, 252, 270
Engaged couple 63
Engagement 11, 126, 215, 217, 226-227, 230, 249, 255, 273-274, 276, 278-281, 285-287, 293, 308-309, 317
England 99, 125, 166, 168, 174, 186
English arrangement 60
Engraving 19, 125
Entourage 35, 120, 170-171, 189, 193, 196, 200, 240
Environment / environmental 23-24, 37, 80-81, 221, 226, 246, 266, 274, 278, 288, 290, 300-301, 306, 319
Envoy 186, 199
Epistemic 83
Equal 46, 49, 51, 59, 107, 188, 208, 221
Equivalent 35, 63, 171
Erasmus, Desiderius 18
Esquire 127
Ethiopia 92
Ethno methodologist 157
Etiquette 17-21, 24, 26, 29, 37, 53, 121, 142, 155, 183, 269, 283, 285-286, 324
Euphemism 158
Eurocorps 119
Europe 22, 25, 34, 41, 119, 121, 125-126, 131, 141, 152, 156, 251, 261, 307, 326
European anthem 119

European Central Bank 118, 120
European Commission 44-45, 120
European Council 28, 49-50, 118, 120, 285
European Court of Auditors 118, 120
European culture 24
European Economic and Social
   Committee 117-118
European Economic Community 117
European flag 119
European monarchies 155, 240
European Parliament 44-45, 50, 117-121
European Union 45, 49-50, 99, 101, 117-118,
   120-121, 180, 273, 311, 323
Evaluation 230, 234-235, 255
Evening dress 134, 141-145, 172-173
Event manager 225-226, 242-243, 300
Exchange of decorations 169, 179, 190
Exchange of gifts 23, 165-166, 187, 190
Exchange of honours 35, 169-171, 196
Execution 119, 204, 225, 230, 233-235
Executive board 138-139, 171, 219, 289-290
Executive Office of the
   Secretary-General 78-80
Expectations 60, 67, 184, 221, 230, 233-234,
   308-309, 316
Expo 2020 Dubai 301-302
Exposure 233, 235
External stakeholders 226, 231
Eyring, Pamela 130

Face mask 282
Facebook 130, 285, 297
Face-to-face 256, 273, 279-280, 294, 297, 305,
   317
Family crest 19
FAO 51
Farewell 131, 226-227, 230, 255, 282
Fatimid 93
FBI 46
Fernández, Marina 297
Fesses, flag element 91
Festival 218, 236, 238, 269-270, 292, 327
Feyenoord 257, 264
Finland 99, 168, 204, 325
First Lady 140, 254
First Marshal of the Court 135
Flag applications 100-116
Flag carrier 109
Flag ceremony 30
Flag code 95-96
Flag element 91
Flag order 98-99, 105
Flag protocol 87-116
Flagpole 33, 88, 90, 97, 100, 102-103, 105-108, 112,
   114-116
Flags in a procession or parade 109
Flags on a car, bus or aircraft 112
Flowers 25, 165-167, 179, 192-193, 197, 216, 251,
   255, 315

Flying flags, fixed dates 96
Follow-up 178, 230, 234-235, 242-243, 255
Fontaine, Nicole 117-118
Food safety 291
Force majeure 292
Foreign community 191
Foreign national flag 98-99, 203
Formal day wear 146
Formal language 152-162
Formality 36, 59, 77, 80, 153, 238, 256
Former 43, 46-47, 92, 205, 212
Forms of address 19, 130-131, 227, 259, 324
Foster, Paul J. 218
Fouquères, Pierre de 179
Frack 141
France 9, 25-26, 37, 44-48, 63, 103-104, 117, 119,
   125, 152, 160-161, 167, 173, 198, 204, 209-210,
   213, 215, 245, 277, 284, 316, 325
Francis, HH Pope 121
Franklin D. Roosevelt Four Freedoms
   Award 240
French arrangement 60
French mandate 245
French Revolution 41-42
Friendship 67, 155, 187, 189, 221
Full evening dress 141
Functional 17, 59, 61, 76, 233, 238, 263
Functionaries 18, 27, 41, 43-44, 46-47, 49, 170, 204
Funeral 70-71, 112, 114-115, 145, 183, 186, 188, 197,
   204-205, 210, 212, 214, 239, 324

Gala 65, 139, 178, 191, 270, 289
Gama, Vasco da 9
Garden Party 137
Garter, Order of the 47, 168, 173
Gaulle, Charles de 179
GCC 99
Gendarmerie 213, 215
General Assembly 45, 49-51, 53, 73, 78-80, 135,
   245, 298, 307
General Debate 69, 79-80
Geneva 51-52, 298
Genocide 83
Geographical outreach 52
George Cross 47, 168
George VI, HM King 169, 205
Germany 24, 44-45, 47, 103-105, 119, 152, 193,
   212-213, 215, 257-258, 261, 292, 315-316, 323,
   327
Gesture 23, 25, 156, 192, 197, 208, 296
Ghana 28-29, 285
Gift(s) 11, 19, 23, 25, 35, 119, 165-167, 171, 178, 187,
   190, 197, 234, 239, 255, 282, 296, 309
Gift-giving 25
Give-away 230
Global quality leadership 256
Globalisation 68, 246
Glory 161
Gloves 119, 142, 146-147, 284, 312, 319

Goebbels, Joseph 154
Gold Star 167
Goldstein, Erik 70, 256
Goodwill ambassador 225
Government guesthouse 191
Government 11, 28, 36, 41, 43, 45-46, 53, 56, 79, 95, 118, 183, 185, 187-188, 204, 216, 219, 239, 250, 253, 256, 258, 279, 285, 290-292, 294, 298, 305, 308, 324, 326
Governor 46, 50-51, 88, 204, 210
Governor-general 133
Gracian, Baltasar 155
Grade 35, 168-170, 172, 174-175
Graduation ceremony 185
Grand Chamberlain 20
Grand Collar 168, 172
Grand Cordon 172-173
Grand Cross 35, 168, 170-172, 175
Grand Master 134, 200-201, 204
Grand Officer 168, 171, 173, 175, 245
Grand opening 251, 295
Grande Entrée 20
Grant Study, the 240
Grave of the Nation's Founder 190
Great Britain 41-42
Great powers 41
Greece 25, 99, 109, 158, 218, 245
Greek cross, flag element 91
Greeting 18, 23, 25-26, 75, 83, 192-193, 195, 198, 203, 227, 238, 282, 296, 305, 307, 318
Grooming 286
Guards of colour 193-194
Guest country 100, 102, 254
Guest list 68, 75, 126, 178, 185, 231, 235, 237, 253-254, 266, 279, 319
Guest of honour 60-62, 64, 68-71, 75-76, 100, 102, 226, 229, 234, 253, 263, 284, 296, 312
Guest 11, 17, 19-20, 22-25, 32, 37, 59-63, 65-70, 73-75, 98, 112-113, 119, 126, 129, 131-136, 139-140, 177-178, 180, 193-196, 208, 212, 215-217, 219-221, 226-232, 235-238, 242, 249-255, 259-260, 262-264, 266, 270-272, 278, 280, 282, 288, 291-292, 295-296, 300, 302, 304, 307, 309, 311-312, 317-319
Guestbook 190
Gulf Cooperation Council 99
Gulf rig 144
Gun salute 23, 192, 205, 208-212
Guyot, P.C. 94

Haiti 77-78
Half mast, flying flags 95, 97, 114-116, 209
Harvard 240
Hashemite 93
Hawaii 50
Head of delegation 199
Head of government 33, 190-191, 285
Head of international organization 45, 204-205
Head of mission 42, 199, 282

Head of protocol 32, 35-36, 79, 117, 119, 121, 262, 295, 301, 325-326
Head of State 24, 27, 41, 43-44, 50, 60-61, 68-70, 73, 75, 78-79, 88, 96, 109, 115, 120, 135, 165, 168, 172-173, 178-179, 186-200, 202, 204, 209-210, 212, 214-216, 219, 251, 275, 285, 290, 302, 313, 323
Head table 22, 65, 68, 70, 263
Health measures 278, 319
Health testing 293
Heerdt, C. Baron van 168
Height of a flag 88
Hellas 99
Heraldic colours 89
Heraldic flag 88
Heraldic symbols 87, 89
Heraldry 88, 169
Hickey, Robert 130
Hierarchical model 258
Hierarchy 20-21, 23, 26, 41, 43, 48, 67, 81, 174-175, 190, 199
Higgins, Dame Rosalyn 53
High commissioner on national minorities 138
High commissioner 50
High society 125
High-ranking 18, 20, 63, 67, 69, 76, 127, 156, 171, 176, 198, 205, 228-229, 233, 261
Hinduism 48
Hirohito, Emperor 70-71
His Excellency 127, 134
His Grace 127
His Holiness 41
His Worship 127
Historical relevance 43
Holbach, baron d' 155
Holland Dance 269-270, 327
Holy Father 178
Holy See, the 41-42, 176
Holyroodhouse, Palace of 168
Honour Escort 196, 214-215
Honour Guard 193, 195, 197, 204, 213-214, 313
Honourable 47, 120, 127
Honours 23, 34-35, 47, 117, 119, 165-175, 179, 183, 192, 196, 210, 212-213, 323-324, 327
Hoop Scheffer, Jaap G. de 28-29
Horizontal tricolour 91
Horseshoe-shape 65
Hospitality 11, 23, 187, 219-221, 227, 231, 234, 249-251, 265, 282, 320, 325
Host city 79, 135, 277
Host country 21-22, 24, 41, 50, 54-56, 69-70, 74, 79, 98-100, 102-106, 109, 178-180, 187, 189, 191-192, 195-196, 218-219, 221, 249, 298
Host 11, 22-23, 25, 30, 37, 49, 52, 60-71, 73-75, 112-113, 126-127, 131-135, 145, 170, 177, 188, 190, 192, 215-216, 226-232, 234-235, 242, 249-255, 263, 290, 296, 308, 312-313, 316
Hostess 60-65, 75, 126, 227-28, 230, 242, 251, 255, 262

INDEX   343

Hotel flag 103
Hotel industry 291
House of prayer 75
House of Representatives 28, 190, 236, 253, 315
Hove, Bartholomeus Johannes van 90
Hungary 116
Husband 62-63, 73, 131, 201, 252
Hybrid 273, 276-277, 282, 288, 291, 294-295,
    298-300, 304, 316-317
Hybridisation 280
Hygiene 283, 286, 291-292, 298, 319

IAEA 51-52
ICC 56-57
Iceland 63, 94, 325
ICJ 53, 57
ICRC 52
ICTY 56
Iftar 129, 252
ILO 51
IMF 45, 51
Immunity 55-56, 153
IMO 51
Inauguration 121, 183, 186, 188, 206-207, 210, 275
Incumbent 30, 206-207
Independence 87, 91, 184-185, 245
India 9, 44-48, 151-152, 209, 225, 275, 286-287
Individual 20, 41-42, 48, 59, 73-74, 82, 84, 88,
    96, 115, 127, 156-157, 160, 167, 169, 183, 203,
    207, 213, 233, 286, 288, 297, 324
Indonesia 151, 165, 325
Infection 303, 319
Informal 31, 81, 83, 126, 130, 147, 150, 202-203,
    229, 231, 251, 276, 286, 306
Initiation 206, 230-231
Innis, Pauline 203, 250
Innovation 82-83, 129, 218, 273, 279, 289, 311
Innovator 84
In-person 277, 281-282, 290, 294-295, 299, 304,
    306, 308-309, 318, 320
Insignia 168-169, 171-174
Inspection of the Honour Guard 32, 193,
    195-196, 199, 212, 244
Institute of Protocol The Hague 264, 324
Institute of Strategic Relationship Management 14, 239, 327
Institutional order 41
Instructions of Kagemni 18
Instructions of Ptahhotep 18
Insult 24-25, 27, 78, 161
Insurance policies 303
Interaction 26, 59, 67, 80, 82-84, 160, 271,
    276-277, 281, 285-286, 288, 296, 305, 308-310
Intercultural understanding 78
Interlocutor 157, 159, 161, 179
International agreement 21, 24, 56
International Court of Justice 44-45, 50, 53-57,
    189, 204
International Criminal Court 51, 56-57, 99

International Olympic Committee 218, 220, 310
International organisation 24, 43-45, 49-50, 52,
    73, 82, 88, 99-100, 115, 136, 138, 156, 204-205,
    285, 297, 304, 324, 326
International Sports Federation 219
International tender 258
Internet connection 300, 316
Internet revolution 239
Interpreter 37, 83, 310
Interpreting 298-300, 310-311, 317
Introductions 22, 195, 227, 229, 255
Investiture ceremony 272
Invitation 11, 69, 124-132, 137-140, 142, 145, 150,
    178, 185-186, 189-190, 201, 231, 233, 235, 255,
    259-260, 278, 283, 311, 315, 319
IOC 217, 219-220
Iran 154
Iraq 53, 161
Ireland 105, 204, 211
Iron Curtain 30
Iron List 253
Islamic community 48
Island casual 151
Israel 44-45, 48
Italy 9, 44-47, 119, 192, 204, 212-213, 215, 217,
    287-290
ITU 51

Jacquet 145
Japan 33, 70-71, 165-166, 168, 184, 325
Jesuit 155
John Paul II, HH Pope 118
Johnson, Boris 272
Jordan 275-276
Juan Carlos I, HM King 132-133
Jubilee 184, 208, 261, 312
Judicial organ 44, 57
Judiciary 43, 45
Juliana of the Netherlands, HM Queen 197
Jurisdiction 54-55, 63

Kennedy, John F. 189
Kenneth-Divine, Patricia 303
Keynote speaker 309
King 9, 18-20, 35, 51, 59, 97, 99, 114, 116, 125,
    132-135, 156, 167-169, 180-181, 188, 190, 197,
    200-201, 205-207, 209-210, 214-215, 240, 246,
    248, 251, 255, 271, 313-315
Kingdom 18, 42, 94, 119, 207
Kingston de Leusse, Martine 156
Klemperer, Victor 154
Knight Bachelor 272
Knight Grand Cross 168, 171-172
Knight 41, 47, 59, 168-172, 174, 210
Knights of the Golden Fleece 41
Koks, Jeroen 236
Kolla 21
Koningsdag 96-97
Koninklijke Marechaussee 192, 204

Koninkrijksdag 97
Kremlin 193-194, 202, 214
Kronborg Castle 210
Kumar, Manoj 286

Lachs, Manfred 189
Lady 69, 140, 204, 254
Lady-in-waiting 216, 314
Laeken 204
Lahoud, Lahoud 245
Language of diplomacy 152-155, 161-162
Language 18, 31, 37, 49-50, 59, 82-83, 99, 109, 128, 130, 153, 155-162, 174, 275, 279, 301, 310, 317
Larche Mele, Maryse 307
Large-scale 68, 205, 274, 276, 293, 311-312, 319
Large-sized enterprise 252-253
Last post, bugle call 197-198, 315
Latecomers 73
Latin Roman tradition 120
Launch of a business 251
Launch of a ship 185-186
Lautenslager, Leslie 304
Le Robert, dictionary 184
Leader of the opposition 45-46
Leader 11, 21, 51, 70-71, 79-80, 82, 89, 188, 193, 218, 225, 243, 251, 273, 282, 307
Lebanon 199-200, 244-246
Lecture 70, 282, 315, 324, 327
Left-hand traffic 76
Légion d'Honneur 117, 173
Legislature 45-46, 190-191
Legrand, Thomas 154
Length of a flag 88
Liberation Day 97, 313, 315-316, 326
Liberation 312-313, 315-316, 326
Liberté, Égalité, Fraternité 41, 216
Linguist 157
Linguistic ability 67
LinkedIn 255, 278, 294
Lintjesregen 34
Lisbon Treaty 120-121
Lisbon 179-180
Lithuania 192, 325
Litote 158
Local authorities 46, 79, 216, 239, 284, 311
LoCicero, Joe 251
Lockdown 275, 286-287, 291, 295, 313
London 21, 53, 182, 211-212, 217, 219
Long evening dress 142, 144-145, 172-173
Long skirt 144, 148
Lopes, Craveiro 177
Lord Steward 134
Lord 42, 47, 89, 125
Los Angeles 218
Lot 49, 73
Louis XIV, HM King 19, 59, 78, 152
Lounge suit 147
Lovette, L.P. 209
Lower house 45-46, 188, 207, 215

Loyal toast 22
Lunch 33, 61, 66-67, 69-70, 80, 121, 128, 132, 134-135, 178, 190-191, 231, 282, 311-312
Lutheran state church 206
Luxembourg 33, 63, 94, 325, 327

Macedonia 77-78
Madrid 179-180, 326
Malaysia 44-48, 51, 151
Malta 117, 204
Management of hospitality 23, 249
Management of relationships 21, 23
Managerial responsibility 43
Mandarin 12, 156
Mandate 43, 52, 120, 243, 245, 249
Marine One 114
Marquis 47
Married couple 61
Master of ceremonies 11, 75, 186, 200-201, 204, 239, 290, 323-324, 326
Master of the Household 134
Mausoleum of Mustafa Kemal Atatürk 198
Mayor 46-47, 51, 135-137, 170-171, 190, 198, 216, 242, 252, 254, 263, 285, 314
McCaffree, Mary Jane 203, 250
Medal of Honour 167-168, 170-171, 174
Medals 169, 218
Media 11, 101, 153, 162, 180, 232-234, 251, 253, 272
Mediaeval Banners 89
Mediation 83, 160, 299
Melbourne 219, 275
Member of an order 171
Member state 37, 45, 51, 69, 78-79, 117-121, 218, 298-299, 311
Memorial Day, National 97, 115, 198, 209
Merkel, Angela 32, 121
Mexico 213
Middle Ages 259
Middle East 11, 22-26, 34, 63, 68, 99, 102, 126, 165-166, 251, 261, 324
Middle Eastern culture 11, 24, 324
Mid-sized enterprise 253
Mikhailova, Gilana 294
Miliccia, Andrea 51, 217, 295
Military aircraft 192
Military District of Washington 205
Military Honours 119, 167, 179, 210, 213
Military police 171, 178
Military protocol 35, 183, 323
Military recognition symbols 88
Military top brass 46
Military William Order 47, 167
Miniature insignia 172
Miniatures 36, 172, 174
Minister of defence 198, 204, 213
Minister of foreign affairs 28-29, 33, 51, 54, 56, 69, 161, 170, 193, 202
Ministry of foreign affairs 43, 152, 159, 176, 245, 204-205, 323

INDEX 345

Mission 31, 34, 42, 50, 54-55, 78, 81, 115, 161, 177-180, 189, 199, 205, 213, 225, 231, 234, 249, 252, 261, 282, 305
Mistress of the robes 200-201
Misunderstanding 25, 81, 127, 157, 222, 235
Modern diplomacy 78, 81
Modern protocol 239-243
Monarch 18, 88-89, 155, 190, 205-207, 210-211, 214
Monarchy 42, 48-49, 155, 167-168, 189-190, 207-208, 211, 216, 240
Monod de Froideville, Gilbert 11, 239, 323-325
Monod de Froideville, Olivier 292
Moore, Sir Thomas 272
Morning coat 145
Morning dress 145-146
Morocco 199-200
Mother tongue 153
Motorcade 30, 79, 121, 193, 196, 204, 215, 261
Motorcycles 129, 194, 196, 203-204
Mõtsla, Anu 283
Movement 226-229, 280, 284
Muhammad, Prophet 92
Muller, D.G. 93
Multinational 48, 73, 139, 171, 252, 258, 294
Munich 257-258
Muslim 166, 296
Mutual interest 67, 229, 249-251, 256
Mutual understanding 83, 249-250, 282

Namaste 282
Nametag 233
Napoleon, Lodewijk 207
Napoleonic Wars 41
National Administration Press 12
National anthem 22, 27, 30, 32, 121, 183, 193-195, 200, 209, 219, 288, 315
National bank 48
National Committee for 4 and 5 May 326
National day 29, 115-116, 128, 131, 186, 209
National dress 134, 140
National flag 74, 94-95, 97-108, 110-112, 114-116, 195, 203, 246, 315
National government 43, 46
National identity 88, 183
National legislature 190
National monument 190, 197-198, 313, 315
National mourning 116, 206, 234
National Olympic Committees 218, 220
National organisation 47, 259, 285, 297, 304, 324, 326
NATO 28-37, 44-45, 49-51, 258, 307-308, 323
Nazi regime 154
Nederlandse titulatuur 324
Nederpel, Ruben 236
Negotiation 26, 54, 82, 154, 157, 159-160, 187, 189, 256, 289, 306-307, 310, 317
Neighbour 50, 189, 265, 281
Neighbourhood 116

Netherlands 9, 19, 22, 25, 28, 35, 44-49, 54-57, 63, 90, 93-94, 96, 99-101, 103-104, 112, 114-116, 119, 134, 136-139, 167, 188, 192, 196-198, 200-201, 204, 207, 210, 212-213, 215-216, 225, 252, 257-258, 265, 292, 312-313, 316, 323-327
Network event 136, 231, 239, 241-243
Network 23, 225-226, 230, 240, 243, 252, 260, 294, 303, 310
Networking strategy 141-142
New York 79-81, 135, 216, 307, 326
New Zealand 33, 44-48, 63, 126, 133, 268, 316
Newspeak 154
NGO 43, 52, 67, 84, 254, 299, 317
Nicholson, Harold 225
Niehe, Eric 225
Nieuwe Kerk, Amsterdam 207, 210, 264
Nobel Peace Prize 120, 289-291
Nobility 19, 42, 47, 167
Noble families 43
Noble title 42
Non-military 52
Non-ranking partner 63
Noor, HM Queen 252
Noordeinde Palace 11, 134, 200-201, 204, 210, 212
Norpois, Marquis de 160
North Atlantic Council 28, 30
Northwest Europe 261
Norway 63, 94-95, 168, 200, 289, 316, 325
Note verbale 130
Nuclear Security Summit 11, 137, 233
Nuncio 41, 44-45

Oath, swears on 206-207
Obeng, Afua 285
Off-campus 81
Officer 171, 174, 177, 326
Official dinner 23, 66-67, 69
Official visit 21-23, 118, 165-166, 175, 180, 189, 191, 194, 214-215, 270, 283, 325
Offline 279, 293
OHCHR 51
OK-sign 25
Olympia 218
Olympic closing ceremony 218-219
Olympic flag 99, 218-219
Olympic Games 51, 99, 109, 182, 185, 217-221, 275, 310
Olympic opening ceremony 182, 217-220
Olympic protocol 218-219, 221
Olympic stadium 219-220
Olympic village 221
Olympic Winter Games 217
Oman 168-169
Online 273, 276-277, 280, 282, 285-291, 293-295, 297, 306-307, 310, 312, 315-319
Orange pennant 90, 96-97
Orange-Nassau, Order of 35, 257, 269
Orb 207
Order of flags 99, 105, 240

Order of precedence 18, 40-52, 57, 67, 76, 120, 199, 221, 301
Order of procession 23, 59, 75-76
Organisation chart 232
Organisational flag 98, 115
Organization of American States 45, 100
Ortiz Pamplin, Rubén 300
Orwell, George 154
OSCE 28-30, 33
Oskam, Eva 306
Oslo 120

Pakistan 44-48
Pales, flag element 91
Palestinian Authority 119
Pall, flag element 91
Pan-African colours 92
Pan-Arabic colours 92
Pandemic 12, 14, 26, 60, 272-321
Panelist 309, 318
Pan-Slavic colours 92-93
Papal inauguration 121
Papal legate 41
Parade 86, 109, 196, 208, 211, 216, 218-218
Paris 18, 46, 152, 216, 218, 284-285
Parliament 28, 44-45, 50, 117-121, 170, 183, 205-207, 211-212, 263, 283, 313
Partner programme 191
Partner 17, 24, 31, 34, 60-61, 63, 74-75, 134, 139-140, 159-160, 165-166, 249-250, 292, 310
PCR test 319
Peace Palace 44, 136
Peacekeeping mission 78
Peacekeeping Operations, Department for 80
Pennant 87, 90-91, 96-97, 114, 116
Pentagon 32
Permanent representative 45, 49-52, 81, 299
Pernis, Martin van 257
Personal accomplishments 59
Personal achievement 67
Personal affinities 59
Personal antipathies 59
Personal attention 32, 225-226, 235, 238-240, 274, 319
Personal flag 88, 98-99, 113
Petit lever 20
Petit Trianon 20
Pflimlin, Pierre 117-118
Philip the Good, Duke of Burgundy 18, 41
Philippines, the 44-48, 151
Philips 261
Photo opportunities 100-101, 296
Physical contact 26, 288, 292, 318
Place of honour 43, 61-62, 75-76, 100, 112
Placement 19, 41, 43, 49, 63, 67, 288
Planning 130, 204-205, 219-220, 230, 232-235, 253, 254, 270, 278, 283-284, 296, 298, 309, 318-319, 321
Plaque et Cordon 141, 172

Plexiglass 292
Plischke, Elmer 189
Plumb, Lord 117-118
Poland 152, 204, 316
Pole 74, 87-90, 97, 102, 106, 112
Policy officer 225-226, 231
Politeness 17-19
Political advisor 46
Political Affairs, Department for 80
Political assistant 46
Political discourse 154, 160
Political language 153, 158
Political mandate 43
Political order 41
Political sensitivities 59
Politics 31, 42, 78, 80, 82-84, 118-119, 118, 235, 251
Polo, Marco 9
Polygamy 63
Pontiff 41
Pope 42, 49, 118, 121, 181, 248
Population 51, 92, 95, 183, 313
Portugal 40, 63, 102, 176-177, 179, 325
Position (status) 20, 30-31, 41-44, 48-49, 55, 59, 63, 67, 71, 82, 127, 131-132, 155-157, 160, 168, 170, 188, 195, 207, 228, 252, 264
Position 60-61, 64, 68, 70, 74-75, 87, 97-98, 100-102, 109, 194, 198, 202-203, 208-209, 228-230, 256-257, 306, 326
Positional flag 97-98, 100-101, 109
Post, Emily 125
Post-COVID 278
Post-event report 234
Post-pandemic 279, 302
Pour condoler 128
Pour féliciter 128
Pour mémoire 126, 128
Pour prendre conge 128
Pour presenter 128
Pour remercier 128
Powell, Colin 35
Power 20-21, 41-42, 52, 81, 87, 153-154, 158, 160, 177, 180-181, 189, 195, 199, 207-208, 218, 256, 286, 304
Prague 135
Precautions 277, 296
Precedence 11, 23, 27, 41-57, 59-61, 66-68, 71, 73, 75-76, 80-81, 88, 98-99, 119-120, 178, 199, 221, 229, 235, 246, 253, 301
Predictability 78, 81, 84
Preferred banking 226
Prefix 127
Prejudice 42
Preliminary announcement 126
Premier 51
Preparation 118-119, 165, 170-171, 180, 187, 190, 230, 232-233, 235, 246, 254, 262-263, 270-271, 307-308, 318, 324
Pre-recorded 288, 317
Préséance 18, 41, 59, 98

INDEX 347

Present 63, 67-69, 71, 119-120, 129, 161, 166, 187, 192, 197, 200-202, 222, 252, 275, 277-278, 290, 295, 307, 318
Presentation of credentials 23, 41-42, 49, 131, 145, 184, 186-188, 199-203, 275, 323
Presidency of the Republic of Lebanon 245
President of the European Commission 118
President of the European Council 120, 285
President of the French Republic 207, 210
President of the International Court of Justice 44-45, 53, 55-56, 204
President of the Norwegian Nobel Committee 120
President of the Russian Federation 194-195, 202, 294
President of the United States 31, 34, 69, 71, 89, 112-114, 118, 203, 205, 207, 209, 212, 214, 253, 275
President 31-32, 34, 43-46, 48-51, 54-57, 69-71, 81, 112-114, 118-121, 133-134, 140, 171, 177-181, 189, 193-195, 198, 202-207, 209-210, 212-214, 219, 244-246, 253-255, 257, 263, 285, 290, 299, 301, 303-304
Presidential flag 203
Presidential palace 193
Presidential protocol 203, 245-246
Presidential standard 88, 112
Press arrangements 233
Press conference 59, 74, 121, 179, 190, 294
Press release 233
Preventive measures 234, 298
Prime minister 32-34, 43, 48, 96, 115, 118, 120, 176, 178, 190-191, 198, 204, 272, 301, 314-315
Prince Consort 210
Prince of Wales 167, 212
Prince 11, 22, 88, 94, 96, 121, 133, 167, 181, 210, 212, 324
Princess Royal 167
Princess 11, 20, 88, 96-97, 114, 133, 167, 181, 210, 324
Principal 50, 53, 57, 71, 286, 303, 305, 307
Principality 42
Prinsenvlag 94
Prinsjesdag 55, 188, 210, 215
Prinsjesfestival 236
Priority 41-43, 49-50, 52, 120, 221, 260, 293-294
Prisse Papyrus 18
Private banking 226
Private sector 36, 67, 73, 82, 128, 184, 225, 261, 265-266, 294
Private visit 187, 191
Private wealth management 226
Privileges 11, 41, 53-56,
Procession 21, 52, 59, 109, 119, 184, 198, 200, 205, 216, 313-314
Programme 11, 51, 128, 175, 191, 196, 226, 228, 231, 243, 265, 270, 276, 278, 285, 319, 325-327
Protocol definition 20-21
Protocol fetishist 240-241

Protocol manager 217, 219
Protocol of the Russian Federation 193, 202
Protocol officer 11, 75, 126, 166, 203, 220-221, 225-232, 235, 240-243, 249, 254, 279, 287, 294, 296-297, 303-304, 307, 311, 320, 327
Protocol service 119, 121
Protocol 9-11, 17-18, 20-27, 29-37, 41-42, 52-53, 59-60, 67, 70-71, 75-84, 97-98, 100, 103-105, 107-109, 111-112, 114, 117-122, 126, 129-131, 145, 150, 160, 165-167, 169-171, 175-180, 183-184, 187, 191-194, 196, 199, 202-203, 205, 209, 211, 213, 215, 217-222, 225-233, 235-243, 245-246, 249-250, 254, 256, 258, 260-266, 269-271, 273-274, 275-277, 279-290, 294-298, 300-308, 310-311, 313, 315-317, 319-320, 323-327
Protocolbureau 11, 58, 236, 239, 241, 257, 264, 326
Protocols of London 21
Protókollon 21
Protos 21
Province 46, 94, 97, 191
Provincial flag 98, 103
Provincial representative 46
Proximity monitor app 293
Prussia 41
Public audience 59, 74
Public health 292
Public interest 43
Public position 43
Public relations 178
Public sector 36, 128, 225, 265, 279
Publicity 233
Putin, Vladimir 31

Qaboos bin Said Al Said, HM Sultan 169
Qatar 116, 121
Quarantine 279
Quarterly, flag element 91
Queen Mother 205
Queen 19, 21-22, 51, 54-56, 69, 94, 99, 114, 121, 125, 132-135, 167, 169, 177, 181, 197, 205-205, 210-212, 219-220, 239, 252, 271-272, 313, 315, 323-324
Queluz 178
Queue 227
Quirinale Palace 212

Raja 51
Ramadan 69, 129, 252
Rank 26, 43, 45, 52, 54-55, 59, 62-63, 66, 89, 98, 120, 127, 130, 157, 159, 166, 168, 170-171, 212
Ratification, order of 51, 99, 105
Ray, Nicolas 156
Recall letter(s) 201
Receiving line 74-75, 142, 278
Reception 33, 74-75, 126, 128-129, 131-132, 135-139, 186, 191, 220, 227-229, 238, 245, 250, 255, 262-263, 317-318, 323, 325
Reciprocity 21, 25-26, 35, 153, 169, 171, 186-188, 235

Recognition 34, 87-88, 155, 165, 167-168, 176, 195, 245, 291
Rectangular table 59, 64
Rectores magnifici 48
Red sea rig 144
Regional authorities 46
Regional 46, 52, 95, 245
Registrar 54-55
Registry 55
Regrets only 126, 129
Relationship management 11, 225-226, 239-243, 327
Religion 24, 32, 34, 36, 183-184
Religious day 231
Religious representative 47-48
Remembrance ceremony 43, 197-198
Remembrance Day 197, 313, 326
Remote interpreting 311, 317
Reply card 126, 129, 140
Répondez sR il vous plaît 126, 128
Representative 26-27, 29-30, 41-52, 66-67, 69, 73, 75, 77, 81-84, 117, 121, 136, 158, 177, 179, 187, 189, 191-192, 199, 201, 204, 228, 238, 252-254, 261, 282, 290, 295, 299, 313, 315
Republic 48, 119, 208-209
Residence 311-312
Respect 9, 17, 20-24, 27, 32, 34-36, 41, 59, 84, 95, 97, 102, 121, 130, 158, 165-166, 169, 186-192, 195, 197, 199, 204, 208-209, 216, 221-222, 227, 240, 246, 255-256, 259-260, 264-265, 271, 284, 296, 303, 313, 315
Restrictive measures 275-276, 283, 287-288, 295, 300, 303, 313
Return cultural event 22
Return dinner 22, 191
Reveille, bugle call 197-198
Ribbons 87, 172-174, 184, 198
Ridderzaal 188, 215
Right-hand traffic 76
Ritual 9, 23, 26, 160, 183-184, 197, 199, 206, 218, 250, 252, 303, 320
Rodday, Deborah K. 308
Roman catholic 49, 118, 167, 206
Rome 21, 51, 212, 217, 219, 289-290
Rotterdam Philharmonic Orchestra 257, 265
Round Table 22, 59, 62-64, 68-69, 262
Row 70-71, 73-76, 168, 228, 259-260
Royal Air Force 28, 205, 272
Royal Army 205
Royal Ascot 145-147
Royal bus 196
Royal Constabulary 204-205, 213-215
Royal Court 11, 240, 252, 323
Royal crypt 204-205, 210
Royal family 20, 22, 48, 69-70, 73, 91, 96, 115, 141-142, 167, 192, 196, 204-205, 209-210, 215, 219, 238
Royal honours 34-35, 183
Royal household 14, 18, 43, 171, 200, 204, 216, 323

Royal Navy 205
Royal Palace, Amsterdam 91, 207, 212, 313
Royal personal flag / standard 88, 91, 98-99, 112-115
Royal regalia 206-207
Royal Victorian Order 47
Royal wedding 186, 188, 214, 237-239
Royal 11, 14, 18, 20, 22, 28, 34-35, 43, 47-48, 53, 69-70, 73, 88-89, 91, 94, 96, 98-99, 108, 112-115, 130, 133-135, 141-142, 145-147, 167-168, 171, 177, 180, 183, 186, 188, 191-192, 196, 198, 200, 204-216, 219, 237-240, 252, 257, 283, 313, 315
RSVP 126, 129
Rüger, Axel 252
Ruler 18, 51
Rules of the game 84
Ruling class 42
Rusk, Dean 189
Russia 25, 30-31, 41-42, 87, 99, 112, 166-167, 193-195, 200, 202, 204, 214-215, 294-295
Rwanda 83

Saint Michael and Saint George, Order of 47
Saltire, flag element 91
Salute, first 208-209
Same-sex couple 63
Sampaio, Jorge 180
Sand, R.M. 203, 250
Sanitary measures 280, 289
Sanitizer 308, 311
Sash 141, 172
Satow, Sir Ernest 250
Saudi Arabia 110, 115-116, 217, 295
Savoir-faire 300
Scandinavia 131
Scandinavian cross, flag element 91
Sceptre 207
Schloss Bellevue 212
Scholar 18, 157, 282
Scholastic achievement 67
Scotland 99, 211
Seating arrangements 11, 26, 37, 52, 59-75, 220, 228-229, 238, 259, 262-263, 296, 312, 324
Seating capacity 296
Seating card 68, 228-229, 233
Seating chart 68, 279
Seating list 228, 230
Secretary of State 35, 45-46, 69, 132, 171, 189, 192, 253
Secretary-general 28-31, 33, 37, 43-45, 51, 69-70, 74, 77-81, 117-118, 121, 135, 159
Secular 34, 49, 206
Security Council 50-51, 69, 78-81, 84, 161, 245
Security officer 233
Security 11, 71, 79, 118, 122, 129, 178, 189, 196, 220, 231-233, 235, 262, 286, 305
Semantic 158
Semi-formal 143, 148
Seminar 226-229, 234, 236-237, 245, 276, 283, 297

INDEX 349

Senate 50-51, 168, 170, 190, 299, 315
Senator 46, 50, 254
Seniority 30, 32, 51, 59, 120, 190
Sennett, Richard 250
Serres, Jean 130, 187
Shahada 110
Shanghai 261
Shield 87
Shiites 34
Short evening dress 144-145
Siemens 257-261, 264
Signing of a treaty 187
Silent procession 216
Silverware 19
Simultaneous 276, 290, 295, 298-300, 310-311, 318
Singapore 151-153
Site visit 232, 307
Skulls of animals 87
Small-scale 274, 319
Smart casual 150-151
SME 251, 253
SMS 130
Snowdon, Sondra 256
Soares, Mário 180
Social distancing 26, 274, 278, 284, 286, 288-289, 293, 296, 298, 301, 303, 307, 312-313, 315, 318
Social manners 17, 286
Social media 130, 188, 233, 239, 281, 290, 294, 320
Social position 42
Social prominence 67
Social secretary 126, 133
Social skills 156, 300
Sociocultural institutions 48
Socio-economic position 42
Sofia, HM Queen 132-133
South Africa 44-45, 47, 63
South American culture 24
Spain 9, 13, 44-45, 47, 63, 91, 94, 102-103, 132-133, 166-168, 180, 200, 245, 297, 325
Spanish 9, 12, 49, 155, 245, 276
Speaker 29, 51, 79, 110-111, 117, 119-120, 130, 154, 157-159, 243, 250, 253, 257, 263, 276-277, 280, 282, 285, 287-288, 291, 301, 309-310, 318-320, 327
Specialised agencies 51-52
Speech 22, 34, 37, 55, 73, 78-80, 120, 153, 157-158, 160-161, 179, 187-188, 191, 202, 207, 215-216, 236, 240, 277, 285, 307, 315, 317
Spouse 37, 61-63, 69, 73-75, 81, 96, 133-134, 165, 170, 178, 190, 192-193, 196, 198, 200-201, 215-216, 311-312
Srebrenica 83
Staff briefing 233
Stag function 62
Stage (phase) 30, 83, 116, 126, 218, 230, 233, 292, 319

Stage (podium) 70-73, 120, 238, 280, 288, 307
Stakeholder management 242, 313, 326
Stakeholder 184-185, 220, 226, 231, 252-253, 273-274, 276, 278-280, 283, 285-286, 289, 293, 303, 305-306, 315-316, 319-20, 326
Standard (flag) 87-91, 98, 112-115, 195-196
Standard (procedures) 21-22, 87, 94, 172, 178, 221, 226, 258, 324
Star 98, 109, 167, 169, 172-173, 209
State banner 90
State banquet 66, 69, 134, 171-174, 187, 253
State budget 49
State decorations 142, 164
State event 71
State funeral 186, 188, 204-205, 212, 239, 324
State minister 46
State protocol 177-178, 220-221
State visit 21-22, 35, 42, 165-167, 169-171, 174-175, 177, 180, 184-191, 194, 197, 199, 210-215, 244, 252, 273, 300, 323
State 9, 21, 46, 50-51, 70, 78, 88, 93, 97, 157, 168, 187-188, 199, 206-207, 209, 246, 256
Status 18, 20-21, 41-42, 52, 59, 73, 117, 130, 170, 215, 233
Statute of the Court 54
Stereotype 154
Stock exchange 48
Strasbourg 117-119, 152
Strategic networking 11, 254, 256, 273, 325-327
Strategic networks 23
Strategic relationship management 14, 239, 241, 327
Strategy 153, 159, 225, 230-231, 234-235, 240-242, 249
Streaming 288, 293, 309
Suavitas 19
Suffix 87, 127
Suleyman, Michel 244
Sultan 51, 169
Sunnis 34
Suomi 99
Supervisory board 28, 73, 252, 257, 259, 263-265, 327
Supplier 233, 292
Supreme Court 46, 254
Surname 51, 131
Sustainability 294
Swallowtail 89-90
Swallow-tailed cloth 90
Swearing-in 183, 206-207
Sweden 23, 63, 135, 168, 172, 200, 211, 214-215, 277-278, 325
Sweeney, Maureen 310
Switzerland 24, 44, 50, 88, 91, 269, 298-301
Sword 95, 168-169, 207-208
Sydney 11, 14, 277-278, 326-327
Symbol of recognition 87-89
Symbol 25, 87-90, 94, 110, 115, 165, 184, 219, 275
Symbolic device 89

Symbolic 59, 91, 95, 114, 157, 165, 167, 184, 208, 218-219
Symmetric cross, flag element 91
Symposium 70

Tabard 94
Table manners 19, 68
Table 19, 22-23, 31, 33, 59-70, 229-230, 262-264, 275, 278-279, 284, 288, 296, 306, 308, 311, 318, 325
Tabouret 20
Tails 141
Tanzania 49
Taptoe, bugle call 197-198, 315
Tea ceremony 184
Technical discourse 154
Telecommuting 293
Temperature checking 278, 319
Tenue de ville 147
Territory rig 151
Tête-à-tête 80, 190, 282
Text chat 317
Thatcher, Baroness Margaret 205
The Hague Institute for Global Justice 77-78, 83
The Hague 11, 28-29, 33, 41, 44-45, 53-54, 56, 86, 97, 99, 136-139, 189, 200, 204-205, 212, 233, 236, 264, 315, 324-326
Think tank 77-78, 82-84, 306
Thistle, Order of the 47
Time management 232
Timelines 232
Timing 126-127, 231
Title 19, 42-43, 68, 127, 130-131, 240, 259, 272
To remind 126, 128-129
Toast 22-23
Tomb of the Unknown Soldier 190, 198-199
Torchbearer 182
Torino 217-218
Totalitarian regime 154
Town 46, 281, 313
Tradition 17, 24, 32, 34, 36, 59, 77-78, 80, 84, 95, 98, 114, 116, 119-121, 125, 156, 178-179, 183-186, 204-205, 218, 246, 249, 252, 262, 272, 289, 291, 312
Traditional dress 140
Transferrable 43
Transmission 21, 188, 319
Travel restrictions 289, 297, 303, 307, 317
Treaty of Vienna 17, 199
Tribe 21, 87-88
Tricolour flag 93-94, 115
Troonrede 188, 215
Trusteeship Council 50
Tryon, Deanna 305
Turabaz, Ehsan 293
Turkey 32, 44-46, 48, 192, 198, 200
Turtle Bay 78, 81
Tuxedo 143-144
Twitter 130

U.S. State Department 249
Umayyad's 93
UN charter 50, 54, 57
UN correspondence manual 130
UN funds and programmes 51
UN organ 49-50, 53, 57, 290
UNCTAD 51
Under-secretary-general 69
UNDP 51
UNEP 51
UNESCO 51
Unforeseen circumstances 234-235
UNFPA 51
UNHCR 51
Unicameral legislature 45
UNICEF 51
UNIDO 51-52
Unilateral 246
Union Jack 88, 99, 110, 114
Union 45, 49-50, 99, 101, 109, 117-118, 120-121, 180, 209
United Arab Emirates 26, 102, 104-105, 198, 275, 301
United Kingdom 22, 25-26, 42, 44-45, 47, 63, 88, 94, 98-99, 103, 105-106, 110-112, 114, 134, 167-168, 170, 173, 196, 200, 204-206, 211, 272, 303, 316, 326
United Nations General Assembly 45, 49-51, 53, 73, 78-80, 135, 245, 307
United Nations Secretariat 50, 79
United Nations 14, 44-45, 49, 51, 53-54, 61, 69, 74, 77-79, 82-83, 99-100, 115, 128, 135, 161, 217-218, 240, 245, 273
United States Institute for Peace 77-78
United States 14, 26, 30-32, 34, 44-48, 50, 63, 69, 79, 94, 99-101, 103-105, 109, 111-112, 125, 132-133, 135, 141, 143, 161, 167, 170, 190, 196, 198, 203, 205, 207, 209, 212, 214, 216, 249-251, 253-254. 304-308, 310-311, 316
Universal 43, 52, 130, 216, 320
University of Leiden 28-29, 33, 138
Unmarried couple 63
UNODC 51
UNOV 52
UNRWA 51
Upper house 45, 188, 207, 215
Uruguay 63
U-shape 59, 65, 69

Vaccin 233, 274, 319-320
Van Gogh Museum 252
Vanderbilt, Amy 125
Vatican 121
Venezuela 244
Verheul, Mark 11, 312, 324-327
Versailles 19-20, 78
Veteran 97, 198-199, 205, 272, 313, 315
Veterans Day 97, 198
Veto power 81

Vexillology 87-89
Vexillum 87
Vice versa 30, 41, 52
Vice-president 51, 53, 56, 69, 119, 253
Victoria Cross 47, 167-168
Videoconference 273, 280, 286, 300, 305, 317
Vienna Convention on Diplomatic Relations 42, 44
Vienna 42, 51-52
Villepin, Dominique de 161
Villiers, Jean Hotman de 155
Vin d'honneur 131
Violence, senseless 185, 216
Virtual reality 300
Virtual 274-277, 279-285, 288-290, 292-293, 298-301, 303-309, 311, 315-319, 326
Viscount 47
Vision 160-161, 225, 231, 234-235, 237, 239, 241
Visit 21-23, 32-33, 35, 37, 67, 79, 118-119, 121, 132-134, 165-167, 169-175, 177-181, 184-200, 210-215, 232, 245-246, 252, 261, 271. 282-284, 289, 302, 307
Visiting country 102, 170, 177-179, 189, 192-193, 195, 200
Visser, Derkwillem 91
Vitart, Thomas 284
Vizier 18
Vliet, Ivo van 14, 236
Voorwaarts, bugle call 197-198
Voting system 317
V-sign 25

Waistcoat 141, 143, 146-147, 173
Wales 99
Washington, DC 77, 205, 214, 254, 275, 311, 324
Weapon 87, 208
Webinar 280, 291, 307
Wedding 11, 65, 145-146, 183, 185-186, 188, 214, 237-239, 280, 324-325
Welcome ceremony 23, 119, 121, 192, 194, 221

Welcome 27, 121, 139, 208, 227-228, 230, 239, 246, 252, 255, 323
Wellink, Barbara 311
Western countries 25, 42, 239
Western Europe 126, 131, 261, 326
WFP 51
Wheeler, Stewart 280-281
White House, the 32, 69, 133, 203, 253-254
White tie 134, 141-142, 171-172, 174, 178, 191
WHO 51
Widow 43, 47
Wife 29, 32, 37-38, 55, 62-63, 73, 76, 125, 156, 192, 200, 259, 264
WiFi 293
Wijers, Jean Paul 14, 239
Wikipedia 184, 205
Wilhelmina of the Netherlands, HM Queen 94
Willem-Alexander of the Netherlands, HM King 97, 190, 207
William of Orange 94
Williams, Abiodun 14, 77
Windsor Castle 69, 168, 272
Winged collar 146
WIPO 51
Wittelsbach, Bavarian House of 93
WMO 51
Working visit 32-33, 191
World Bank 45, 51
World War II 88, 97, 125, 167, 197
Wreath, laying of 23, 183-185, 187-188, 190-191, 197-199, 215, 323
WTO 51
Wuersten, Samuel 14, 269

Xi, Jinping 121

York 48

Zeeland 94
Zhou, Dr Jiali 282